The Essential Family Guide to
Borderline Personality Disorder

"This indispensable book is compassionate to all involved and avoids blame, jargon, and oversimplification."

Freda B. Friedman, PhD
Dialectical Behavior Specialist

"With exquisite understanding of the disorder and empathy for both those who have it and their family members, Randi Kreger offers valuable 'Power Tools' to help readers endure the ravages of BPD."

Jerold J. Kreisman, MD, coauthor of *I Hate You—Don't Leave Me: Understanding the Borderline Personality* and *Sometimes I Act Crazy: Living with Borderline Personality Disorder*

"Randi Kreger uncovers the marvelous symmetry of the borderline relationship, in which both participants experience similar self-doubts, irrational guilt and shame, wavering identity, helplessness, anger, and fear of abandonment. Those with BPD and their loved ones will, together, benefit from the tools she provides."

Richard A. Moskovitz, MD, author of *Lost in the Mirror: An Inside Look at Borderline Personality Disorder*

"Randi Kreger masterfully breaks down BPD to help people more easily understand this complex subject."

Barbara Oakley, PhD, author of *Evil Genes: Why Rome Fell, Hitler Rose, Enron Failed, and My Sister Stole My Mother's Boyfriend*

THE ESSENTIAL FAMILY GUIDE TO

Borderline Personality Disorder

New Tools and Techniques
to Stop Walking on Eggshells

· Randi Kreger ·

HAZELDEN

Hazelden
Center City, Minnesota 55012
hazelden.org

Library of Congress Cataloging-in-Publication Data

Kreger, Randi.
   The essential family guide to borderline personality disorder: new tools and tech-
niques to stop walking on eggshells / Randi Kreger.
      p.   cm.
   Includes bibliographical references and index.
   ISBN 978-1-59285-363-2 (softcover)
   1. Borderline personality disorder—Treatment.   2. Borderline personality
disorder—Patients—Family relationships.   3. Antisocial personality disorders—
Treatment.   I. Title.
   RC569.5.B67K73838 2008
   616.85'852—dc22

                           2008036456

Editor's note

The BPD stories quoted in this book are either composites or used with permission.
In some instances, names, details, and circumstances have been changed to protect
anonymity.

   This publication is not intended as a substitute for the advice of health care
professionals.

12 11 10   4 5 6

Cover design by Theresa Jaeger Gedig
Interior design by Ann Sudmeier
Typesetting by BookMobile Design and Publishing Services

Dedication

This book is for those who walked with me hand in hand—and sometimes carried me—in my own journey along the yellow brick road. It is also dedicated to the libraries in and around Saint Louis Park, Minnesota. The children's novels there, more precious than any ruby-red slippers, made both me and this book possible.

When we are no longer able
to change a situation . . .
we are challenged to change ourselves.
▪ Viktor E. Frankl ▪

Contents

Foreword

The Essential Family Guide to Borderline Personality Disorder is a very useful addition to the growing literature on *borderline disorder* (the term most acceptable to my patients and readers). The author's first book, *Stop Walking on Eggshells* (with Paul T. Mason), has been an international best seller in this field since its publication in 1998. A brief overview of the history and current status of borderline disorder will provide context for this guide.

Borderline disorder has been surrounded by many myths that leave people with the disorder and their family members feeling very hopeless. This should not be so because there are many actions that can be taken to markedly reduce the effects of borderline disorder on those who have it and on their families.

For almost a century, borderline disorder has been referred to as a "wastebasket diagnosis," reserved for those patients whose presenting symptoms are often so complex that they do not fall cleanly into a single diagnosis, thereby frustrating the clinician, the patient, and the family. Borderline disorder is resistant to treatment with conventional uses of traditional treatment approaches, and it was not listed in the American Psychiatric Association's *Diagnostic and Statistical Manual of Mental Disorders* until 1980. According to the latest research, this devastating disorder has an estimated prevalence of almost 6 percent in the general population.

The many years of neglect of borderline disorder have resulted in a high prevalence of underdiagnosis, disability, continued suffering, premature death by suicide, and a deep sense of hopelessness. These overwhelming emotions pervade not only those with the disorder, but also their family members, whose lives are terribly affected. In short, borderline disorder is an overlooked, devastating disorder of tragic proportions.

Today, however, there is new hope as a convergence of factors are causing dramatic strides forward. The first factor is represented, in part, by the reports of neuroimaging studies that demonstrate clear differences in the brains of people with borderline disorder compared with those of control subjects. Other studies have demonstrated a high degree of heritability of borderline disorder, further underscoring the fact that the disorder has a significant biological basis. These studies provide clear and visible evidence that borderline disorder is associated with anatomical and functional abnormalities of the brain, and that the disorder should be viewed no differently than medical disorders affecting other organs.

The second factor is the emergence of research on the effective use of a new generation of antipsychotic agents, antidepressants, mood stabilizers, and psychotherapeutic and psychosocial interventions specifically developed for borderline disorder. Treatment programs have also been significantly effective for patients with the disorder, and they have provided highly useful information and new skills to patients' families.

The third factor has been the development of two national advocacy organizations focused solely on borderline disorder: the Treatment and Research Advancements National Association for Personality Disorder (TARA APD) and the National Education Alliance for Borderline Personality Disorder (NEA-BPD). These organizations are dedicated to educating patients and their families about the disorder and how to cope more effectively with it.

The other mission of these organizations is to increase awareness of the disorder on a national and even international level and stimulate public and private funding for research and education. As a result of the efforts of the leadership of NEA-BPD, people with borderline disorder, their families, and professional experts in the field, the U.S. House of Representatives passed a resolution (H. Res. 1005) on April 1, 2008, designating the month of May as Borderline Personality Disorder Awareness Month.

In addition, other organizations have added significantly to the increase in activity in the field. For example, the National Alliance on Mental Illness (NAMI) has recently named those with borderline disorder as one of their "priority populations." The Borderline Personality Disorder Resource Center has been recently established to help those affected by borderline disorder "find the most current and accurate information on the nature of BPD, and on sources of available treatment."

Two new important private resources for research funding of borderline disorder have begun to have a positive effect on the field. Founded in 1999, the Borderline Personality Disorder Research Foundation (BPDRF) "has mobilized research centers in the United States and Europe to investigate whether BPD is a recognizable distinct entity, and, if so, what the defining characteristics of the disorder are." Initially, it selected and funded four centers to investigate borderline disorder from varying scientific and clinical perspectives. In addition, it has awarded research grants to twenty-two investigators.

During the past decade, the National Alliance for Research on Schizophrenia and Depression (NARSAD) has expanded its original focus from schizophrenia and affective disorders to other prevalent mental disorders such as anxiety disorders. Since 1987, this donor-funded organization has awarded more than $180 million in grants to senior and new meritorious researchers involved in brain research focused on psychiatric disorders. Recently, it has included borderline disorder in its areas of interest.

A final critical factor has been the marked increase in the amount of information readily available about borderline disorder. During the past decade there has been an increasing number of books written for the nonprofessional about borderline disorder, and there has also been a comparable number of Web sites launched. One of the most successful of these books has been *Stop Walking on Eggshells,* coauthored by Randi Kreger, the author of this guide.

In *Stop Walking on Eggshells,* Kreger focused her attention on the families of those who do not acknowledge their borderline disorder, do not seek treatment, and blame their difficulties on others. The success of this book attests to the large number of people who fall into this group—whom

Kreger calls "higher-functioning invisible BPs" in this book—and the devastating effect their behavior has on their families and others close to them.

In *The Essential Family Guide to Borderline Personality Disorder*, Kreger significantly expands the scope of *Stop Walking on Eggshells* and her accompanying workbook by providing a current and understandable description of the symptoms, nature, and treatment of the disorder by using numerous helpful examples. She also provides much useful advice to families on how to effectively help and how to cope with a family member with borderline disorder.

To do so, Kreger has read broadly in the area and has consulted with a number of leading experts to ensure, to the highest degree possible, the accuracy of her content. This represents no small amount of investigative work, as scientific knowledge in the field is expanding rapidly.

In *The Essential Family Guide to Borderline Personality Disorder*, Kreger utilizes a markedly different approach to educate her readers. Using novel concepts and approaches, she integrates a comprehensive amount of information about the disorder and its treatment.

Kreger does so in a writing style that neither "talks down" to the reader nor expects a high level of knowledge of psychology and neuroscience. Kreger achieves her formidable task in a very impressive fashion. In *The Essential Family Guide to Borderline Personality Disorder*, there is much to be learned by family members who are affected by loved ones with borderline disorder, and also by professionals who strive to help them.

Robert O. Friedel, MD
Distinguished Clinical Professor of Psychiatry
Director, Borderline Personality Disorder Program
Department of Psychiatry, Virginia Commonwealth University
Richmond, Virginia
Author, *Borderline Personality Disorder Demystified*
www.bpddemystified.com

Acknowledgments

When someone asked a songwriter I know how long it took her to compose a song, she said, "my whole life." In the same way, this book took my whole life—the years I spent in my own BP/non-BP relationship, the dozen years I spent managing my online community for family members, and the three years of intensive research and writing that went into this particular book, the third of my trio of books for those who are struggling to love someone who keeps painfully pushing them away.

On the publishing side, the heavy lifting was done by my good friend and literary agent Scott Edelstein and former Hazelden editor Rebecca Post. Few agents provide the hand-holding and "rah-rahing" that Scott does, and no one else could have been such an excellent sounding board. He has been with me from that day in the early 1990s when he said, "So, do you think you're ever going to do that book on borderline personality disorder?"

Rebecca Post actually initiated this book when she asked me whether I was interested in writing something for Hazelden—a memoir, perhaps. That seed of an idea grew into the book you now hold in your hands. She nurtured this book in a way that few editors do today. Sid Farrar and the staff at Hazelden stepped in after Rebecca left and have been positive forces in shaping the manuscript, ensuring accuracy, and promoting the book to a wide audience.

Because of the success of my previous books, *Stop Walking on Eggshells* and *The Stop Walking on Eggshells Workbook,* I had access to some of the top BPD clinicians, researchers, advocates, and other professionals when writing this book. They all share my passion for helping those with this insidious disorder and for helping their friends and family.

At the topmost level is Robert O. Friedel, MD, Distinguished Clinical Professor of Psychiatry at Virginia Commonwealth University and the author of *Borderline Personality Disorder Demystified*. He kindly wrote the foreword and spent hours teaching me how impairments of the physical and chemical brain can lead to BPD behaviors. He also lent his insights to the chapters on treatment and finding a clinician. Thank you.

Another important contributor is Blaise Aguirre, MD, the medical director of the Adolescent Dialectical Behavioral Therapy Center at McLean Hospital in Belmont, Massachusetts. He is a child-and-adolescent psychiatrist recognized for his work in the treatment of BPD and is the author of *Borderline Personality Disorder in Adolescents*. Dr. Aguirre managed to do interviews with me despite his hectic schedule, sometimes fitting me in by cell phone as he walked through the hospital corridors. If you are the parent of a borderline child, you *need* his book.

Jim Breiling, PhD, from the National Institute of Mental Health, is the clinical cornerstone of all things BPD—a kind of real-life "BPDCentral." He has been supportive of my work for many years and answered a multitude of questions during the time we've worked together. He is the greatest.

Other clinicians and professionals who gave me in-depth interviews or significant content include the following (in no particular order):

- Beverly Engel, MFCT, a psychotherapist and the author of eighteen self-help books.
- Barbara Oakley, author of *Evil Genes: Why Rome Fell, Hitler Rose, Enron Failed, and My Sister Stole My Mother's Boyfriend*. At the last minute, I asked Barbara to apply first aid to the brain chemistry section in chapter 4. She assisted me in writing it and came up with the analogy of tree pollen.
- John Gunderson, MD, Professor of Psychiatry at Harvard Medical School and Director of Psychosocial and Personality

Research at McLean Hospital in Belmont, Massachusetts, and Cynthia Berkowitz, MD.

- Sharon, founder of the online community NUTS (parents Needing Understanding, Tenderness, and Support to help their child with borderline personality disorder).
- Perry D. Hoffman, President of the National Education Alliance for Borderline Personality Disorder and cofounder of the Family Connections Program.
- Floyd Koenig, who served as an impromptu research assistant, gathering information on topics at my request.
- A. J. Mahari, a recovered individual with BPD who has authored several electronic books and maintains the Web site Borderline Personality Disorder from the Inside Out (www.borderlinepersonality.ca).
- Debra Resnick, PsyD, President of Psychological Services and Human Development Center, Inc., in Fort Washington, Pennsylvania. Debra, a psychotherapist who specializes in dialectical behavior therapy (DBT), uses my workbook in a great deal of her work with families.

Furthermore, I am honored that these leading clinicians known for their work with individuals with BPD reviewed chapters of this book for accuracy (although I take all responsibility for the content). These notable people are

- Robert O. Friedel, MD: chapters 1–6
- Marlene Schwartz, RN, MSN, PhD, ANCC, APNP: chapter 8 (Power Tool 2: Uncover What Keeps You Feeling Stuck)
- Debra Resnick, PsyD: chapter 9 (Power Tool 3: Communicate to Be Heard)
- Freda Friedman, PhD (DBT psychotherapist and coauthor of *Surviving a Borderline Parent*): chapter 10 (Power Tool 4: Set Limits with Love)
- Blaise Aguirre, MD: chapter 11 (Power Tool 5: Reinforce the Right Behavior)

Other professionals whom I interviewed or whose work inspired me include Byron Bloemer, PhD; Annette Boehm; Andrea Corn, PsyD; Carolyn DeRoo; William Eddy, attorney, mediator, and clinical social worker; Kathryn Jane Gardner, PhD; Mary Gay, PhD, LPC; Jan Hargrave; and James Holifield, LCSW.

Also Patricia A. Judd, PhD; Anne Katherine, MA, CEDS; Janet Klosko, PhD; L. Allison Langlois, PsyD; Daniel Mattila, MDiv, LCSW; Bennett Pologe, PhD; Karen Pryor; Rachel Reiland; Kimberlee Roth; Kwan Soo, MD; and Amy Sutherland. The founding mothers of the fundamental premise of all three of my books have been Harriet Lerner, PhD, and her book *The Dance of Anger,* and Susan Forward, PhD, and her book *Emotional Blackmail.*

I would also like to thank two singer-songwriters for the use of their lyrics: John Forster ("Codependent With You," page 158) and Carrie Newcomer ("Closer to Home," page 242). I found Carrie's lyric about going "to the edge of my blindness, and then a little more ways" to be a perfect definition for a leap of faith.

All writers have something we must deal with called "real life," which occurs in those brief moments when we're not stewing about the book, researching the book, writing the book, rewriting the book, or incessantly talking about the book until everyone around us becomes thoroughly sick of hearing about it. My husband, Robert, has kept me fed these past three years (twelve years, if you count the first two books) and seen to things like changing the oil in my car while I had my nose in a book, was staring at my computer, or looking blankly at nothing while my mind was churning out the solutions in the second half of this book. He is the one who avidly scans the Internet and sends me new book reviews, articles, and the URLs of Web sites he thinks I might be interested in.

Lisa Radtke, the manager of my Welcome to Oz (WTO) online family community, took over after the death of a dearly beloved volunteer and has, for the past several years, kept the WTO community a safe, sacred place for all 16,000 members in fifteen Listserv "neighborhoods." Assisting Lisa is another longtime volunteer, Rita Closson, MA, who scans the list and sounds the alert when something needs attention. Rita missed her true calling as a stand-up comedian.

In 2007, computer programming whiz kid Robert Bauer tried to help me keep my technically challenged message board on www.bpdcentral.com in one piece. When it became apparent that, like the *Titanic,* it was sinking fast and all I could do was rearrange deck chairs, he gave the message board new life at his "Facing the Facts" board at www.bpdfamily.com. He has been generous with his time and expertise in all sorts of matters.

Also in 2007, Leslie Steis assisted me by setting up interviews and doing research. I learned a great deal from her about the challenges facing grandparents, who are so often villainized and prevented from spending time with their beloved grandchildren.

Finally, I would like to recognize Edith Cracchiolo, a good friend whom I sorely miss. She and I worked together on the WTO community for ten years. For several of them, she dedicated more than eight hours a day to assisting people on the WTO, especially her beloved adult children. In 2005, she traded in her earthly guardian angel wings for real ones up in heaven. How I wish she were here so I could give her this book. She would have taken it in both hands, looked up at me with a grin, and exclaimed, "Yes!"

The author gratefully acknowledges the following sources:

Kay and Doug's story, pages 11–13, reprinted with permission from *Hope for Parents: Helping Your Borderline Son or Daughter Without Sacrificing Your Family or Yourself* by K. Winkler and R. Kreger (Milwaukee, WI: Eggshells Press, 2000). Richard and Laurie's story, pages 13–15, reprinted with permission from *Love and Loathing: Protecting Your Mental Health and Legal Rights When Your Partner Has Borderline Personality Disorder* by R. Kreger and K. Williams-Justesen (Milwaukee, WI: Eggshells Press, 2000). All material from A. J. Mahari's Web site articles reprinted with permission of the author. Material from June People's radio interview reprinted with permission of *The Infinite Mind* produced by LCMedia, Inc., ©1999. Material on schema therapy reprinted with permission of Jeffrey E.

Young from www.schematherapy.com—this material also appears in *Schema Therapy: A Practitioner's Guide* by Jeffrey E. Young, Janet S. Klosko, and Marjorie E. Weishaar (New York: Guilford Press, 2003). Material on medications for mental health conditions, page 80, taken from www.drjoe carever.com, "The Chemical Imbalance in Mental Health Problems," by Joseph Carver, PhD, reprinted with permission. Medication chart, pages 81–82, taken from www.bpddemystified.com, reprinted with permission of Robert O. Friedel, MD. E-mail from Rachel Reiland, pages 101–102, reprinted with permission of Rachel Reiland. Material on the Stockholm Syndrome, page 149–150, taken from www.drjoecarver.com, "Love and Stockholm Syndrome: The Mystery of Loving an Abuser," by Joseph Carver, PhD, reprinted with permission. Material from www.aboutpsychotherapy.com reprinted with permission of Bennett Pologe, PhD. Material from the National Association of Cognitive-Behavioral Therapists Web site (www. nacbt.org) reprinted with permission. "Codependent With You" music and lyrics by John Forster, page 158, ©1991 Limousine Music Co. (ASCAP), all rights reserved, reprinted with permission. Chart on boundaries, page 199, reprinted with permission of Donna Bellafiore, www.drbalternatives. com, © by Simmonds Publications. "To the edge of my blindness, and then a little more ways," lyric adapted with permission on page 242, from *Closer to Home,* lyrics by Carrie Newcomer.

About This Book

The information in this book reflects the best of three types of research: an exhaustive, three-year survey of the latest scientific studies related to borderline personality disorder (BPD), interviews with more than two dozen top mental health clinicians and researchers, and the collective experiences of thousands of people affected in one way or another by BPD. All these individuals are members of the Welcome to Oz Online Family Community located at bpdcentral.com or the Facing the Facts message board at www.bpdfamily.com.

Welcome to Oz, or WTO, has provided an online home for more than 65,000 family members since it started in 1996. It functions much like a real-life support group, except that members communicate via e-mail instead of face-to-face. Current membership stands at 16,000, with members gathering by type of relationship (parents, siblings, stepparents) or similarities in their situations (partners who want to stay in the relationships versus those who have decided to separate). Facing the Facts—with 7,000 members—offers the same support. There, members post their thoughts on an online message board.

In part 1 of this book, you'll learn exactly how BPD impairs an individual's thoughts and feelings, which in turn triggers behaviors such as raging, perceived manipulation, suicide threats, and excessive blame and criticism. Since the bane of every family member is finding effective professional help, chapter 6 provides hard and soft qualities to look for in a clinician and seven questions that separate neophyte BPD providers from those with the necessary experience.

Then, armed with new insight about how your borderline family member experiences the world, you'll be introduced to five powerful tools that will help you organize your thinking, learn specific skills, and focus on what you need to do to avoid becoming overwhelmed. They will help you become more confident and clear about who you are, and they will show you steps to take to improve the quality of your life.

Many self-help books are written so readers can skip from chapter to chapter as needed. This book isn't one of them. The chapters in *The Essential Family Guide to Borderline Personality Disorder* are like Russian dolls—you open a big doll, and inside there's a smaller doll, and inside that a smaller one, and so on. Many of the concepts and terms used are unique to this book. So, start at the beginning and read straight through. The one exception is the chapter on finding a therapist.

If you feel trapped, this book will teach you how to get unstuck. If you feel burdened, you'll learn how to ask for help from others. If your self-esteem is in the pits, you'll learn how to climb up, step by step. And perhaps most important, you'll come to realize that you have a right to your own feelings and your own beliefs, and the right to pursue your own goals.

Psychiatrist Milton Erickson said, "There are so many things you know. It's just that you haven't always known that you know them." After you're done reading this book, you'll know.

Terms You Need to Know

To keep it simple, we use the following terms throughout this book.

"Borderline" and "BP"

Because the diagnosis of borderline personality disorder (BPD) has been so stigmatized, it's much more acceptable to say, "He's bipolar" or "She's a diabetic" than to say, "He's borderline." In effect, there is a double standard. Just the word *borderline* conjures up such negative stereotypes that many people avoid the term altogether or use a substitute.

One popular alternative is *consumer,* as in consumer of the mental health system. However, a large percentage of people with BPD are not in the mental health system. They are in as much denial of their illness as an active, untreated alcoholic. They not only don't seek treatment, but also forcefully repel any suggestion to do so.

People with BPD are finding their own solution. Just as people who are gay or lesbian have adopted the word *queer* as their own, individuals with BPD use the term *borderline* or *BP* for short. This book will follow their lead.

"Family Member" and "Non-BP"

A similar problem surrounds the term *family member*. Like the term *consumer, family member* is limited. The effects of BPD are far-reaching: in addition to the immediate family, the disorder impacts the lives of extended relatives, co-workers, friends, in-laws, stepparents, those who emotionally support family members, and even therapists. For this reason, the term *non-BP* refers to *anyone* who is in a situation in which the behavior of a BP affects him or her.

Non-BPs may have their own mental health issues, too, from depression to a personality disorder. In fact, it's common for some non-BPs to have either BPD or narcissistic personality disorder (NPD). You'll read more about narcissism on pages 46–47. *Stop Walking on Eggshells* has an appendix called "Tips for Non-BPs Who Have BPD."

The terms *BP* and *non-BP* are not a philosophy meant to divide loved ones and family members into separate camps. They're just shorthand, like saying "scuba gear" instead of "self-contained underwater breathing apparatus."

Part 1

THE ABCs OF BPD

Chapter 1

Welcome to Oz

Be true to yourself despite being misunderstood.
It is painful but not fatal.
▪ I Ching ▪

Do you feel as though you're walking on eggshells around someone important in your life? Does this phrase immediately strike not just a chord but a whole piano concerto? If so, someone in your life may have either borderline personality disorder (BPD) or borderline traits.

Take a look at the following questions. If you answer "yes" to most of them, your loved one might have BPD:

- Does she see you in one of two modes: either a hateful person who never loved her or a source of blessed, unconditional love?
- Does he continually put you in no-win situations? When you try to explain that his position is the opposite of what he said earlier, does it bring on more criticism?
- Is everything always your fault? Are you the target of constant criticism?
- Are there times when everything seems normal and you're on her good side—even idealized—but then for no obvious reason everything falls apart?
- When he's angry, does it degrade into a take-no-prisoners, vicious attack that leaves you reeling?

- Does she use fear, obligation, and guilt to get her way? Do you feel so manipulated that you don't trust her anymore?
- Are you starting to doubt your own sense of reality? Has constant exposure to his skewed sensibility, combined with isolation from family and friends, made you feel like Dorothy confounded in the strange Land of Oz?

What Is Borderline Personality Disorder?

Borderline personality disorder is a serious mental illness that causes those who have it to see people and situations as all good or all bad; to feel empty and without an identity; and to have extreme, blink-of-an-eye mood swings. People with BPD act impulsively; their self-loathing and extreme fear of abandonment can cause them to lash out at others with baseless criticism and blame. Some practice self-harm or see no other option than suicide as a way to end their pain.

People with borderline personality disorder experience the world much differently than most people. For reasons we don't entirely understand, the disorder distorts critical thought processes, resulting in emotions and actions that are out of the norm.

If we could look inside the heads of people with BPD to see the way they think, we'd find out they live in a world of extremes. To them, people and situations are all good or all bad, with nothing in between. They don't just admire or respect someone—they elevate that person to an impossible standard and then knock him down when he inevitably disappoints them. They see themselves this way, too, so that one small misstep leads them to think, *I am a worthless person.*

If you could snap your fingers and, by magic, experience what a BP feels, you would be overwhelmed by self-loathing, an intense fear of being abandoned, and a relentless sense of emptiness. Irritability and depression would be there, too, a steady drumbeat blocking out feelings of joy and even simple satisfaction. "BPD is a cancer that eats away at my body, mind, and soul," says one woman with the illness.

It's easy enough to observe how BPs act. Actions, unlike thoughts and feelings, are obvious. They're what make people with BPD so hard to live with. BPs behave impulsively, not thinking things through. Some deliberately hurt themselves—they make themselves bleed or they attempt suicide. They may spend too much money, engage in dangerous sex, abuse drugs or alcohol, drive recklessly, shoplift, or eat in a disordered way.

People with BPD repeatedly pull people toward them—often desperately—and then brusquely shove them away through bitter criticism, unappeasable rages, and fits of irrational blaming. They elevate people onto a lofty pedestal and then push them off. Some BPs put people into no-win situations and make absurd accusations.

What's difficult for loved ones to understand isn't the *what* of borderline behaviors, but the *why*.

What Is It Like to Have BPD?

Helen is a twenty-two-year-old borderline woman who just transferred from a small community college to a large university, miles away from friends and family. Other people see her as talented and bright, though a little standoffish. She sees herself as defective and keeps to herself because people terrify her.

To assuage the loneliness, she sometimes sleeps with men she doesn't know very well just to feel their bare skin on hers. She is a binge eater now; in high school she was anorexic. She keeps a journal, from which the following entry is taken (spelling and grammar are preserved).

> I want to be dependent sometimes, i want to be taken care of i
> want to be loved no matter what i want complete understanding
> from everyone (at all times, no less, ho ho ho). i wants someone
> who makes love to me, to love me, to understand how I FEEL be-
> sides this journal, I want to really touch someone and I want them
> to touch me. I don't know where to go, I doubt myself so much
> I don't respect myself i don't have confidence I can do whatever.
> I WANT TO BE LIKE A NORMAL PERSON I WANT TRUE
> LOVE, i feel insecure and tired.

I AM AFRAID OF MYSELF AND MY FEELINGS I AM
AFRAID, HORRIFIED THAT OTHER PEOPLE WILL HURT
ME, I CAN'T ACCEPT MYSELF I DON'T FEEL INCONTROL
OF MY BEHAVIOR I CAN'T CONTROL MY EATING. I think
if I let it all out I could scream and cry and rage and fear and dis-
appointment, anger, hurt. I feel like a little girl. i want someone
to come along to take control and enfold me and tell me I will be
ok. I feel tired of living sometimes. I want to help myself and my
room is so messy I can't stand it . . . I feel like I alternate be feeling
so dead inside and feeling so much such rage I would rather be
dead! Why do I feel so self-conscious around my roommate? She
tells me my feelings are too intense, I'm too spacey, I take everything as criticism. Why do I feel so angry when someone tells me
to open up and share my feelings? Why do I let them manipulate
me? I am so very hungry . . . I am me my name is Helen Helen
Helen Helen Helen Helen Helen

What Is It Like to Care about Someone with BPD?

Loving someone with BPD is a full-time job. Family members describe
it as living on an emotional roller coaster or walking on eggshells. They
feel alternately pursued and rejected, as if they're constantly being tested
for something, but unsure of what it could be. Over time, people who are
close to someone with BPD become so accustomed to living with abusive
behavior they start to think it's normal. Family members frequently experience feelings of guilt, shame, depression, exhaustion, isolation, and
helplessness.

People affected by the behaviors of someone with BPD come in two
categories: "chosen" and "unchosen." In the chosen category are partners
and friends. The unchosen category encompasses parents, siblings, in-laws,
stepparents—both blood family and those who find themselves in this
situation because of their relationship with someone else, for example, a
wife whose husband's father turns out to have BPD.

If you have someone in your life with BPD, you may

- be angry a great deal of the time at yourself, your loved one, fate, and the healthcare system
- be drained of emotional energy; your inner resources tested to the limit
- grieve for the loss of your dreams of the happy child, loving partner, close sibling, or loving parent
- fear for your physical safety
- question your own self-worth and your ability to be a good parent, partner, relative, or friend
- experience strain in other family relationships
- experience financial difficulties
- constantly walk a tightrope, balancing your needs and the needs of the rest of your family against those of your BP
- deal with the social stigma of having a mentally ill person in your family
- lose contact with family and friends
- worry about being responsible for keeping your family member alive and healthy
- have your spirituality tested—some people question their religious faith or their ability to see life as promising and good

Different types of relationships pose different challenges. The following stories, which are composites of actual family members, display the similarities and the differences of various relationships involving someone with BPD.

Parents and Grandparents

Parents of those with BPD receive a double whammy: the anguish from having a disturbed child; then, when they search for help, the shame and shock when most professionals hold them responsible for their child's suffering.

Jill was a beautiful baby. "I looked at her and I could feel the tug at my heart," says Kay, Jill's adoptive mother. Grade school wasn't easy for Jill;

she clung to Kay like rubber cement, refusing to get on the yellow bus: "Don't make me go, Mommy! Let me stay with you!" She had a hard time making friends, and teacher after teacher complained of her being uncooperative. The school counselor was certain that Jill would most likely grow out of it. But she never did.

At fourteen, Jill became introverted and rebellious. "We thought it was just adolescent rebellion, but she never came out of it," says Kay. Years of misery followed: drinking, rebellious friends, and skipping school. Jill's screams of defiance were punctuated by slamming doors and flashing anger. She dated a boy who slammed her into her locker, leaving bruises up and down her arms. She yelled at her parents and demanded they get off her back.

As soon as she turned eighteen, Jill moved in with an equally rebellious girlfriend, the friend's hard-drinking mother, and the mother's drug-dealing boyfriend. The mother moved out of town, leaving the two girls and the boyfriend alone in the apartment. Jill's new boyfriend, Sam, quickly moved in.

A few months later, Jill announced that she was pregnant. Her parents rallied to her side and met Sam, the child's father. Jill and Sam wanted to get married, so Kay quickly put together a lovely wedding. Jill was radiant.

After baby Alicia was born, Jill seemed grateful for her parents' love and support. Alicia quickly became the joy of all their lives. But then Jill felt restless again and rebellious; she began seeing other men behind Sam's back. When she met Trevor, she divorced Sam and married her new love just a few months later. Cozying up to her parents, Kay and Doug, Jill convinced them to pay for another wedding. Then Jill ignored them the entire day of the wedding. She had no photos taken with her family, only with Trevor's family. She called them her "real" family now.

Jill started using her daughter and stepchildren to control her parents. For example, one day Jill told them they could spend time with Alicia only if they took her husband's two boys as well. Kay and Doug agreed. After all, they wanted to establish a relationship with their new step-grandchildren, too. But even though they treated all three children equally well, Jill raged at them for showing favoritism toward Alicia. "You'll never see any of the children again," she threatened.

Kay and Doug found that it was much easier to see Alicia when she was visiting her father, Sam. They knew that Jill wouldn't like it, but they felt they had no other choice if they were to have a positive and loving relationship with their granddaughter. Unfortunately, when Jill found out about the visits she became so enraged that she accused Sam and Doug of sexually molesting Alicia. Careful examination by a doctor and psychologist found no basis for the accusation, and the charges were dismissed. The psychologist recommended counseling for Jill, but she refused.

Kay and Doug are now in the process of getting court-ordered visitation rights so they will still be able to have some relationship with Alicia. "We don't want to abandon her because I think she's already had a lot of emotional damage from the things Jill has subjected her to," Kay says. "I think we are the only people in her life who show her constant, unconditional love." Their only hope is that the court will see through Jill's lies. Yet they know how convincing she can be.[1]

Partners

Richard met Laurie at a party and was immediately taken by her stunning brown eyes. After dating for eighteen months, Laurie began pushing Richard toward marriage. Her demands for his time and attention grew steadily until she became almost threatening.

Not long after the couple married, Laurie announced that Richard should spend more time with her and less time with his friends. He did to keep her happy. "She kept exploding over things, and it was always all my fault," he says. "I twisted and turned to please her, but it was never enough. I'd move out. She'd go into her 'I'm going to kill myself' song, and I'd come back and try to make it better."

After two years, he told her that perhaps they should separate for a while. He recounts what happened next:

> She started screaming at me about me wanting to divorce her so
> I could sleep around. She said really ugly things about how I

couldn't "make her happy." I was so devastated that I just stood there with my mouth hanging open. Then she picked up a plate and threw it at me. It hit the wall. I picked up my gym bag and left.

I was staying with my parents and Laurie called me there all hours of the day and at work to get me to come home. Finally, she started threatening to kill herself if I didn't come back. I gave in and moved back, sure my love could heal her. Then she became pregnant. When she suffered a miscarriage, she blamed me because she said I didn't love her or the baby. She said that this was how God was punishing me. My self-esteem had dropped so low that I was struggling at work and drinking a lot. I was spending more and more time away from home with my friends so I could avoid her anger and her rages.

I vowed to get the hell out. Laurie said that she felt terrible about what she had done. She was so sweet and seemed so sincere. She promised to change. She said how sorry she was and kept telling me that no one would ever love me as much as she did. We made love that night and conceived our son.

The day my son was born was one of the happiest and most difficult days of my life. When Michael was two weeks old, I came home from work to find the locks changed. Laurie screamed at me through the door that I would never see my son again and that she was going to have my parental rights revoked. I drove to a friend's house and sat on the front steps trying to figure out what to do next.

Laurie contacted a therapist who specialized in family and child sexual abuse. She convinced the therapist that I posed a threat to my son because of my "abhorrent sexual behavior" and the therapist wrote a letter to her attorney suggesting that I be placed on restricted, supervised visitations.

Early one morning, Laurie dropped Michael off at the sitter and said she had to go to work. She never showed up. She began calling everyone she knew and telling them that she was killing herself. After a six-hour search, paramedics found her in a hotel room trying to overdose. She survived and was put into psychiatric care. Her diagnosis was borderline personality disorder.

My attorney filed for immediate, temporary custody of Michael. It took two and a half years and a lot of money, but I finally won full custody. Laurie is now on supervised visits with our son. She has been on medication and in and out of therapy for the past five years. I wish her the best, because that's what's best for my son.[2]

Children

Kellie wrote (but never sent) this letter to her borderline mother, Ruth.

For most of my life I have been afraid of you. It is almost like I grew up with two mothers: the Good Mother and the Bad Mother. The Good Mother is very supportive and nurturing. She encourages me to get better at chess, stands up for me, worries about my future, and tells me she loves me.

But when the Bad Mother appears, everything the Nice Mother does gets wiped away. The Bad Mother's anger is out of control, 'cause she can only feel better once she has destroyed. I'm thirteen or so and the Bad Mother doesn't like the way I eat. She thinks it's impolite. She tells me, "You'll never have any friends if you eat like that."

I'm a teenager and once a week I am supposed to take out the trash and clean my room. Sometimes I don't and it's okay. Then sometimes the Bad Mother comes out and screams and yells and rages because the trash overflowed and egg yolk hardened on the floor. She tells me what a jerk I am and says I can't watch TV for a week. "You're ruining the family," she screams at me.

When I grow up, I try desperately to find someone who will love me. I keep on re-creating my relationship with my mother by choosing men who ultimately reject me. When my husband gets irritated at me and doesn't want to talk, or if he says no when

I initiate sex, I am convinced he no longer loves me and we argue. When I return to reality, I don't understand what made me doubt his love. But I keep testing him 'cause I just can't stop.

Siblings

Perry Hoffman, PhD, who is cofounder of the Family Connections program of the National Education Alliance for Borderline Personality Disorder, says that parents and siblings tell her that having a borderline sibling can be devastating.

> The parents of an eighteen-year-old borderline daughter just told me that their other daughter, who is fifteen years old, has been so traumatized by her older sister's nonstop verbal barrage they are seeking psychiatric treatment for her.
>
> Some siblings take on an enormous amount of responsibility and end up being the caretakers of their borderline sibling. They make life decisions based on the fact that they have a relative with BPD. For example, I've heard some siblings say that they will never have children of their own because the disorder may be passed on, and they don't want a child of theirs to suffer the way their borderline sibling has suffered.
>
> Siblings also worry about the impact the borderline sibling may have on their marital relationship. They're unsure of how to explain that the entire family is organized around the ill child's behavior.[3]

Specific issues siblings face include

- losing out on a great deal of their parents' time and attention.
- feeling guilty and wondering if they did something to cause their sibling to be ill.
- fear of bringing their friends home.
- fearing for their own safety and the safety of their parents.
- feeling enormous pressure to be good to make up to Mom and Dad for the problems caused by the borderline sibling.
- problems with self-esteem. "I didn't have much self-esteem until I went away to college and got away from her," Mary says

about her sister. "At college I got some positive attention, and I really used that to build a sense of self-esteem."

- dreading family gatherings and holidays because their sibling's behavior is usually disruptive, dampening the celebratory mood.
- being influenced by the friends, sometimes from a rough crowd, of the borderline child.

Other Relationships

Stepparents have tremendous problems dealing with family members and ex-spouses with BPD. This is especially true with women in second marriages when their husbands have children from a previous marriage and an ex-wife with BPD. These women are the main support for their husbands, who are usually embroiled in terrible conflicts with their ex-wives about their children. They see the suffering of their husbands and stepchildren and are drawn into the morass. Many become a target of a vengeful ex-wife.

Friends and extended family members who support the immediate family member of the BP often end up on the roller coaster, too, if only because they're holding the family member's hand. These relationships often become strained because of disagreements about how to handle the chaos that BPs can ignite.

BPD in Society

Borderline personality disorder is a complex mental illness that has far-reaching effects. It's common for people with BPD to suffer from depression, substance abuse, eating disorders, and other serious co-occurring mental health conditions. The disorder can underlie domestic abuse, high-conflict divorce, lost work productivity, sex addiction, gambling, self-harm, criminal behavior, and more. In this way, it's more than a ripple in a pond; it is a tsunami, an undersea earthquake that sends ninety-foot waves miles past the shore and destroys much of what's in its path.

Despite its far-reaching and damaging effects, BPD is largely unknown and frequently ignored—especially compared to more publicized yet less common conditions such as anorexia and bipolar disorder. Because of its complex, multifaceted nature, BPD is likely the most misunderstood and stigmatized mental illness listed in the *Diagnostic and Statistical Manual of Mental Disorders* (more about that later). The vast majority of clinicians haven't been trained to treat people with BPD, resulting in misdiagnosis and improper treatment. It's common for clinicians to miss the diagnosis in higher-functioning patients and drop lower-functioning patients because the clinicians haven't been able to set proper limits.

But over the last decade, a lot of progress has been made. The widespread belief that BPD is always caused by childhood abuse is being challenged by sophisticated brain scans of BPD patients that reveal that the brains of people with borderline personality disorder function markedly different from those without the disorder.

This research has been key to putting BPD on par with other brain disorders, helping to bring about a wealth of new resources, including nonprofit organizations dedicated to helping patients and families, providing education, and bringing in research dollars. It's also been a compelling reason why other public and private mental health organizations have begun making BPD treatment part of their mission. Public attention has blossomed with more than a dozen new books on BPD, features in the *New York Times* and *O, The Oprah Magazine,* and even characters with BPD on television and in the movies.

Key Principles

Keep these principles in mind as you read this book. These thoughts need to become a permanent part of your mind-set when dealing with someone with BPD.

To Help Your Family Member, You Must Help Yourself First

Your intuition may tell you that it should be the other way around—that the health of your relationship is dependent on your family member's willingness to get help, and your job is to ignore your own needs and concentrate on fixing the other person. Wrong.

People spend years trying to please their borderline family member by twisting themselves into a pretzel to avoid conflict. Even if it works, the price is high. Family members suffer from depression, isolation, help-lessness, low self-esteem, sleep deprivation, and even physical illnesses (especially adult children of people with BPD). Predictably, the relation-ship begins to degrade, which is exactly what family members are trying to avoid.

This means that, paradoxically, the long-term health of your relation-ship partly depends upon your willingness to look after your own needs, such as taking time away, setting limits with love, and having a hearty life of your own separate from your borderline family member.

This curious paradox is many family members' undoing. They may hear it but not believe it; they may have lost the ability to take care of themselves (or never had it to begin with); or they may be unwilling to accept that giving, giving, and giving some more is just not helping the situation. Of course, that doesn't have to happen to *you*.

BPD Thoughts, Feelings, and Behaviors Are Not Different, Just Exaggerated

We all have traits associated with borderline personality disorder. At times, we all let our feelings overcome logic, blow things out of propor-tion, and act impulsively in ways we later regret. If we didn't, we wouldn't be human.

Two key differences between what is "normal" and what veers into per-sonality disorder territory are *extremity* and *frequency*. When these traits, thoughts, feelings, and behaviors become so intense and so frequent they greatly interfere with jobs, relationships, and other aspects of daily life, one or more personality disorders may be present.

You Can Improve Your Life Even If Your Family Member Doesn't Change

Right now, you probably feel trapped, confused, and powerless. But it doesn't have to be this way—at least to the extent it is right now. It may seem hard to imagine, but by the time you're finished with this book, you'll have learned tools and techniques that will enable you to feel better and more in control of your life regardless of what your loved one does or doesn't do. You control your own destiny much more than you think you do, though it takes learning, planning, and practicing.

It Takes Only One Person to Fundamentally Change a Relationship

It takes two to have a relationship. But each person is in charge of 50 percent. Right now, you may think that your family member has power over you and can "make" you do and feel things you don't want to do and feel. This is false. When you take more control of your own reactions and make decisions true to yourself, the dynamic of your relationship will change.

Borderline Personality Disorder by the Numbers

Some of these statistics, provided by the National Education Alliance for Borderline Personality Disorder, were derived through research of borderline individuals within the mental health system or other institutions.[4] It does not include the hundreds of thousands (probably millions) who do not seek treatment and are a large focus of this book.

Prevalence in Adults

- Officially, four million American individuals have BPD (2 percent of the general public). Cutting-edge research is showing that this number is much higher.
- BPD is more common than schizophrenia.
- BPD is twice as common as the eating disorder anorexia.[5]
- Twenty percent of people with psychiatric hospital admissions have BPD (more than for major depression).

Suicide and Self-Injury

- Ten percent of adults with BPD commit suicide.
- A person with BPD has a suicide rate 400 times greater than the general public.

- Thirty-three percent of youth who commit suicide have features of BPD.

Treatment Challenges

- No FDA-approved medication exists for BPD (although many medications are used to treat the symptoms).
- BPD can co-occur with other illnesses. Most people with BPD also have depression.
- An overwhelming number of clinicians do not have the training or experience to effectively treat those with the disorder. Research-based therapies for BPD are not widely available and are only appropriate for a sub-section of those with the disorder. Eighty percent of psychiatric nurses believe that people with BPD receive inadequate care.[6]
- A thirty-year-old woman with BPD typically has the medical profile of a woman in her sixties.

Economic Impact

- Up to 40 percent of high users of mental health services have BPD.
- More than 50 percent of individuals with BPD are severely impaired in employability, with a resulting burden on Supplemental Security Income (SSI), Social Security Disability Insurance (SSDI), and Medicaid and Medicare.
- Twelve percent of men and 28 percent of women in prison have BPD.

Chapter 2

Understanding Borderline Personality Disorder

Do I contradict myself?
Very well then I contradict myself,
(I am large, I contain multitudes.)
▪ Walt Whitman, "Song of Myself" ▪

We're going to cover a lot of ground in this chapter. First, we'll look at the nine traits that make up the formal definition of BPD. Then, we'll rearrange these traits to give you a better idea of how and why people with BPD act the way they do. Next comes:

- Other common characteristics of people with BPD
- The three subtypes of BPD
- BPD in children and adolescents, men, and older adults
- Other mental health problems that often go along with BPD

But first, following are answers to a few commonly asked questions:

1. Does "borderline" mean that people with BPD are on the border of something?

   The short answer is "no." The long answer: A century ago, psychiatrists observed that some patients who generally functioned well got much worse when they talked while lying down on the couch. At the time, psychiatrists believed that all patients were either neurotic (think Woody Allen) or psychotic (a man who thinks he's Jesus). Borderline personality disorder, they theorized, existed right in the middle, or on the "border."

Today, the mental health profession categorizes mental illnesses differently than it did a century ago, and there is no "middle" or "border." But like many names that no longer hearken back to their original meaning, the name "borderline" remains. It may change one day, but don't expect any action for many years to come.

2. What is a "personality disorder"?

A personality disorder is a pattern of inner experience and behavior that differs markedly from the expectations of the individual's culture. It involves the way an individual responds to people and leads to significant distress. The traits must
  - be extreme, significantly affecting a person's life
  - be enduring, a long-term pattern (years) of looking at the world and relating to other people
  - show themselves in a wide range of contexts[1]

3. Is BPD considered an "official" illness?

Yes. The American Psychiatric Association added borderline personality disorder to its diagnostic bible, the *Diagnostic and Statistical Manual of Mental Disorders* (DSM), in 1980, after obtaining input from experienced clinicians and professional organizations. The DSM provides descriptions of thinking, feeling, or behaving that fit the various diagnostic categories. Psychiatrists and other mental health professionals then use these DSM categories to diagnose mental disorders.

The Nine Traits for Borderline Disorder

Following is a very simplified interpretation of the nine criteria the DSM-IV-TR uses to describe borderline personality disorder. According to the

DSM-IV-TR, an individual only needs to meet five of the nine criteria to qualify for a borderline diagnosis.

1. strong reactions to fear of abandonment, whether real or imagined
2. a history of troubled relationships with extremes in behavior and attitude
3. poor sense of self
4. impulsive and self-destructive behavior by at least two means (for example, substance abuse, self-mutilation, eating disorder)
5. repeated suicidal tendencies
6. intense and frequent moodiness and irritability
7. an ongoing feeling of emptiness
8. intense and uncontrollable anger
9. persistent feelings of detachment

Criterion 1: Fear of Abandonment

Everyone fears abandonment to some extent. But the borderline brand of fear is more pronounced. Also, while most people generally respond only to real threats, people with BPD react to real or *imagined* threats. And they have a good imagination.

Just as those with hypochondria consider a slight cough a harbinger of the black plague, people with BPD are hypersensitive to anything that smacks of abandonment. Once triggered, the over-the-top expression of fear cannot be easily assuaged. That's because it originates from within, not from without.

Susan Anderson, author of *The Journey from Abandonment to Healing*, says:

Abandonment is about loss of love itself, that crucial loss of connectedness. . . . Sometimes it is lingering grief caused by old losses. Sometimes it is fear. Sometimes it can be an invisible barrier holding us back from forming relationships and reaching our true potential.[2]

Abandonment doesn't have to be physical, like walking out the door or slamming down the phone. It can be emotional distance or too much space in your "togetherness," as author Kahlil Gibran would say.

Most of us are healthy enough to handle it when important people in our life don't agree with us about important things, or when they do things differently than we would. With people who have BPD, however, differences of opinions—even about something small—have an impact not unlike how it must feel when devout parents learn their child has decided to switch faiths. Not only is it a sort of abandonment; it can also be interpreted as a put-down of one's most cherished beliefs.

Recovered BP A. J. Mahari explains:

> Emotional distance can be caused by nearly anything. To be truly intimate without it being threatened, one has to be able to tolerate the distance (as well as the closeness). People with BPD are different in that they experience this distance as rejection. That causes them to desperately defend themselves against the very one they love and want to be close to. This distances the borderline's partner and leaves the borderline feeling abandoned once again.[3]

A woman with BPD reflects:
During an argument, my boyfriend was trying to get away in his car. I stood behind him, trying to prevent him from leaving. When he maneuvered out of the way, I banged my fists on the back of the car. I ran to the door and tried to force it open, as he reached over and locked it. After he started down the street, I ran as fast as I could to catch up with him, begging him to stop.

Criterion 2: Unstable Relationships Characterized by Alternating between Extremes of Idealization and Devaluation

Because unstable relationships are at the core of this book, let's take a look at the crucial second half of this trait: the BP's pattern of idealizing and devaluing people. This thought process, called *splitting*, is insidious, affecting the way BPs see the world, themselves, and their closest relationships. As such, it lurks behind most of the troubles in a relationship.

Most people can integrate their positive and negative feelings about a person and come to a place in the middle. BPs, however, cannot reconcile the two. They elevate others to an impossible standard and then knock them down when they inevitably disappoint. They see others as either their champions or as out to get them—and then can switch their opinion in a moment, not recalling that they ever felt differently.

Rachel Reiland, who wrote about her recovery from BPD in *Get Me Out of Here,* split her psychiatrist, Dr. Padget. When he empathized with her, she fantasized about actually being his daughter. When he seemed too distant from her, that sense of belonging was destroyed. Once she threatened to punish him by making false allegations about sex. When Dr. Padget switched back, all was forgiven—until the next time.

A man with BPD says:
When you are deep in the disorder, splitting is a complete and fundamental reality shift—you can remember that you felt the opposite way, but you can't for the life of you understand why. It's like someone who gets drunk, does something stupid, and wakes up the next morning saying, "What on earth was I thinking?"

Criteria 3 and 7: Unstable Self-Image and Feelings of Emptiness

In adolescence, we are still uncertain about our core values and beliefs. As we mature, most of us develop a sense of a stable, authentic self. But BPs never do. Playing a role—such as husband or mother—fills some of the emptiness. But when these roles are threatened—for example, a child becomes more independent, a spouse threatens divorce—the shell starts to crumble. This is why some BPs take extreme measures to keep the status quo: for example, accusing a partner of child abuse to prevent losing custody.

People with BPD do have one core belief about themselves: They are unworthy. A borderline woman says, "My life is a nonstop struggle to be 'good enough.' I always think no one wants me around, no one cares about me, and my only hope of having people like me is to be perfect. When someone likes me, I wonder what they see in me that I don't see in myself. When they go do things with their other friends, it hurts like hell, and I have to pretend that I don't care. And that happens all the time."

Criterion 4: Impulsivity

In an interview, Robert O. Friedel, MD, author of *Borderline Personality Disorder Demystified,* explains,

> People with BPD feel intensely in response to little things. Then *boom,* their emotions take over and the part of the brain that controls impulse is unable to moderate the intensity of their emotions. Anxiety and depression feed into the impulsivity. People with a reasonable amount of anxiety and good impulse control can say, "I'm going to make it; I'm going to be okay." But the person with BPD doesn't have that restraint.[4]

Impulsivity is also associated with the rest of the DSM traits for BPD. When BPs are distressed, they can't sit with it or think through the problem—especially adolescents. Instead, it becomes an immediate crisis calling for a dramatic 911 response, like taking mind-altering drugs or running away from home to meet someone you met on the Internet.

Criterion 5: Self-Harm and Suicidality

Michelle, a teenager, hates the way she looks. She hits her leg until it turns blue. Maggie pours boiling water on her arms to distract herself from her agony. Rod scratches his head until it bleeds and forms a scab.

Self-harm can occur on a spectrum, from simple picking at the skin to making razor cuts so deep they require stitches. Other forms of self-injury are burning, branding, picking at scars, and piercing. Self-mutilation becomes a compulsion because it works. Tension builds up and is relieved by giving in to the urge.

Self-injury is not an attempt to die. People engage in it to distract themselves from emotional pain, punish themselves, bring on numbness, relieve stress, maintain control, express anger, and communicate their pain to others. Cutting also seems to release endorphins, chemicals in the brain that promote a sense of well-being.

According to Blaise Aguirre, MD, medical director of the Adolescent Dialectical Behavioral Therapy Center at McLean Hospital, Belmont, Massachusetts, adolescents who cut generally tend to describe themselves as being more sensitive than other kids their age, feeling things quicker than other people, and taking longer to get back down to their normal state than others. They may make excuses when their parents see injuries ("the dog bit me"). These signs, he says, may indicate self-harm activity:

- consistently wearing long-sleeve shirts
- spending too much time in the shower
- isolating themselves after a fight or other stressful event
- increasing substance abuse
- hoarding sharp implements such as razor blades, tacks, and knives, as well as antiseptic solutions, bandages, and other first-aid paraphernalia[5]

Suicide is another matter. For some, the concept of death serves as an escape fantasy. Like most people who make suicide attempts, they don't really want to die. They're just desperate to end their pain.

A woman with BP says:
My incredible sense of hopelessness made me feel like annihilating myself. I would continually up the ante. If I wasn't satisfied with how people reacted to me because I overdosed on 200 pills, then the next time I would try 400 pills. I had an overwhelming and irrational need to somehow punish myself, destroy myself. It was my one purpose in life. The sense of emptiness and loneliness was very hard to tolerate.[6]

Criterion 6: Affective Instability (Unstable Emotions)

Affective instability has three components:

- Intense feelings that are out of proportion to the triggering event.
- These intense emotions go up and down much more quickly than those of a nondisordered person.
- Once these intense emotions are triggered, it takes the BP a long time to return to a normal emotional level.

A woman with BPD reflects:

I'll get irritated if I have to stop by the grocery store on the way home because it's always crowded. I get home, and my daughter asks me if I'm in a bad mood. That irritates me more, so I snap at her. She snaps back. I seethe for the next sixty minutes until my TV program comes on. Five minutes later I am in a good mood, and I can't understand why she's so crabby. Doesn't she know the argument's over?

Criterion 8: Intense Rage

A BP rage is much more terrifying, shocking, and inexplicable than a normal rage. There is a change in the air, something palpable, before it erupts. Following is how one non-BP eloquently explains his partner's rages.

When in a rage, it seemed like she was channeling an evil spirit. Her eyes had no life in them: just a blankness. She didn't see who I was or how she was hurting me. There was no way to negotiate, no way to reason or argue. She did not understand rational arguments.

Her voice would become more rapid, accusatory, demeaning, patronizing, irrational, and paranoid. Her tone was very fast—rat-a-tat-tat—like she was offensively firing at me. She would pace and become very menacing, growing closer and closer as I became more and more afraid.

She was no longer someone I knew, though I tried with all my power to talk her out of the fog. But it never worked. The rage seemed to need to run its course until she felt relief, no matter how much it killed me.

A contributing factor of the intensity of the BP's anger is that words aren't enough to make others understand the depth of her emotions. Here's an analogy: Imagine visiting a country where you don't speak the language. Suddenly your chest hurts, and you're having trouble breathing. You spot a police officer and urgently cry out, "I'm having a heart attack! I need an ambulance now!"

Her response is a quizzical look and "Quijibo oompa loompa snoo-snoo?" You'd panic. Frustrated and frantic, you'd raise your voice and gesture more emphatically. "I could be dying!"

In essence, sometimes BPs and non-BPs speak in different languages. The BP's frenzied wrath becomes a way to try to get across her immediate needs—kind of a cry for help. Another explanation: dependency breeds anger. People with BPD feel that others have the power to define who they are. What's even harder for them is that other people can give or withdraw love at any moment. That's why small actions of others can make them feel good or out of control.

Criterion 9: Dissociation

People who dissociate feel detached, as if they were observing their body from the outside. Familiar objects look strange. Have you ever found your-self unaware that you were reading the same paragraph over and over, or while you were driving, suddenly realizing that you missed the right turn a mile back? That's dissociation. Focusing on the physical world (such as "my glass of iced tea is right here, in a blue glass with three ice cubes") helps people stop dissociating.

Alice, a BP, explains:

Much of a borderline's time is spent in oblivion, when the mind is so chaotic that the real world is very far away. There are periods of time I can't remember at all, and I spend so much time in a blanked-out state. Even at work, I just go through the motions. I'm not really there.

An Integrated Approach to Explaining BPD

The DSM definition was developed to assist clinicians in making a clinical diagnosis. To better grasp the disorder and see it in action, we need a more integrated approach. We can do this by reorganizing the traits into three groups: traits that control *thinking,* traits that control *feeling,* and traits that control *acting.* These normally happen in sequence, one following the other like falling dominoes (although our emotions impact our perceptions).

Let's say you see a friend walking across the street. You yell "hi" and wave, but he ignores you. You feel hurt and a bit miffed, so you don't invite him to your annual Fourth of July picnic. Later, you discover he's hard of hearing. You *thought* he ignored you, you *felt* angry and miffed, and your *action* was to not invite him to your party.

BPD Traits Organized by Thoughts, Feelings, and Actions	
	DSM Traits
THINKING: Impaired perception and reasoning	• Splitting (extremes of idealization and devaluation) • Brief moments of stress-related paranoia or severe dissociative symptoms (being very "out of it")
FEELING: Poorly regulated, highly changeable emotions	• Intense, unstable moods and strong reactions to shifts in the environment. Irritability or anxiety, usually lasting for a few hours or days. Feelings of acute hopelessness, despair, and unhappiness • Frantic efforts to avoid real or imagined abandonment • A feeling of emptiness and a lack of identity, which complicate moods and emotions
ACTING: Impulsive behaviors	• Impulsiveness in at least two areas that are potentially self-damaging (e.g., spending, sex, substance abuse, reckless driving, or binge eating) • Inappropriate, intense anger or difficulty controlling anger (e.g., frequent displays of temper, constant anger, or recurrent physical fights) • "Pain management" behaviors such as overspending, aggression toward others, suicide, self-harm, substance abuse, and eating disorders

This 1-2-3 punch results in patterns of unstable and intense interpersonal relationships characterized by splitting.

Impaired Thinking

Splitting, of course, is the key cognitive flaw. Other cognitive distortions come in second. What myopia (nearsightedness) is to eyesight, cognitive distortions are to thinking. They shape our reality and dictate how we respond to people and situations. They are automatic, habit-forming, and invisible. It's important to note that we all grapple with cognitive distortions. But as the chart on page 34 shows, in BPs, they can be much more extreme (be sure to note the distortion "feelings equal facts" because it will appear later in the book).

Cognitive Distortion	Cognitive Distortions in BPs
Feelings equal facts: Emotions color interpretations of people and situations	The BP makes jaw-dropping interpretations, assumptions, and inferences that may bear little resemblance to reality.
Jumping to conclusions: Negative interpretation without supporting facts	The BP jumps to conclusions even when past experiences with the person/situation have been positive. The BP dismisses contrary supporting facts.
Mind reading: Assuming others think badly of you	The BP assumes others think she's scum on the garbage scow of the world.
Catastrophizing: Thinking the worst-case scenario will occur and nothing can be done to help the situation	The BP's catastrophizing can lead to poor, rash decisions or dangerous actions, such as self-harm or suicide attempts. Small molehills become Mt. Everest.
Blame: Holding others totally accountable for negative situations	The BP not only dismisses contrary supporting facts but also thrashes, mutilates, and pummels them into submission. The BP will not be held accountable for anything.
Discounting the positive	In a way similar to splitting, some BPs discount anything good in themselves and in others.
Mental filter: Dwelling on criticism of the self while repelling compliments	For the BP, the soaking in is deeper—to the bone instead of the pores. Compliments are repelled faster and further away.

Impaired Feelings

The DSM traits having to do with feelings—emotions—are intense anger; unstable, irritable moods; fear of abandonment; and an overwhelming, constant sense of emptiness.

People with BPD feel the same emotions that we all do. The difference is the intensity of their emotions. On a scale of 1 (extreme negative feelings) to 10 (extreme positive feelings), the scale runs from an impossible 0 to 11.

Shame, a hallmark of BPD, is an inner sense of being completely diminished or insufficient as a person. A shame-based person feels fundamentally inadequate, defective, and unworthy—not for anything they do, but just for existing.

Impaired Behavior

The DSM traits having to do with actions are impulsivity in areas that are potentially self-damaging; recurrent suicidal or self-harming behavior; and difficulty controlling anger.

Add to this putting others in no-win situations, criticism, blame, creating chaos, and all the other behaviors that make you feel as though you're walking on eggshells, and you have the king of BPD traits: DSM-IV-TR number 2, "A pattern of unstable and intense interpersonal relationships characterized by alternating between extremes of idealization and devaluation."

Other BPD Traits

Some other BPD traits are as follows:

Not Telling the Truth

While no one has done formal research on people with BPD and lying, anecdotally, family members say it is a major concern—especially for parents. One non-BP blogger found that 20 percent of the searches on the site for family members had to do with lying.

People with BPD may tell lies consciously (as we all do, sometimes), unconsciously, or somewhere in between. Some statements start out as deliberate lies; over time, they're recollected as the truth. Some statements may not be lies as much as they are blowing the truth out of proportion. They seem to happen more when the BP is under stress. Lying might serve to

- deflect shame when something might make them look bad, thereby increasing their shame. Angelyn Miller says, "People who feel unworthy believe they have to say all the right things, true or untrue, so they can appear better or different than they really are. People with high self-esteem don't feel like they have to create a cover. If they make a mistake, their own sense of worthiness allows them to admit it because they know everyone makes mistakes."[7]
- quell the fear that if non-BPs knew the truth, they would reject the BP.
- create drama and gain attention.
- mask real feelings and put up an impressive facade.
- help make sense of why things happen to them in their mixed-up reality.

> A husband says:
> After denying it for months, she finally admitted she had gotten us seriously in debt. When I asked her follow-up questions, I was met with more lies. Once she realized I had the actual bills, they turned into partial lies. Then she told me she promised to never lie again. When she did lie again, I totally lost my trust in her.

Need for Control

People with BPD try to seize control of situations and other people to make their own chaotic world more predictable and manageable. Things that threaten the BP's sense of control—as irrational as that sense of control may be—will be met with resistance. If you refuse to go along with your family member's wishes, she may accuse you of wresting control from *her*. And she believes it. This dynamic ensues quite frequently when non-BPs try to set limits or to respond to provocation, even in a healthy way.

Non-BPs everywhere experience these controlling tactics as manipulation. Dictionaries define *manipulation* as the intent to influence others by indirect, insidious, or devious means. The key word here is *intent*, which implies that the "manipulator" has thought through what he wants ahead of time and devised a clever scheme to get it.

But BPs don't think that far ahead. They're much too impulsive to plan—they need what they need *right now.* They are not in stealth mode, either: they come right out and try their best to get what they need, while a true manipulator would work behind the scenes.

Some BPs, after the immediate crisis is over, don't realize the effects of their behavior on others. In a long "why-I-broke-up-with-you" letter to her BP ex-girlfriend, Terry, Chris writes:

> You think you have the right to be hostile to other people and treat them badly. But if they respond in anything but a kind manner, become upset or get angry back, you see it as further proof that you shouldn't have been nice to them in the first place. You did this repeatedly to me—suddenly snapping at me for unclear or unjustified reasons, and then completely refusing to take any responsibility when I became upset.[8]

Others look back and are ashamed of their actions. Their emotions are too overpowering, though, because the next time a similar situation comes up, they feel compelled to act that way again. That furthers a cycle of self-loathing.

Types of BPs: Lower-Functioning Conventional, Higher-Functioning Invisible, and Combination

BPs come in two overlapping categories, and which type you're dealing with determines which struggles you will likely face. To be flip about it, individuals in the first category seek therapy and individuals in the second category provoke *others* to seek therapy. (See the chart on page 40.)

Lower-Functioning Conventional BPs

These are the classic borderline patients who result in the statistics you read about in chapter 1. Here are some characteristics of lower-functioning conventional BPs:

1. They cope with pain mostly through self-destructive behaviors such as self-injury and suicidality. The term for this is *acting in.*

2. They acknowledge they have problems and seek help from the mental health system, often desperately. Some are hospitalized for their own safety.

3. They have a difficult time with daily functioning and may even be on government disability. This is called *low functioning.*

4. If they have overlapping, or co-occurring, disorders, such as an eating disorder or substance abuse, the disorder is severe enough to require professional treatment.

5. Family members' greatest challenges include finding appropriate treatment, handling crises (especially suicide attempts), feelings of guilt, and the financial burden of treatment. Parents fear their child won't be able to live independently.

Because lower-functioning conventional BPs seek mental health services, unlike the higher-functioning invisible BPs we'll talk about next, they are subjects of research studies about BPD, including those about treatment.

Higher-Functioning Invisible BPs

Unlike lower-functioning conventional BPs, higher-functioning invisible BPs have the following characteristics:

1. They strongly disavow having *any* problems, even tiny ones. Relationship difficulties, they say, are everyone else's fault. If family members suggest they may have BPD, they almost always accuse the other person of having it instead.

2. They refuse to seek help unless someone threatens to end the relationship. If they do go to counseling, they usually don't intend to work on their own issues. In couples therapy, their goal is often to convince the therapist that they are being victimized.

3. They cope with their pain by raging outward, blaming and accusing family members for real or imagined problems.

4. They hide their low self-esteem behind a brash, confident pose that masks their inner turmoil. They usually function quite well at work and only display aggressive behavior toward those close to them. Family members say these people bring to mind Dr. Jekyll and Mr. Hyde.

5. If they also have other mental disorders, they're ones that also allow for high functioning, such as narcissistic personality disorder (NPD).

6. Family members' greatest challenges include coping with verbal, emotional, and sometimes physical abuse; trying to convince the BP to get treatment; worrying about the effects of BPD behaviors on their other children; quietly losing their confidence and self-esteem; and trying—and failing—to set limits. By far, the majority of Welcome to Oz (WTO) members have a borderline partner.

Recovered BP A. J. Mahari explains how higher-functioning invisible BPs live in denial:

A borderline's frantic search for a way to meet their needs and avoid pain creates layers and layers of defense mechanisms— [which leads to] an unstable identity. That's why borderlines are not aware they need help. To them, life is just as it has always been. The hurts, the problems, the torments are everyone else's fault and/or responsibility. Many borderlines do not have any understanding or self-awareness from which to "know" that they do indeed need help.[9]

Two Overlapping Categories of Individuals with Borderline Personality Disorder

	Mostly Lower-Functioning Conventional BPs	Mostly Higher-Functioning Invisible BPs
Coping Techniques	*Acting in:* Mostly self-destructive acts such as self-harm.	*Acting out:* Uncontrolled and impulsive rages, criticism, and blame. These may result less from a lack of interpersonal skills than from an unconscious projection of their own pain onto others.
Functioning	*Low functioning:* BPD and associated conditions make it difficult to live independently, hold a job, manage finances, and so on. Families often step in to help.	*High functioning:* The BP appears normal, even charismatic, but exhibits BPD traits behind closed doors. Has a career and may be successful.
Willingness to Obtain Help	Self-harm and suicidal tendencies often bring these BPs into the mental health system (both as inpatients and outpatients). High interest in therapy.	A state of denial much like an untreated alcoholic. The BP disavows responsibility for relationship difficulties, refuses treatment; when confronted, he or she accuses others of having BPD. May see a therapist if threatened, but rarely takes it seriously or stays long.
Co-occurring (Concurrent) Mental Health Issues	Mental conditions such as bipolar and eating disorders require medical intervention and contribute to low functioning.	Concurrent illness most commonly a substance use disorder or another personality disorder, especially narcissistic personality disorder.
Impact on Family Members	The major family focus is on practical issues such as finding treatment, preventing/reducing BP's self-destructive behavior, and providing practical and emotional support. Parents feel extreme guilt and are emotionally overwhelmed.	Without the diagnosis of an obvious illness for the BP, family members blame themselves and try to get their emotional needs met. They make fruitless efforts to persuade their BP to get professional help. Major issues include high-conflict divorce and custody cases.

Recovering BP Alice says:

BPs can perform flawlessly, as if on stage, because they put themselves in different roles for different situations. In public, [a higher-functioning invisible BP] becomes a different person; a person who is in control and would never let borderline behaviors show because at that time, that other part of her personality doesn't exist. The BP really believes she's in control, so she acts in accordance with that personality.

The performance, however, doesn't always fool everyone forever. Something triggers the other personality, and if that trigger is strong enough, it will take precedence and the BP's sense of control will be lost.

BPs with Overlapping Characteristics

Many BPs possess characteristics of both lower-functioning conventional BPs and higher-functioning invisible BPs. Author Rachel Reiland is typical of a BP with overlapping characteristics. When she insinuated she was going to shoot herself, her psychiatrist admitted her to a psychiatric hospital. Yet she held a job as a full-time mother and was active in church. Although she acted out toward her husband and psychiatrist, she was able to appear nondisordered toward most people outside her family.

BPD in Children and Adolescents

Dr. Blaise Aguirre, medical director of the Adolescent Dialectical Behavioral Therapy Center at McLean Hospital, Belmont, Massachusetts, says that the DSM allows for a BPD diagnosis in childhood if the patient has had the symptoms for more than a year. He has seen children as young as thirteen meet criteria for the diagnosis. Parents often identify BPD traits beginning at puberty.

BPD symptoms in adolescents aren't that different from those of adults with the disorder: self-injury (including piercing), drug abuse, promiscuity, rages (especially when the child doesn't get his way), extreme overidealization and devaluation of friends and family, and ongoing thoughts of suicide or suicide attempts.

Today, leading clinicians say that the best early intervention is predictable and consistent caregiving. Caregivers need to be aware of how the environment may be invalidating. For example, there might be a mismatch between how the caregiver sees the world and how the child sees the world. The most important thing is to close this gap—not by blaming the parents or the child, but by recognizing the problem and working with a family therapist who is familiar with BPD dynamics. This message desperately needs to get out to the rank-and-file therapists who are out of date with current research.

BPD Diagnosis in Men

The DSM says that the percentage of men with BPD is 25 percent, or one out of every four people with BPD. The percentage may be higher—half of the non-BPs on the WTO groups for partners are women. (Frequently, their male partner has BPD with co-occurring narcissistic personality disorder.) Yet we know very little about how BPD expresses itself in men or if treatment programs designed for women are as effective for men. Why do we know so little about borderline men? Several reasons:

Men Seek Professional Help Less Often

Research has shown again and again that men won't even seek treatment for less complex but equally serious mental health problems such as depression, let alone a stigmatized disorder like BPD. Many men see it as "unmanly" to acknowledge feelings, especially the vulnerability and abandonment fears associated with BPD.

Clinician Bias

One study found that when fifty-two professionals from a mental health agency in California assessed patient vignettes, they were unable to accurately diagnose the presence of BPD in males—even though the symptoms were identical to those in vignettes of females.[10]

These results help explain the way anger is interpreted differently depending upon whether it comes from a man or a woman. "For the most part, when women are angry they are classified as irrational, frenzied, or too emotional," says therapist Andrea Brandt. "On the other hand, men's anger is sometimes recognized as strength and aggressiveness."[11]

Cultural Influences

Men are socialized not to expose their fear of abandonment or other emotional vulnerabilities, which are hallmarks of BPD. They are supposed to be macho and fearless, sexual studs seeking the maximum number of sexual conquests with a minimum of commitment. And if he does get "roped" into marriage, he's the one who's supposed to be on top, for fear of being called "whipped."

Most of all, if he's not as confident as he "should" be, or if he's feeling alone, depressed, or scared, by the Male Code he is not supposed to let these feelings show. He is, however, permitted anger. In some circumstances, beating someone up is even the righteous thing to do.

Borderline Men and Domestic Violence

Imagine you're a man whose greatest fear in the world is being abandoned, second only to the terror of looking into the mirror and seeing an empty, worthless self looking back. Imagine how hard it would be to share these emotions with the people you fear will reject you, let alone to admit you need professional help.

Those feelings have to go somewhere. Some men use the same outlets as borderline women do, such as making suicide threats. A great many of them (perhaps even more than women) anesthetize themselves with alcohol and drugs such as cocaine or methamphetamine. A subset, however, channel their feelings into their more socially acceptable cousins, rage and aggression.

Both men and women can express their fear of abandonment as physically aggressive rage toward the "cause" of their distress. However, men's level of violence is often more lethal. A perceived betrayal or a real or imagined act of abandonment may trigger acting-out activities such as kicking down a door, forcing sexual activity, blocking the partner's escape, and threatening the partner with a weapon. Some are involved in controlling and stalking behaviors, such as tapping phones, installing secret cameras, and hiring private detectives.

This aggression often results in a misdiagnosis of antisocial personality disorder (sociopath) or, in adolescents, a conduct disorder. As a result, these men don't get the right treatment. What they *do* get is incarcerated. As a matter of fact, so many males with BPD have been incarcerated that a form of therapy for BPD, dialectical behavior therapy, has been adapted for male offenders in correctional settings.[12]

Sexual Acting Out

Mary Gay, a therapist who treats many men with BPD, finds that borderline men frequently engage in addictive, sexually compulsive behaviors, including regularly hiring prostitutes, having serial affairs, going to strip clubs, obsessively viewing pornography, engaging in voyeurism or exhibitionism, and compulsive masturbation.[13]

One borderline man used high-risk sex as his form of self-harm. He says:

> The out-of-control sex was something I hated myself for, it was obsessive, it felt like an invisible hand grabbing me by the collar and dragging me off to do whatever. I needed to cause enough pain and degradation to myself. The incredible guilt of the risks I was exposing my partner to really destroyed something inside me. But when the inner loneliness was strongest, sex was the only thing that would quiet the fear.

Older People with BPD

Experts differ on whether people with BPD "grow out of BPD" when they get into their fifties and above. The popular thinking is that they do. But that is not the last word. Jim Breiling, PhD, from the National Institute of Mental Health, says that while some studies show that age has a mellowing effect, much more research needs to be done.[14]

Co-occurring Disorders

Most people with BPD have what is known as a co-occurring illness; that is, another brain disorder in addition to BPD. Each complicates the other.

According to the National Alliance on Mental Illness, depression is the most common co-occurring disorder (up to 70 percent; however, other sources believe it's almost universal). Following are substance abuse (35 percent), eating disorders (25 percent), narcissistic personality disorder (25 percent), and bipolar disorder (formerly called manic-depression) (15 percent) and histrionic personality disorder (unknown).[15]

Depression

Depression, which is nearly universal in those with BPD, can make BPD more difficult to treat, especially if it is severe. Symptoms of depression include feelings of overwhelming sadness; fear of abandonment; loss of energy; and intense feelings of guilt, nervousness, helplessness, hopelessness, and worthlessness.

Substance Abuse

Nearly one-third of people categorized as having a substance use disorder (abuse of or dependence on alcohol or other drugs) also have BPD. Conversely, more than half of those with BPD also have a substance use disorder. Their drugs of choice can include everything from alcohol and prescription drugs to illegal drugs such as cocaine and crystal methamphetamine.

Substance abuse and dependence are disorders unto themselves, but they are also part of the DSM-IV-TR definition of BPD (trait 4, impulsivity in at least two areas that are potentially self-damaging). BPs may use alcohol and other drugs to temporarily relieve emotional pain. Many clinicians who specialize in substance use disorders see the primary problem as the substance abuse or dependence and may not be aware that BPD is an underlying factor.

BPs who abuse chemicals have a marked decrease in the effectiveness of both medications and psychotherapy and an increased risk of suicide attempts and other severe psychiatric problems.[16] If borderline patients undergo treatment only for substance dependence and not the underlying BPD, they may be more prone to relapse or may put another unhealthy coping mechanism in its place. In a presentation to Congress, psychiatrist Robert Friedel said that patients should first get treatment for substance dependence before addressing BPD. Otherwise, there is little to no hope of gaining control over BPD.[17]

Eating Disorders

While substance abuse is significantly more common among borderline men than women with the disorder, eating disorders (particularly bulimia) are more prevalent among women.[18]

People with anorexia starve themselves to dangerous levels. Some experts see it as an alternative type of self-harm and another way to capture control. A BP says, "When people said I was so thin that something must be wrong with me, it pushed me to lose even more weight. This was *mine,* something that only a few can accomplish. It was *my* control."

Those with bulimia binge then rid themselves of the food by vomiting, taking enemas, exercising obsessively, or abusing laxatives. The long-term effects can include stomach rupture, tooth loss, and even death.

Narcissistic Personality Disorder

In a popular television cartoon series, a young girl gives her father a lovingly crafted drawing for Father's Day. Dad says "thank you," but his daughter starts complaining when he makes it obvious that he prefers his son's present: a "real" gift from a store. To mollify her, he puts her picture on the refrigerator. But it's too heavy and slips off, quickly becoming a water-soaked glob of paper. As the daughter runs off, crying, the puzzled father asks his wife how it is possible that his daughter can be unhappy when she knows that this is his very special day.

It may be a cartoon, but it's not an exaggeration of the way people with narcissistic personality disorder (NPD) behave. Based on the experience of Welcome to Oz members, especially partners and adult children, it's quite common for higher-functioning invisible BPs to have NPD or NPD traits, especially the men. In fact, roughly 75 percent of the women partners on WTO have husbands or boyfriends with traits of both BPD and NPD.

While BPs depend on close relationships with others to meet their insatiable need for love, narcissists (NPs) don't need real relationships as much as they need a supply of unceasing adulation, special treatment, and confirmation of their superiority. A hallmark of the disorder is that they don't have empathy for other people; that is, they can't put themselves in another person's place. To the person with NPD, other people are objects whose function is to meet their needs.

People with NPD may come off as quite charming and confident, even arrogant. They may overestimate their abilities and inflate their accomplishments while devaluing accomplishments of others. But don't let that fool you. When it comes to their inner experience, both BPs and NPs have much in common.

According to www.mentalhelp.net, underneath the NP's image of grandiosity is an insecure person with very low self-esteem and underlying feelings of emptiness and worthlessness. The arrogant image is a way to protect others from finding out that the NP has weaknesses and imperfections.[19]

"Narcissistic individuals are actually needier than most people," says Beverly Engel in her book *The Jekyll and Hyde Syndrome*.[20] "To admit that a relationship is important to them forces them to face feelings of deficiency. This, in turn, creates intolerable emptiness, jealousy, and rage. If anyone crosses them or challenges them in any way, there will be hell to pay for whoever forces them to face themselves or face reality."[21]

Bipolar Disorder

Because both people with BPD and those with bipolar disorder experience dramatic mood swings, the disorders are often mistaken for one another. The situation gets even more confusing when someone has both disorders.

Bipolar disorder causes dramatic mood swings—from overly "high" and/or irritable to sad and hopeless, and then back again, often with periods of normal mood in between. Severe changes in energy and behavior go along with these changes in mood. The periods of highs and lows are called episodes of mania and depression.[22]

A *cycle* is the period of time it takes for a person to go through one episode of mania and one of depression. The frequency and duration of these cycles vary from person to person, from once every five years to once every three months. People with a subtype of bipolar, *rapid-cycling bipolar,* may cycle more quickly, but much less quickly than people with BPD.

According to Dr. Friedel, director of the BPD program at Virginia Commonwealth University, there are two main differences between BPD and bipolar disorder:

1. People with BPD cycle much more quickly, often several times a day.
2. The moods in people with BPD are more dependent, either positively or negatively, on what's going on in their life at the moment.[23]

Marsha M. Linehan, professor of psychology at the University of Washington, says that while people with bipolar disorder swing between all-encompassing periods of mania and major depression, the mood swings typical in BPD are more specific. She says, "You have fear going up and down, sadness going up and down, anger up and down, disgust up and down, and love up and down."[24]

Histrionic Personality Disorder

Adult children frequently describe their BP mother as having traits of histrionic personality disorder (HPD). These traits include striking self-centeredness or seductiveness, over-the-top emotional displays, and a need for attention that's so excessive it's beyond borderline. Those with HPD may charm people and use their appearance to draw attention to themselves; they're often the life of the party—until they can't get something they want.

Chapter 3

Making Sense of Your Relationship

People leave me. Everyone does. I know it and you know it. Why?
Because the only people I hurt are the people I love. It's as if I'm
driven to give them a reason to leave, even though being
abandoned scares me more than anything.

▪ Mary Ann, a woman with BPD ▪

When non-BPs join the Welcome to Oz Family Community, they immediately discover that their story is not unique. It's not just that their loved ones with BPD act alike—that is to be expected if they all meet basically the same diagnostic criteria. What astounds new members is the similarity of the *dynamics*—the psychological interplay—within the BP/non-BP relationship. For example, phrases heard again and again include

- "I keep telling my BP I don't hate her. I love her. But she refuses to believe me."
- "My borderline husband is one of the smartest people I've ever met. But when it comes to him understanding my feelings, he doesn't have a clue."
- "If I want to spend any time by myself, she thinks I'm rejecting her and starts to cry."
- "My husband works in an emergency room and can keep calm under pressure. But when someone makes him mad, he yells and lashes out at me and says he just can't help it."

- "She keeps saying, 'You never loved me, not really,' and when I assure her that I do, she just shakes her head and refuses to believe me."
- "My borderline mother always turns things around so she's the victim and I'm the nasty, unreasonable person who's hurting her."

This chapter will explain the BP/non-BP relationship: the dysfunctional interaction patterns that keep people walking on eggshells and feeling stuck. Please read this chapter carefully. The terms and concepts discussed here are fundamental to understanding the interpersonal conflicts going on between you and your family member and will appear many times in other chapters.

Most Borderline Behavior Isn't Deliberate

Without education about BPD, family members take their BP family member's behavior personally—especially if the BP is of the higher-functioning invisible type. This leads to much unnecessary suffering, because BPD behavior isn't willful. Think of it this way: Why would anyone choose to be in situations that make them angry, unhappy, or otherwise in distress?

Look at your BP's face the next time you're having a conflict. Does she look cheerful and satisfied with the way things are going? Does his jealously, anger, criticism, and general crazy-making actions seem to make *him* happy? Quite the contrary—after all, one out of ten BPs commit suicide. You can't get much more miserable than that.

The following empathy exercise will give you a glimpse into what's really behind borderline behavior.

See the World through BPD-Colored Glasses

This empathy exercise will take two months to complete. You will need to buy a thick blank journal or lined notebook. IMPORTANT: Begin this exercise only after you have read it in its entirety.

Week one: Sit down with your notebook and recall every time you ever felt publicly humiliated or ashamed, starting with grade school. For now, hold off on recording incidents having anything to do with your family.

Week two: Go over your life, from as early as you can remember. Think about times when each member of your family did or said something that caused you a great deal of pain. Then conjure up all those feelings you had at that time. Next, do the same thing for all your love relationships.

Week three: Take note of the times you felt enraged at someone. Did you ever feel like throwing something at the wall—or even at the person—during a major free-for-all?

Week four: Repeat as before, focusing on the following issues: Did you ever feel as though you wanted to die—really die? Are there any areas of your life you can't control, like eating or drinking too much? Make a list of all the things you hate about yourself.

Week five: Think of all the times you've hurt others. Did you ever break a promise to a child or give an unfair punishment?

Week six: Go through your notebook. In each instance, no matter how absurd it seems, find someone or something else to blame for each incidence, as a higher-functioning invisible BP might do. Chant to yourself, "It wasn't my fault. It was her fault (his fault)." Feel the relief that acts as a blessed sunburn balm that takes away the pain on your emotional skin.

Go back through each week casting blame and criticism. For example, for the previous week, blame the other person for making you hurt him. Do the same type of thing for week two. When you're done, reward yourself to compensate for having had to deal with such crazy people.

Week seven: Now do what some lower-functioning conventional BPs do: blame yourself for every painful incident. If your parent forgot your birthday, believe it was because you did something bad or were so worthless that you didn't deserve to have your birthday remembered.

Week eight: Now it's time for the most complex assignment yet: spend a few hours with your notebook and put all your notes equally at the top of your mind—even the ones that contradict each other, such as blame yourself and blame everyone else (in fact, especially those). You may find that you can think of little else, making it hard to function. Feel free to cry liberally.

Interpreting the Exercise

Now that you're prepared to run out and buy your blank journal, don't. Hopefully, just reading the exercise has given you insight into what it is like to have BPD. Imagine living with this emotional turmoil 24/7 and put yourself in the following situations. How would you react?

- You're at work, and your boss criticizes something about your job performance.
- Your daughter says she hates you.
- You miss the bus, and it's raining.
- You interview for a job, and they pick somebody else.
- Someone you're interested in says he or she "just wants to be friends."

Just facing the daily challenges of life and maintaining self-esteem and good humor can be difficult for anyone, let alone someone with BPD. Individuals with BPD often feel—for the lack of a better word—wounded. When they believe they've been deliberately hurt, part of their pain is from wondering why someone who is supposed to love them would want to hurt them.

When you swoop in to rescue them—for example, with the intense "love-at-first-sight" Romeo and Juliet type of heroic and undying love, they see a chance (unconsciously so) to escape from their horrifying mental prison. No wonder they fall in love so far so fast and cling to it with all they have.

BPD Features That Challenge Relationships

BPD is characterized by the following four features, all of which make relationships difficult:

1. *Childlike characteristics and defense mechanisms:* Non-BPs say that having a discussion with a borderline adult can be reminiscent of arguing with a small child. That's because in a developmental sense, they *are* arguing with a small child.

2. *Low emotional intelligence:* There's more than one way to be smart. In addition to the kind of intelligence you can measure on an IQ test, there's *emotional intelligence*. Emotional intelligence is about monitoring emotions—both your own and those of the people around you—and then using this knowledge to guide your thinking and actions.

3. *Rejection sensitivity:* In addition to fearing abandonment, people with BPD are overly sensitive to rejection. They anxiously await it, see it when it isn't there, and overreact to it whether it's there or not. This is why small slights—or perceived small slights—can cause major messes.

4. *Impulsive aggression:* Impulsive aggression is what ensues when the other shoe drops, when the eggshells break, and the emotional roller coaster takes a 180-degree turn. The aggression can be turned inward (self-injury, suicide) or turned outward (raging, verbal abuse, domestic violence).

Childlike Characteristics

People with BPD may seem as mature as any other adult in social or professional situations. But if you could do a Star Trek Vulcan mind-meld, you'd know that on the inside they feel as vulnerable, scared, and needy as a small child left alone by his parents for the first time.

Modes or Feeling States

Jeffrey Young, PhD, the founder of schema therapy (pages 91–92), believes that people with BPD can fall into four different childhood modes: the abandoned or abused child, the angry and impulsive child, the punitive parent, and the detached protector.

The Abandoned or Abused Child: The abandoned child feels lonely, sad, misunderstood, unsupported, defective, deprived, overwhelmed, needy, frightened, anxious, victimized, unlovable, weak, excluded, and pessimistic.

The abandoned child is easy to spot in lower-functioning conventional

BPs. It's that quality exuded by Marilyn Monroe and Princess Diana Spencer—both people who were said to have suffered from BPD.

The Angry and Impulsive Child: The angry child is infuriated, frustrated, and impatient because core emotional and physical needs aren't being met. These children are self-absorbed and out of control, acting on their desires to get their own way.

The Punitive Parent: The punitive parent punishes the child for expressing needs and feelings and for making mistakes. As a result, the BP is full of self-hatred, self-criticism, and self-denial and may self-mutilate.

The Detached Protector: BPs protect themselves emotionally by cutting off their needs and feelings and by detaching from others. The result is emptiness and boredom, which lead to substance abuse, bingeing, and self-mutilation.[1]

Primitive Defense Mechanisms

Defense mechanisms are psychological strategies that protect us from being consciously aware of thoughts or feelings that could make us feel bad, especially about ourselves. A common one is rationalization, where we make up good reasons for a course of action we wish to take. ("I might as well eat this last piece of cake so I can put the plate in the dishwasher.")

We begin using defense mechanisms as children, when our methods are fairly primitive. Primitive defense mechanisms include splitting, dissociation, denial, and acting out.

As we grow older and become more sophisticated about social situations, most of us move from these "primitive" defense mechanisms to more mature and complex ones, like rationalization. People with BPD, however, keep using primitive defense mechanisms even in adulthood. That's why interacting with a BP can be reminiscent of dealing with a child.[2]

Low Emotional Intelligence

Emotional intelligence (EI) is a measure of qualities such as self-awareness, personal motivation, empathy, and the ability to love and be loved by friends, partners, and family members.

The concept of emotional intelligence helps explain why people with BPD can have multiple doctorates and be Mensa members in good standing, yet be unable to sense what other people are feeling. EI theories weren't developed with BPD in mind. Nonetheless, it sure looks as if the social scientists who theorized about EI and those who formulated the concept of BPD must at least have been connected by two tin cans and some string.

The best seller *Emotional Intelligence: Why It Can Matter More Than IQ* revolutionized the way we think about why some people live happy, successful lives and some don't. In the book, the author, Daniel Goleman, explains that EI falls into five domains:

1. Knowing one's emotions
2. Managing emotions
3. Motivating oneself
4. Recognizing emotions in others
5. Handling relationships[3]

BPD seems to diminish a person's skills in all five domains.

Knowing One's Emotions

Some people with BPD are self-aware and can articulate their emotions, but others have trouble. For one thing, their emotions can shift so radically and so quickly that it can be tough for anyone to keep up—even them. Second, some BPs have a tough time separating their own emotions from the emotions of others. Knowing what you *feel* is essential to knowing who you *are*. BPs who become enmeshed with others suffer from identity issues.

Managing Emotions

"Emotional dysregulation," as clinicians call it, is a hallmark of BPD and needs no further explanation.

Motivating Oneself/Impulsivity

A portion of motivation has to do with the ability to control impulsive actions, especially those driven by intense emotions.

"There is perhaps no psychological skill more fundamental than resisting impulse," Goleman writes. "It is the root of all emotional self control, since emotions, by their very nature, lead to one or another impulse to act." An experiment designed to test children's ability to resist temptation at age four found that the four-year-olds who were able to delay gratification were, as adolescents, more socially competent, personally effective, and better equipped to handle frustration.[4]

Recognizing Emotions in Others

As we just discussed, some BPs have trouble identifying their own emotions, let alone anyone else's. BPs can misread cues: For example, they will see somebody who's angry and they'll think the anger is directed at them, even when it isn't. Then they will assign too much significance to it, as if the anger means that the person is going to abandon or hurt them.

Mostly, though, BPs are so fearful of any distance between themselves and others—and so needy of other people's attention—that it's all too easy to forget that other people have their own needs. This proves to be the most problematic in BP parent/non-BP child relationships (the roles become reversed, to the detriment of the child) and romantic relationships (non-BP partners expect a more equal give-and-take).

Handling Relationships

Being able to manage one's emotions is necessary to having close relationships. Emotional self-control includes the ability to be patient and moderate impulses, anger, and distress. It takes self-knowledge and the ability to see both the good and bad in others and to recognize they have needs, too. We want to be around people who make us feel good about ourselves.

Feeling safe around someone, comfortable enough to show our vulnerabilities and sensitive spots, engenders trust. Trust is sacred. It is the currency of relationships of all kinds, from the plumber to the psychiatrist. We tend to trust people who

- accept us for who we are
- make us feel safe and secure

- won't hurt, betray, or ridicule us
- don't expect us to be perfect
- are consistent and dependable
- are truthful and fair
- respect our boundaries
- let us say what we really think and feel without repercussions

Borderline personality disorder is incompatible with some of these qualities. The ultimate tragedy of this illness is that it makes those who have it crave close, safe relationships, and then robs them of the qualities they need to have such relationships.

Rejection Sensitivity

Part of being human is to experience rejection, from the other kids in kindergarten who won't share their Play-Doh to not being asked to dance at the senior citizen's ball. Rejections can be small, like those just mentioned, or large: being fired or learning your partner wants a divorce. Even trivial snubs can cause a world of hurt and send our self-esteem into a tailspin.

Rejection sensitivity exists along a continuum, from the office boor who never notices people don't like him to—unsurprisingly—people with BPD. Just as BPs are more fearful of abandonment than most people, they're also more sensitive to rejection. Already depressed and suffering from low self-esteem, they *expect* to be rejected. Like giraffes at a watering hole in the African veld on the alert for predators, they continually scan their environment for any hint of disapproval or exclusion, seeing intentional slights in the smallest things.

Once a rejection-sensitive person is convinced someone is rebuffing her, she'll come up with her own reasons why this is so and then react in a hostile way without checking out the facts.

A borderline man describes it like this:

I have a constant edge-of-your-seat alertness for little clues that might mean someone hates me or doesn't want me to be with them anymore. With my boyfriend, when we would be together doing something quiet like reading, every so often I would interject with a pleading and submissive, "Are you mad at me?" until it annoyed him so much he really would get angry! For me, though, the impression that he was displeased with me was so real. All it takes is silence to make me feel like I've been rejected, and this fills me with panic.

Impulsive Aggression (the Border-Lion)

Please read this section closely, as the concept of the "border-lion" (impulsive aggression) will appear multiple times in part 2 of this book.

Impulsive aggression is widely acknowledged by Larry J. Siever, MD, professor of psychiatry at Mount Sinai School of Medicine, and others as a core feature of BPD that can be triggered by immediate threats of rejection or abandonment paired with frustration. Impulsive aggression:

- comprises verbal hostility, physical hostility, or both, with the purpose of hurting another person or self.
- can be turned outward (such as outbursts, rages, hitting objects, or violence toward others) or inward (such as suicide attempts or self-injury).
- is impulsive, unplanned, and reckless (that is, the person gives no thought to the consequences of his actions).
- is linked to several BPD traits, including rage, emotional instability, impulsivity, suicidal thoughts, and self-injury.
- is associated with a biological "tug-of-war" between the logical and emotional aspects of the brain, in which the logical side loses. These aggressive tendencies can be inherited.[5]
- is not exclusive to BPD, but a component of several impulse control disorders such as intermittent explosive disorder.

Think of impulsive aggression as a "border-lion," a ferocious beast that is uncaged when BPs' emotions are so strong and overwhelming they can no longer be contained. The border-lion also protects the "abandoned or abused child" inside the BP (more about that in chapter 4).

Whether the border-lion is turned inward or outward, it is one of the top barriers keeping BPs and those who love them from developing the close, trusting relationship each partner yearns for.

It's going to be tough, but try to hold fast to the notion that your family member and the border-lion are not one and the same. The border-lion comes from within your family member and can be tamed with the right treatment.

The Five Dysfunctional Dances

Having a borderline loved one means having that "it's déjà vu all over again" feeling much of the time. You may feel stuck in these frustrating "dances" with no clue about what's happening, how you got there, or how to get out.

The "It's Your Fault Fox-Trot"

By blaming others, BPs try to avoid taking responsibility for their own behavior. Shame and splitting play a part, as well.

For BPs to admit to themselves or others that anything about them is less than perfect would be admitting that they are defective. But this strategy alienates others, blurs reality, and ultimately doesn't reduce the BP's shame. In a long good-bye letter to her BP ex-lover, Chris, a non-BP, wrote:

> One morning after we had had a fight the night before, I realized that I had been wrong and wanted to apologize. I felt awkward and ashamed, and I said, "It's hard for me to say I'm sorry." This was a brutally honest statement. The reward for my honesty was you snapping at me, "How come it's so hard for you to say you're sorry!?"
>
> You were constantly irritated at me. If I complained, you would simply become nastier. Once you snapped at me for looking through some DVDs the wrong way. I asked you in a very even tone of voice, "What are you getting upset about?" For the rest of the day you sulked, gave me the silent treatment, wouldn't talk to me, wouldn't look at me—in fact, you simply walked away from me without responding when I tried to talk to you![6]

The "No-Win Waltz"

You know you're in a no-win scenario when you're damned if you do and damned if you don't. Chris gives us more examples:

> You were a master of double-binds. Whenever I got back home to my apartment at the end of the day, I never knew when to call you. It seemed that sometimes when I called you right away, you'd be in the middle of dinner or doing chores, and would be short and rude. But if I waited until later in the evening to call you, you would say in an accusatory manner, "You've been home for *how* long? And you didn't call me?"
>
> When you were feeling depressed about something and I tried to comfort you, you pushed me away with anger and the seething silent treatment. However, if I just tried to leave you alone during these situations I again got—surprise!!—anger and the seething silent treatment!! Just what the hell was I supposed to do?[7]

The "Projection Polka"

People often try to avoid feeling bad about their own unpleasant traits, behaviors, or feelings by attributing them (often in an accusing way) to someone else. This is a common defense mechanism called *projection*. As with everything else, people with BPD take it to the extreme.

Sam, a non-BP, and his BP friend Hank were good buddies. Hank was on his second marriage to a woman, Beth. Sam knew things weren't the best, but didn't know why until late one night when Hank's lips loosened.

One of the main problem areas, it seems, had to do with their sex life. Sam listened in a companionable way because he knew Hank needed to talk, but it was definitely more graphic than he was comfortable with. Sam listened, nodded, made a few polite comments, and heaved a sigh of relief when Hank decided to go home. A few days later, Sam came home from work and found Hank and Hank's wife, Beth, sitting at the kitchen table with his wife, Manjula. Sam says:

> Hank had some book with him about boundaries that he'd been reading. It was all underlined and highlighted like a textbook or

something. He and Beth sat there and explained that Hank was going to have to set some boundaries with me because I was interfering with their marriage and was, in fact, the cause of many of their problems! What? How?

He hung his head dramatically as he told my wife that he had already "confessed" to Beth that he had "betrayed" her by telling me their private matters. But then he twisted it all around as though I had been intrusive and had pried into their affairs and was telling him what they should and should not be doing in their marriage. It was all so backward from reality, like a mirror with everything appearing the opposite way.

We had no contact until a few months later, when Hank called and asked if I wanted to watch Sunday football at his house. He chatted about work and such like the whole thing had never happened. I couldn't believe it.

The "I Hate You—Don't Leave Minuet"

When people get too close, people with BPs feel engulfed. In turn, they distance themselves to avoid feeling controlled. But then BPs feel neglected, even abandoned. So they try to get closer again, and the cycle repeats.

For example, Agnes doesn't understand her BP lover, Bernice. Since they live far apart, they only get to see each other every few months. Bernice writes Agnes beautiful love letters and tells her on the phone that she can't wait to see her.

But when Agnes actually comes to visit, Bernice picks fights and continually criticizes her. Finally, they have a big blowup. Bernice yells and says the relationship is over. Agnes cries and flies home, mourning.

The next day, Bernice calls Agnes, begging her to take her back. She does. It happens again the next two times they're together. By the third time, Agnes swears to herself that this is it—she will *not* take Bernice back one more time. But then she receives this letter:

My sweet baby,

I can't imagine living the rest of my life without you. When I "go crazy" sometimes it's because I know how truly madly in love I am with you and that scares me. My hands are shaking as I write this letter. I feel so vulnerable, but you need to know that you are it for me, my one, my own, my soul mate. I will keep trying to work on my issues. Please forgive me. It will never happen again. I am nothing without you.

Me

With tears in her eyes, Agnes calls Bernice and they both cry, swearing their undying love. They even plan Agnes's next visit.

A few months later, a joyful reunion ensues. Some twenty minutes after the makeup sex, Bernice starts screaming at Agnes because Agnes forgot to pick up the half-and-half Bernice takes with her coffee.

The "Testing Tango"

Does it ever seem like your BP's behavior and demands of you just get more and more outrageous? Do you find yourself tolerating conduct you never thought you would—maybe even some things you wouldn't want other people to know? If so, you're on the dance floor doing the Testing Tango.

No matter how many times non-BPs say it or show it, people with BPD don't trust that others really love them and won't abandon them. Elizabeth, a recovered BP, says, "How were they seeing things in me that I wasn't? I really did want to be loved and accepted. I just didn't know how to let in the love because I didn't feel worthy of that love and acceptance."

Life is stressful when you know that the people you love are going to grab your heart and walk out the door, but you don't know when it will happen. So you do what kids do—you act out a bit to see if your behavior will be tolerated. If it is, next time you take it up a notch to see if the other person will take that, too. Elizabeth says:

I'll never forget the first time I uttered the words, "I'm just testing you to see when you'll leave me because everyone does. I know it's wrong, but I just can't help myself." What might start out as a casual gripe about finances would eventually become a three-day rage-fest over money management. I became a screaming, ranting, raging mess.

I knew that I couldn't start with a full-blown BP rage. So I started softly and slowly. With each test I set forth and the person passed, I upped the ante and said, "If you loved me, you would do this or that." People usually accepted the most outrageous and inappropriate behavior to maintain the relationship.

You might think that once the non-BP passes the tests, their borderline family member would feel more secure. But that doesn't happen. Instead, people with BPD begin to question the sanity and character of the other person. They think, "Why would a healthy, normal person accept this kind of abuse? There must be something wrong with him to put up with these things from me."

Family Dynamics

Families are systems of interconnected and interdependent individuals, none of whom can be understood in isolation from the system. One popular model is called the Karpman Triangle, after its founder, Stephen Karpman, MD. The Karpman Triangle happens in all families, even in relatively healthy ones (see page 210). The roles in this drama are

- the "victim"
- the "persecutor," who bullies the victim
- the "rescuer," who swoops in and saves the victim

In the following example of the triangle, two sisters discuss their problems involving child care arrangements. Eleanor, a single parent, has BPD.

Person	What They Say	Role
Louise (non BP)	"You keep on calling me at the last minute to babysit. I have to drop all my plans, and I don't like it."	Louise feels like the victim, and Eleanor is her persecutor.
Eleanor (BP)	"I can't help it! Sometimes things come up and I can't plan!"	She sees *herself* as the victim, and her sister is the persecutor.
Louise	"You really could plan better. Did you *really* have to rush over to your boyfriend's house on Tuesday?"	Same as before: she's victimized by her sister.
Eleanor	"No! I couldn't plan better. He was upset, and he threatened to take drugs if I didn't come right at that moment." (Cries)	Same as before: *she's* the victim of her sister.
Their father, Harry	(Walks in) "I heard you two arguing with each other. Louise, do you have to argue? Just back down to keep the peace."	To Louise, her father is another *persecutor*. To Eleanor, he is a *rescuer*.
Louise	(Sighs) "All right, all right. Please stop crying. Just *try* not to do it again, okay?"	Feeling pressured, she drops her request for more notification. In effect, she has *rescued* Eleanor, which leaves her still feeling like the *victim*.
Eleanor	"Thank you, thank you. Okay, I'll try. Thanks, Dad."	Comes out of victim mode—for now.
Their mother, Thelma	(Comes in) "Will you all just come sit at the dinner table? I've been cooking all day, and everything's getting cold, and no one appreciates me."	A new victim is created, with Harry, Eleanor, and Louise as persecutors.

During disputes, the participants wear each other down, each trying to claim victimhood and to slap the other with the persecutor label. This constant tug-of-war is exhausting. The roles constantly shift. Eleanor, a single parent, has BPD.

Two can play the game just as well. For example, let's say that Harry wasn't at home, and Eleanor's pleas made Louise back down instead of setting clear limits. If Louise sighed and said, "Never mind, just call me whenever you need me," Louise would then be acting as the rescuer. This is a frequent occurrence in families with members who have BPD. You'll learn more about this in chapter 10, Power Tool 4: Set Limits with Love.

The Karpman Triangle game inhibits real problem-solving. It creates confusion and distress, not solutions. No matter who "wins" each fight, both sides are miserable. This becomes a second layer of upsetness—one layer is the never-ending fights; the other is whatever the disagreement is about.

When someone with BPD is one of the parties, this dynamic becomes more intense and dangerous. Metaphorically, the tug-of-war game is held over a river full of crocodiles and piranhas. Reread the BP-point-of-view empathy exercise and recall the general feeling of victimhood you might have felt. Additionally, the thinking, feeling, and acting impairments (especially splitting) of people with this disorder make finding a middle ground unlikely.

The bottom line: you can't "out-victim" your BP. Although you can't change the way your loved one relates to you, you *can* choose to stop dancing altogether.

Chapter 4

Risk Factors of BPD

The prevailing thought is that there is not one "cause" of BPD. Instead, there are many *risk factors* that create the likelihood that the disorder will develop. A risk factor is just what it sounds like: something that, when present, increases the risk that something else will happen. Risk factors can be both biological and environmental. The more risk factors that a person has for some type of physical or mental illness, the greater the chance he will develop that condition.

As an example, consider heart disease. Imagine a man whose grandmother and uncle died of a heart attack. His parents own a bakery, so he grows up appreciating the buttery taste of croissants and chocolate-covered cream puffs. As an adult, he eats high-fat, high-cholesterol meals and doesn't have time to exercise.

Suddenly, on his sixtieth birthday, he dies of a heart attack while shoveling a heavy, wet snow. What caused his death? Was it his genetic history? The high-fat diet? The lack of exercise? The shoveling? The answer is all four factors (and perhaps others) working together.

Now let's extend that example as it applies to developing BPD. Let's take four people: Julius and Nelson, two brothers, ages thirty and thirty-two, and Terri and Sherri, identical twins separated at birth and adopted by different families.

Terri and Sherri are both biologically vulnerable to BPD. However, they grew up in different environments. Terri grew up in a high-conflict household. At ten years old, she was sexually abused by a neighbor. She develops BPD. Sherri was luckier. Her home life was stable and with no major trauma. She never develops the condition.

Julius and Nelson grew up in a reasonably stable and pleasant environment, just like Sherri. In Julius, the mix of genes is such that, even with good parenting, he still develops BPD. His brother Nelson doesn't, because his genetic heritage is just different enough.

In the rest of this chapter, we're going to look at the two kinds of risk factors that lead to the development of BPD: biology and environment. The argument about which is dominant has been going on for decades. One might as well debate about which came first: the chicken or the egg. Increasingly, research is finding that it's not one or the other. It's both.

That's not to say that the two are always equal. If many biological risk factors are present, only a few environmental aspects are needed to develop BPD. The fewer the biological factors, the more the environmental factors. Whichever dominates, the result is the same: lots of splattered eggs and a whole lot of crunched eggshells.

First, we'll take a look at the biological risk factors: the physical brain itself, brain chemistry, and genetics. Even though we'll be looking at them separately, they're interwoven. We can't separate them any more than we could separate the sugar, eggs, and flour from a piece of cake.

Biological Risk Factors

The following is a greatly simplified explanation of how the brain works.

1. Our brain controls the way we think, feel, and act.
2. BPD is characterized by impairments in thinking, feeling, and acting.
3. To a large extent, these biological impairments in the brain contribute to the skewed thoughts, emotions, and behaviors characteristic of people with BPD.

Even when we intellectually understand the chemical causes of BPD, it's hard to accept that a three-pound organ and a complex chemical imbalance can cause a learned professor to become completely illogical or a child from a loving home to try to commit suicide. But once this notion truly settles in our bones, it becomes easier to empathize with a loved one, to depersonalize the behavior, and to use the power tools that make up the second half of this book.

Our brains are divided into three sections: the *primitive brain,* the *limbic system,* and the *cerebral cortex.* Imagine an upside-down golf club: That's the primitive brain (the clubhead) joined with the spine (the shaft). Now cover the clubhead with a sock. That's the limbic system. Top it off with a bike helmet (the cerebral cortex). This is a model of the brain as it might appear in a Girl Scout project.

Each part has a specialized job:

- The primitive brain controls functions like breathing, digestion, and heart rate. When someone is labeled "brain dead," this is the only part of the brain that is working.
- The limbic system, which includes the powerful *amygdala,* has a hold over our emotions. This is the *feeling* brain.
- The cerebral cortex is our *thinking* brain. It's the part measured by an IQ test, or what you might glimpse during an autopsy in an episode of *CSI.*

The Physical Brain

We've known for more than a century that our wrinkled gray cells have a large role in shaping personality. This was demonstrated in the mid-1800s when an unfortunate railway worker named Phineas Gage was the victim of a freak accident that's still discussed in science books today. (Warning: the next paragraph is graphic.)

Gage was packing a load of explosives into the ground when the charge accidentally went off. The iron tamping rod he was using (4 feet long and 1¼ inches in diameter) was propelled though his left cheek and brain and exited through the top of his skull. Incredibly, he walked away from the accident and lived another thirteen years.

But the accident radically altered his personality. Gage's physician, John M. Harlow, wrote:

> Before his injury, Gage possessed a well-balanced mind and was looked upon by those who knew him as a smart businessman, energetic and persistent. After the accident, Gage was fitful, irreverent, indulging in the grossest profanity (which was not previously his custom), exhibiting little deference for his fellows, and at times impatient, obstinate, capricious, and vacillating. . . . His mind was so decidedly changed that his friends said he was "no longer Gage."[1]

To figure out why Gage's personality changed so radically, in the 1990s scientists examined the accident's impact on the brain using the latest technology. They discovered that the rod had damaged structures in Gage's cerebral cortex, the thinking part of the brain.[2]

So, specifically, what's wrong with the brain that can lead to BPD? Part of the story lies in a horseshoe-shaped organ called the hippocampus. It's associated with memory and emotional sensitivity. A glitch in how the hippocampus operates may explain why BPs can get so angry in a short time, why their memories can be so unreliable, and why simple events and innocuous statements trigger extreme rage.[3]

The Feeling Brain

Our amygdala, which lies within the limbic system (the sock), is the heart of our emotions. Although it's only the size and shape of an almond, it packs a mighty punch. (By the way, even though we say *the* amygdala, there are actually two of them: one on the right temporal lobe, and one on the left. That's also true of the hippocampus.)

When a person experiences an event, her cerebral cortex tells her objectively what's happening. (For example, "I just spied my old classmate Charlie Richards at my high school reunion. I see his hair is gone, and he's gained a little weight. I hear his wife left him, too.")

But her amygdala helps produce the emotions that hit her as she watches Charlie belly up to the bar. If Charlie was a good friend, she may feel sympathetic. If he once deliberately tripped her in the hall, she might smirk. That's the cognitive part of the brain connecting with the amygdala in twelve thousandths of a second.[4]

The amygdala also controls the intensity of our emotions. If Charlie was a close confidant, her sadness may turn to sorrow. If he ditched her at the senior prom, her smirk might turn into a wide grin. Even a chuckle.

Although we'd all like to think we base our decisions on logic, our emotions often hold a larger sway than we think. A striking example: A few decades ago, a television series featuring a family living in a small town ended its run on a sad note. The town's citizens learn that a corrupt man is going to take over their community. Unable to stop this, they blow up their homes so he won't get them.

For years afterward, the actor who played the swindler had strangers come up to him on the street and scold him for being so evil. And that's not even the unusual part. It's that the series was *Little House on the Prairie,* starring Michael Landon, and the fictional event was supposed to have occurred in 1901.

The Teenage Physical Brain

Although parents have instinctively known this since the Ice Age, research has confirmed that the parts of the brain that weigh risks, make judgments, and control impulsive behavior are still developing through the teen years and don't fully mature until about age twenty-five.[5]

Young people process emotions differently, which makes talking about feelings more difficult for them. In one experiment, researchers scanned a subject's brain activity with an MRI while the person identified the emotions of faces on a screen. Researchers found out that adults use the frontal lobes (the reasoning part of the brain) to perform this task, while young teens used the amygdala.[6]

The Chemical Brain

Most people have a vague notion that BPs have some kind of chemical imbalance in their brain. While this is true, it's an oversimplification. You might as well say that buses work because the wheels go 'round and 'round.

To better understand the complexity, imagine a dense forest with flowering maple trees, leaves shimmering in the summer sun. The maple trees "talk" to one another by emitting clouds of pollen that waft through the air on puffs of wind. Pollen is a chemical messenger of sorts that helps one tree interact with another despite the air gaps between the branches.

The mass of neurons tangled in our brain is like a forest. Like trees, neurons have branchlike shapes to help them reach out to catch chemical messages called neurotransmitters. Neurotransmitters, like pollen, carry information across the synapse from one neuron to the next—or sometimes even to neurons that are very far away.

Little pulses of voltage, like wind, help waft neurotransmitters off one neuron so they can float to the next. In this way, different parts of the brain set up a conversation with one another.

So far, scientists have identified about fifty neurotransmitters. Each carries different messages. For example, norepinephrine involves memory and the fight-or-flight response. Dopamine is linked to feelings of being rewarded. And serotonin is associated with both impulsivity and mood. Neurotransmitters can combine together in different ways to carry still more messages.

Problems arise when there are too many or too few neurotransmitters, or when changes in the neurotransmitter system happen too quickly or slowly. The neurons can have trouble "talking" to one another. This can then build on other difficulties in a person's neurological makeup, and the mental and physical health consequences can be severe.

For example, very low levels of dopamine in the motor areas of the brain are known to produce Parkinson's disease, with its symptoms of muscle rigidity and loss of coordination. An imbalance of serotonin is associated with depression, chronic fatigue, and social withdrawal. Frequent, uncontrollable panic attacks are associated with quirks in the amount of norepinephrine.

Glitches in neurotransmitter systems help underpin the three core dimensions of BPD: faulty thinking (cognitive abilities), feeling (emotional dysregulation), and acting (impulsivity). It would be marvelous if we could describe exactly how that happens. But the reality is that the neuroscience involved is so complex that researchers are just beginning to understand what's going on.

So why do some people have problems with their neurotransmitters and other parts of their brains, like the hippocampus and amygdala, while other people don't? The answer lies partly in genetics.

Genetics and the Brain

One gene alone is responsible for a rare, incurable disorder called Huntington's disease. If you have the gene, you'll come down with Huntington's eventually. But most inherited medical problems need several genes to converge before the disease develops.

For example, more than twenty genes can play a role in diabetes. Typically, someone who inherits four or five of them becomes diabetic. The different ways in which those genes combine can influence how severe a particular person's diabetes is, how easily it can be treated, and so on.

BPD itself isn't passed from one generation to the next. What are inherited are two to four traits that define this complex disorder. Two parents, neither of whom have BPD, might still have some of the genes that can lead to traits associated with BPD, such as

- aggressiveness
- depression
- excitability
- quickness to anger
- impulsivity
- a susceptibility to addiction
- cognitive (thinking, reasoning) impairments

Is genetics a form of destiny? Yes and no. Psychologist Pierce Howard sees genetics as a seed, and personality as something that develops from that seed in response to its environment—sun, water, fertilizer, and so on. So genes play a role, but environment and lifestyle choices have a great impact as well.[7]

Environmental Risk Factors

The following environmental factors play a role in the development of BPD.

Abuse: Myths and Realities

If you've researched borderline personality disorder for any length of time, you've read that abuse causes BPD. This belief partly comes from the *Diagnostic and Statistical Manual of Mental Disorders* (DSM), which states that 75 percent of people with BPD have been abused.

The data, however, have a few flaws. First, if abuse causes BPD, then how do you explain the fact that one out of four BPs has not been abused? Second, a *correlation* is not necessarily a *cause*. Robert O. Friedel, MD, director of the BPD program at Virginia Commonwealth University, says, "None of the environmental risk factors I've discussed [early separation or loss, trauma, ineffective parenting, and adverse social customs] has been shown to *cause* borderline disorder. Many people who are exposed to the same abuse, separations, and bad parenting do not develop borderline disorder, and some borderline patients have not experienced any of these environmental risk factors."[8]

Third, the 75 percent figure is based on self-reporting, meaning that it was compiled by asking adult patients if they have a history of abuse. The assumption is that the responses are 100 percent accurate, and that there is a consensus of what, exactly, constitutes "abuse," be it emotional, sexual, or physical.

However, as a method of data collection, self-reporting is considered to be unreliable. Dieters are notorious for underestimating their food intake, and food is a pretty simple thing to measure compared to "abuse." Plus, the subjects have a disorder that, by definition, is characterized by faulty perception and reasoning. These cognitive defects, added to the vagueness of the term *abuse* and the limits of the methodology, mean that the 75 percent abuse statistic should come with a disclaimer.

There is a middle ground here. Clinician Harriet Lefley, PhD, explains, "People biologically predisposed to develop BPD are hypersensitive to, and more intensely experience, the slights, criticisms, and punishments endured by most children in the process of growing up. And if parents are raising an exceptionally difficult child, these criticisms and punishments are likely to be frequent and generate tension in family dynamics—and later be recalled as abusive."[9]

Sharon is a mother of a child with BPD and maintains an online support group for parents of children with this disorder. Her group is called NUTS (parents Needing Understanding, Tenderness, and Support to help their child with borderline personality disorder). She says:

> Throughout my ten-plus years of running NUTS, I have seen very few families pass through where abuse, neglect, trauma, etc., have been an issue. I realize that abusive parents probably won't be joining a group and talking about it. Still, our little sampling of the world of BPD does indicate that there are many of us out here struggling with BPD where there isn't the trauma/abuse cause involved.
>
> In addition, about 70 percent of our children in NUTS have falsely accused someone of abuse; my own daughter accused me, and we were under investigation. My other daughter denied that we were abusive.[10]

Perry Hoffman, cofounder of the Family Connections program of the National Education Alliance for Borderline Personality Disorder, is concerned about the same issue. She says:

> We have to educate clinicians not to fingerpoint family members. Certainly we know there's abuse that goes on. But I certainly know that the family members I interface with or who have come through our Family Connections program are not the parents who have abused their children. And these are the families who are feeling so terrible when they read about abuse and [its association with BPD].[11]

Family and Peer Influences

Many other environmental circumstances favor the development of BPD.

All our personalities are shaped by the surroundings we grew up in. Some influences are positive, such as a caring older brother, a good school system, and a family with good financial resources.

Then there are negative influences: losing a grandfather, getting pneumonia, or living in a dangerous neighborhood—not to mention the "normal dysfunction" we all grow up in. Our culture—its norms and expectations—influence us, too.

Some life circumstances may present a higher risk for the development of BPD. Some doctors refer to these as "environmental burdens" that can trigger the condition. They include

- emotional, physical, or sexual abuse.
- ineffective parenting—or *perceived* ineffective parenting—of the borderline individual. This can mean anything from poor parental skills to a parent's mental illness or substance abuse.
- an unsafe and chaotic home situation.
- a poor match between the temperaments of parent and child.
- the sudden loss of a parent or a parent's attention (sometimes perceived by the child as abandonment). This can arise from the death of a parent, a divorce, or even the birth of a new baby.

You might be thinking that this describes 99 percent of families. (About 50 percent of marriages end in divorce.) It probably does, so don't feel guilty if this looks familiar. Also keep in mind that many people who are exposed to the same abuse, separations, and ineffective parenting do not develop BPD.

Research is beginning to tell us that relationships with peers are crucial to the development of our personality—interesting, considering that most parents in the Welcome to Oz community say their child had a hard time making friends and lacked social skills. This could be because, compared to others seeking psychological help, people with BPD are especially likely to misinterpret or misremember social interactions.[12] With their deep fear of abandonment, people with BPD may need and expect more from friendships, even at a young age.

"Invalidating Environments" as a Factor in BPD

Marsha M. Linehan, the creator of dialectical behavior therapy (DBT), a method used to treat BPD and other disorders (see page 87) developed a "biosocial" model about the causes of BPD. The "bio" refers to biology and the "social" to the environment.

She agrees with research that shows that people with BPD are hard-wired to react more intensely to stress. Their emotional peaks are more pronounced. Once the stress is over, they take a longer time than most to calm down. Linehan calls this tendency "emotional vulnerability." BPD, she says, can develop when an emotionally vulnerable child is raised in an "invalidating environment." An invalidating environment is one in which caregivers

- tell children that their feelings and experiences are wrong or untrue
- find fault with children who fail to perform to the expected standard, and make comments such as "you weren't motivated enough"

Children raised in this environment learn not to trust their own gut reactions and look to others to tell them how to feel and to solve their problems for them.

A Poor Parent/Child Fit

Perry Hoffman, who is also the president of the National Education Alliance for Borderline Personality Disorder, says that one risk factor for BPD is a poor match between a biologically vulnerable child and her caregivers, who, for whatever reason, find it overwhelming to meet the child's needs.

For example, perhaps the mother develops post-partum depression or the family's going through a crisis. Another example is a single mother who, for economic reasons, takes two jobs that limit the time she can spend with her child.

All of this helps us to realize an important point. We may *believe* that people with BPD are consciously choosing to act the way they do—and in a sense, they are. But in another sense, if we had the same genes and environmental influences as a person with BPD, we might be surprised to find ourselves acting in precisely the same way.

Chapter 5

Treating BPD

When faced with a complex situation, realize it cannot
be solved quickly or with one simple solution.

▪ I Ching ▪

First, let's address the $64,000 question: Can therapy help motivated individuals with BPD overcome the disorder? The answer is unquestionably "yes." New medications and innovative types of psychotherapy have led to measurable improvements. Anecdotal evidence shows the same results; when an author put out a call on the Internet for people who felt they had largely recovered from BPD and wished to share their experiences, she received more than a dozen replies.

Medications

Distinguished clinical professor of psychiatry Robert Friedel says that scores of mental health workers—even those experienced with BPD—don't know that medications play a dramatic role in treating borderline symptoms. Yet just as many studies show the effectiveness of medications as those that report positive therapy outcomes. Medications can provide the stability that people with BPD need to get the most out of therapy.

What Medications Can and Cannot Do
No medication can change someone's personality, save that heady potion that transformed Dr. Jekyll into Mr. Hyde. What medications *can* do is

reduce BPD symptoms such as depression, mood swings, dissociation, aggression, and impulsivity. Medications do this by normalizing the brain's neurotransmitter functioning, just like another medication might change the levels of "good" and "bad" cholesterol.

On his Web site, psychologist Joseph Carver explains how medications work:

- Some imitate neurotransmitters, triggering a response as though the original neurotransmitter were present.
- Some make neurotransmitters more available in the synapses (those all-important spaces between the neurons).
- Some force the release of neurotransmitters, causing an exaggerated effect. (Some street drugs do the same thing, which is one reason why taking these drugs is called "self-medicating.")
- Some increase the supply of certain neurotransmitters; others reduce or block their production.
- Some affect the storage of neurotransmitters, which makes them lose their potency.[1]

Finding the Right Medications

Even though we know a great deal about the medications, each person's biology is unique. The same drug in the same amount may affect different people in a variety of ways. Frequently, patients use two or more medications at the same time, because different drugs work on different brain chemistry problems.

Therefore, there's a period of trial and error to discover which medication (or combination of medications) and dosage provide the best results. The goal is to use the lowest dose possible to treat the symptoms effectively while minimizing the chance of side effects. Depending on how much medication a patient is taking and how long it takes to reach maximum effectiveness, this can be a lengthy process.

And the trial-and-error period isn't fun, either. Clients want relief *now*, and some drugs take six weeks to take effect. On the positive side, we're lucky to have so many medications to choose from. The key is to work closely with the doctor and to monitor symptoms on paper. In the end, it's usually worth it. Many people with BPD have found that the proper medications turn their life around.

Medications Studied and Used in the Treatment of Borderline Disorder[2]

Drug Class	Medications	Symptoms Improved by One of More Medications in the Class
Antipsychotics		
Neuroleptics	thiothixene (Navane)* haloperidol (Haldol)* trifluoperazine (Stelazine)* flupenthixol*	anxiety, obsessive-compulsivity, depression, suicide attempts, hostility, impulsivity, self-injury/assaultiveness, illusions, paranoid thinking, psychoticism, poor general functioning
Atypica	olanzapine (Zyprexa)* aripiprazole (Abilify)* risperidone (Risperdal)° clozapine (Clozaril)° quetiapine (Seroquel)°	anxiety, anger/hostility, paranoid thinking, self-injury, impulsive aggression, interpersonal sensitivity, low mood, aggression

* placedbo-controlled studies   (continued)
° open label studies
SSRIs—selective serotonin reuptake inhibitors
MAOIs—monoamine oxidase inhibitors

Drug Class	Medications	Symptoms Improved by One of More Medications in the Class
Antidepressants		
SSRIs and related antidepressants	fluoxetine (Prozac)* fluvoxamine (Luvox)* sertraline (Zoloft)° venlafaxine (Effexor)°	anxiety, depression, mood swings, impulsivity, anger/hostility, self-injury, impulsive aggression, poor general functioning
MAOIs	phenelzine (Nardil)*	depression, anger/hostility, mood swings, rejection sensitivity, impulsivity
Mood stabilizers	divalproex (Depakote)* lamotrigine (Lamictal)* topiramate (Topamax)* carbamazepine (Tegretol)° lithium°	unstable mood, anxiety, depression, anger, irritability, impulsivity, aggression, suicidality, poor general functioning

* placedbo-controlled studies
° open label studies
SSRIs—selective serotonin reuptake inhibitors
MAOIs—monoamine oxidase inhibitors

If a psychiatrist proposes using a medication, ask

- What is the drug used for? Many medications have a primary and a secondary effect. Some are "helper" drugs that intensify the effects of another drug.
- What is the beginning dosage? The maximum allowable dosage? Psychiatrists start at lower doses to minimize side effects and then go up as necessary. This process is called *titration*.
- How long does the drug take to work? Popular drugs that affect

the transmitter serotonin (such as Paxil and Prozac) can take six weeks. In contrast, some anxiety-reducing drugs such as alprazolam take effect right away.

- Is a generic version available? The newest ones are the most expensive—often ridiculously expensive. Some pharmaceutical companies have patient assistance programs that provide meds to people who can't afford them. Find out more at www.rxassist.org.

- What are the side effects? Drowsiness and dry mouth are two common ones.

- What are the side effects of discontinuing the drug? This is an important question that is often missed, and the pharmaceutical companies are not free and easy with this information.

- If the medication is for a minor child, ask if any research has been conducted with children.

Over time, the number of medications a person is taking can add up, especially if he's seen more than one psychiatrist. Each health care provider, including family doctors, needs a list of all the medications the patient is taking, including what the drug is for, what the dosage is, and when it's taken.

The Internet is chock-full of Web sites about medications. Consult one that is reputable. Pharmaceutical companies may paint very rosy pictures, so make sure you look at some unbiased ones as well. Another great way to find out about any medication is to ask a pharmacist. Because drugs are their only business, they can be just as informed about the drug itself as your doctor—sometimes even more so.

Medications in Hospitalization

Blaise Aguirre, MD, who specializes in children and adolescents with BPD, says that borderline patients often enter the hospital taking a mixture of medications.

Often, at each of these hospitalizations, the treating psychiatrist is presented with a single part of the whole picture: We call this the "admitting symptom": for example, the patient is "depressed," "manic," "anxious," or "psychotic."

Usually, past psychiatrists prescribed a medication for each of these symptoms. In subsequent hospitalizations, medications were seldom removed, so we see kids on all the meds from previous hospitalizations.

Often, our approach is to be clear as to the clinical criteria that make the diagnosis of depression or psychosis. If there is no clear sense that these diagnoses are correct, we gradually remove the medication. Often, the problem behavior began after a relational conflict, and, unfortunately, there is no medication that can cure a broken heart.[3]

Psychotherapy

Some people enter therapy because they want to figure out why they feel so stuck in certain areas of their lives. Some want to work on specific issues, such as overeating or an inability to control their anger. Some just would like to feel happier, less anxious, or more relaxed.

Therapy is especially helpful for people who find themselves falling into the same unsatisfying patterns over and over again: for example, getting into destructive relationships, losing job after job, or acting in self-destructive ways. Often people try to get out of these patterns by themselves. But they can't get *out* of them because they don't know how they got *into* them.

Whatever the reason, the purpose is the same: to help people enjoy their life more, feel better about themselves, improve their relationships, and achieve their goals.

Clinical "Orientations"

Throughout the decades, different schools of thought, or "orientations," have emerged about how to best treat people with mental illnesses. There are hundreds of them: psychoanalysis, solution-oriented therapy, brief therapy, psychodynamic therapy, and cognitive-behavioral therapy, to name just a few.

Most therapists, however, combine bits and pieces from different schools of thought and then draw from their education, training, personal experiences, and personal style. This is called the *eclectic approach*. (*Eclectic* is a word that means composed of elements drawn from various sources.) In essence, each eclectic clinician's approach is unique. In these cases, evaluating the clinician and the approach is essentially the same thing.

With *standardized treatments,* practitioners undergo the same education and training, and the therapists trained in that method will use similar techniques and approaches, whether the therapy takes place in Buffalo or Beijing. This consistency allows researchers to conduct studies that measure the outcomes of these therapies.

Eclectic Therapy

Although there are probably hundreds of different types of theoretical orientations and techniques, most eclectic clinicians use techniques largely from two schools of thought: psychodynamic therapy and cognitive-behavioral therapy.

Psychodynamic Therapy

In psychodynamic sessions, the therapist and the client work together to uncover and examine the client's feelings and past experiences. The goal is to see if unresolved conflicts and old business are triggering the client's counterproductive behavior.

For example, a man who loses job after job because he can't handle authority figures might discover in therapy that his anger and unresolved issues with his authoritarian father are costing him well-paying and interesting jobs. Armed with that knowledge, the client can begin to look at his boss more objectively, and he and his therapist can work on his father issues during sessions.

Bennett Pologe, a clinical psychologist in New York City, says:

> What you want most from a session is the experience of insight. You will know when it happens. It is not like intellectual learning. You will find yourself suddenly feeling clearer, saner, more

hopeful, more decisive, more energetic, and your symptoms will clear up. This is the one magic that psychotherapy offers. When you feel the things you've been trying not to feel, when you become aware of things you've avoided, you feel better, and you function better.[4]

Cognitive-Behavioral Therapy (CBT)

One drawback of psychodynamic therapy, some say, is that insight doesn't necessarily lead to any changes in thoughts, feelings, and actions. This is where cognitive-behavioral therapy (CBT) comes in. The National Association of Cognitive-Behavioral Therapists explains CBT in this way:

> Our thinking causes us to feel and act the way we do. Therefore, if we are experiencing unwanted feelings and behaviors, it is important to identify the thinking that is causing the feelings/behaviors and to learn how to replace it with thoughts that lead to more desirable reactions and behaviors instead of depending upon external things like people, situations, and events. This way, we can feel better even if the situation does not change.[5]

CBT is essentially the thought-feeling-action approach presented throughout this book.

The Eclectic Combination

Merging psychodynamic and cognitive-behavioral therapy (and, in some cases, others as well) to create an eclectic approach allows for a lot of flexibility. The therapist can provide what the client needs when the client needs it.

For example, let's say an overbearing boss is making life miserable for a man in therapy. The boss makes unreasonable demands on the man's time, and his family is complaining that they never see him. The therapist and patient might discuss how the boss reminds the man of his own demanding father, which gives the man insight into why it's so difficult to set boundaries with his boss. Armed with that insight (thinking), the therapist might help the patient feel more confident (feelings), thus enabling him to improve his practical limit-setting skills (actions).

Most clinicians use eclectic therapy, though they may call it something else (or not call it anything).

Standardized Therapies

Three structured therapies used to treat BPD are dialectical behavior therapy (DBT), Systems Training for Emotional Predictability and Problem Solving (STEPPS), and schema therapy.

Dialectical Behavior Therapy

Dialectical behavior therapy (DBT) is one of the fastest-growing forms of treatment for lower-functioning conventional BPs, because it significantly reduces the rate of self-injury and suicide, as well as lowers emergency room and inpatient hospital visits.[6]

The word *dialectical* means that two opposite things can be true at the same time—in this case, that patients need to accept themselves, warts and all, yet recognize that by changing their destructive coping methods and by learning new skills, they can have lives worth living.

Dialectical behavior therapy combines elements of CBT and Zen concepts of radical acceptance and mindfulness. These ideas, which we'll talk about later, anchor the program in place. "People who meet the criteria for borderline almost always hate themselves," says DBT originator, Marsha M. Linehan, PhD. "So I figured that I needed to accept them myself, and then teach them how to accept themselves, because if you don't accept yourself as you are, you actually can't change. It's kind of a paradox but true."[7]

FUNDAMENTAL DBT CONCEPTS

- *Patients are motivated and willing to change.* DBT patients have tried to conquer their pain and loneliness on their own. But it's all been too much for them. They're tired of feeling like failures, fearing abandonment, and taking impulsive actions that end relationships or put them in the hospital. Thus, they have a strong and conscious commitment to change.
- *Radical acceptance is essential to recovery.* Radical acceptance means that before you can move toward positive change, you

must accept yourself as you are right now, without judgment or blaming. Radical acceptance is a lifetime project and a key tool for all of us, not just those with BPD.

For example, let's say that every time a young man loses a romantic partner, he falls apart for months, sobbing, panicking at the thought of being alone, and needing to rush into another relationship—and, at the same time, he hates himself for doing it. Everyone tells him to get over it already and "be a man" about it. He suffers both the end of the relationship and the shame of his vulnerability.

Radical acceptance, Linehan says, will release him from the shame. "This is the way I was made," he could tell himself calmly. "I wish it were not the case, but it is." Ironically, once we release our judgments about ourselves, we can truly move forward.

- *Mindfulness is the key to managing emotions.* Anger, frustration, grief, and other emotions often involve the past or a potential future. Mindfulness enables us to step back for a moment, observe what's happening inside us and all around us, and live and breathe *in that moment,* not the past or the future. "You'd be amazed how much suffering is due to thinking about the future or ruminating about the past," Linehan says.[8]

Let's revisit the high school reunion we talked about in chapter 4. In addition to Charlie, you spy your first love, Chris, who broke up with you many years ago. You notice the familiar pangs in your stomach. You even recognize other emotions— for example, the thankfulness and the sorrow that you'll never be that young and innocent again. You notice your feelings at a bird's-eye level and observe them rather than get caught up in the emotions. (No one said this was going to be easy!)

Mindfulness also means living in the moment during the good times. It's taking a walk through the park and being totally in the moment, soaking in the beauty of nature instead of being absorbed in the past or the future.

Mindfulness is for everyone, not just people with BPD.

- *People with BPD need validation.* Briefly, validation is listening empathetically to a BP's feelings and accurately reflecting back what he said without necessarily agreeing with him. It's avoiding phrases that tell BPs how to feel, such as "There is no reason to get angry about this." An alternative validating phrase might be "I can see you feel really angry about this." Note that you're not agreeing with the reason for the anger.

PROGRAM COMPONENTS

At the heart of the program are (1) a two-hour weekly group skills training session led by a therapist, and (2) a weekly hour-long session with an individual therapist. Telephone crisis management is available if needed.

Group skills training sessions follow a strict schedule and cover four interrelated topics: distress tolerance, core mindfulness, emotional regulation, and interpersonal effectiveness.

- *Distress tolerance.* "I tell clients that distress tolerance is about getting through a crappy moment without doing something to make it worse," says social worker Michael Baugh. "DBT offers a large collection of ways to distract attention that are more positive than planning suicide attempts, taking street drugs, or jumping into abusive relationships."[9]
- *Emotional regulation.* The goal of emotional regulation is to decrease the intensity of patients' anger, fear, shame, and sadness. To fit in with less emotionally sensitive people, some people with BPD ignore their emotions. They don't know how they are feeling until the emotion overwhelms them.
- *Interpersonal effectiveness.* The aim of this training is to decrease patients' interpersonal chaos and lessen their fear of abandonment. To do this, the skills trainer teaches them to have a more positive outlook about their environment, their relationships, and themselves. The content is very similar to that of an assertiveness training class, with lessons in the following: asking others to meet their needs in a more positive manner, asserting their limits, and proactively doing things to keep relationships going well.[10]

- *Individual sessions.* Once a week, each patient meets with her private therapist, preferably one affiliated with the DBT program. During sessions, the therapist's first priority is to discuss self-injury and suicidal behaviors during the week. The second priority is "therapy interfering behaviors," such as coming late to sessions and phoning the therapist at unreasonable hours. The next priority is troubles that lessen the patient's quality of life, such as depression and substance abuse. Finally, the therapist finds out how well the patient is progressing with skills training.

LIMITATIONS OF DBT

DBT offers great hope and a way to counter the oft-repeated (and demonstrably false) maxim that there is no treatment for BPD. Many patients say DBT has improved their lives tremendously. However, DBT is not a miracle cure. As you evaluate treatment alternatives, keep these limitations in mind:

- DBT has been shown to lessen suicidal thoughts and reduce instances of self-harm. Studies have not shown that it relieves depression or makes clients happier (although many individuals say it does).
- DBT is appropriate only for patients who acknowledge their illness, want to learn about it, and will work hard in therapy. Higher-functioning invisible BPs do not meet this criteria.
- DBT is demanding. Each day, patients fill out diary forms, and most patients spend many hours each week in therapeutic activities. To benefit from the therapy, patients must be highly motivated.
- DBT is not available in all locations. Also, it can be costly (we'll take a closer look at insurance in the next chapter).

FINDING A DBT THERAPIST

DBT therapists come in two flavors:

1. Those who have completed the official training and work in (or run) a formal DBT program
2. Those who have taken some DBT training or who use some

of Linehan's patient education materials and techniques. DBT adherents caution that clinicians in this second group may not produce the positive results shown in the studies of DBT.

The Behavioral Tech Web site (www.behavioraltech.com) has a database of clinicians by state.

STEPPS Group Treatment Program

STEPPS stands for Systems Training for Emotional Predictability and Problem Solving. It is popular in the Netherlands and has recently spread to other countries. STEPPS is meant to be used in addition to, not a replacement for, traditional therapy.

Like DBT, STEPPS is a cognitive-behavioral, skills-training approach. Clients learn specific emotion and behavior management skills. Family members learn how to reinforce and support the newly learned skills by developing a common language to communicate clearly about the disorder and the skills used to manage it. In STEPPS, family members are a crucial part of the team and help their loved one receive help for the disorder.[11]

The basic skills program consists of twenty, two-hour weekly meetings that focus on skills such as managing problems, setting goals, and self-care. Clients use a notebook to track the intensity of their thoughts, feelings, and behaviors each day. The program emphasizes personal responsibility, and members of the treatment team are available after hours.[12]

Schema Therapy

Schema therapy is based on the principles of cognitive-behavioral therapy, but also includes techniques and concepts from other psychotherapies. Schema therapy offers patients relief from self-destructive acts while focusing on deeper personality changes. Preliminary research suggests it leads to recovery in about half of all patients with BPD and shows significant improvement in two-thirds.[13]

A *schema* is an entrenched, self-defeating life pattern. A *schema mode* is the moment-to-moment emotional states and coping responses that we all experience. In this book, we've been referring to the abandoned or abused child and the angry and impulsive child. These are schema therapy terms. The punitive parent, who punishes the child for expressing needs and feelings, and the detached protector, who cuts oneself off from needs and feelings, are also part of schema therapy.

An underlying assumption of schema therapy is that patients were emotionally damaged during childhood and can benefit from reparenting. Schema therapy emphasizes the bond between the therapist and patient. Mutual respect and genuineness is essential. Patients attend intense therapy two times a week for three years. But the therapy's founder, Jeffrey Young, PhD, of the Cognitive Therapy Center of New York, says that while DBT aims for just changes in behavior, the goal of schema therapy is to help patients feel better, too. "With Schema Therapy, patients are, in addition, breaking free of lives of chaos and misery and making deeper personality changes," says Dr. Young.[14] More information is available at www.schematherapy.com.

Comparing Individual Treatment Programs

Comparing therapies isn't easy because people with BPD experience the disorder in so many different ways. Psychiatrist Dr. Robert Friedel says, "The notion that one can develop any 'cookbook' therapy for BPD is contrary to our understanding of the [environmental and biological differences] that place people at risk for the disorder. I know of no study performed to date that takes into account these patient differences. Until we do, discussions [about what treatment is best] will continue."[15]

In the end, the health and happiness of your family member—and your own happiness and sanity—are what are most important. How other people respond to treatment X is not as crucial as how *your* loved one responds to it. No study can predict how one particular person will respond to one particular type of treatment.

Keep in mind that treatment takes time—several years, depending on the method. Personality disorders are woven tightly within an individual. A more complicated treatment plan, which can take additional time, may be needed for those who have a co-occurring disorder.

"Clients with BPD take a long time to realize what they are feeling," says therapist Andrea Corn in an interview with the author. "They almost always want to say, 'The other person made me feel that way, it was *her* fault, or it was *his* fault—he did it.' It's very hard for them to take the ownership. It could take years to tease this stuff out."[16]

Couples Therapy

In couples therapy, you're not the patient. Neither is your partner. The "patient" is the relationship itself (although you get to pay the bills). The therapist's role is *not* to serve as referee but to improve the relationship in ways that are meaningful to both partners.

The primary objective is improving the couple's communication skills. Therapy becomes effective as couples apply their new knowledge to break ineffective communication patterns and develop more useful ones. Other goals include reducing criticism, defensiveness, and derision.

Many people who have partners with BPD suggest couples therapy after they've been unsuccessful in convincing their partners to get help on their own. They usually hope that the therapist will back them up in the face of their partner's unreasonable demands and irrational behavior. The borderline partner, of course, sees this as an opportunity to do the same in reverse.

In the face of severe BPD, especially when the BP is unwilling to look at his contribution to marital difficulties, the value of couples therapy is limited. If the therapist doesn't recognize this limitation—which is not unusual—the therapist may validate the BP's misperceptions and drive a deeper wedge between the couple.

Some therapists are aware of the BP's deeper pathology; however, they may discourage the non-BP from bringing up sensitive issues out of fear that the BP may bolt. Non-BPs end up feeling invalidated, and therapy can actually make the situation worse. For this reason, if you do choose couples therapy for yourself and your partner, proceed with the utmost caution.

Another problem with couples therapy, according to therapist James Holifield, is that many people only enter therapy when there's a crisis and they're forced to do something different. A good example is when one partner threatens to end the relationship unless the other person changes. A BP partner may agree to therapy, but then find an excuse to drop out once the immediate threat is over and the non-BP is hooked back into the relationship. At this point, typically, their behavior goes back to what it was before.

"That's something very different than real therapy," Holifield says. "So usually one of my first goals is to establish a motivation for engagement in the process, a sort of a contract between us that the purpose of therapy is not what they thought they came in for, but to consider other ways of relating to each other that is beyond their comfort level, but more beneficial to the relationship. Otherwise it just doesn't work very well. You never get past a certain level if someone feels coerced into the process."[17]

Couples counseling may not change the fundamental relationship, but it can provide a safer place to try out the new communication and limit-setting skills you'll learn in the second half of this book. Sometimes a structured setting and the presence of a third person can make a big, positive difference.

Hospitalization

Hospitalization may be necessary if your family member is a danger to others; has a co-occurring disorder that requires intensive treatment; feels suicidal; has made suicide attempts; is becoming psychotic; or has severe symptoms that aren't getting better with outpatient therapy. Lower-functioning conventional BPs often enter the hospital from the emergency department, where they are rushed after a suicide attempt.

Insurance companies are not eager to pay for hospitalization, and some clinicians believe that hospitalization should be a last resort for borderline patients because it can encourage dependence.

Once a patient has been admitted, her psychiatrist controls what happens next: the appropriate number of days in the hospital, the medications the patient will be taking, whether the patient can leave the unit to go to the cafeteria, what activities the patient will participate in, when she can be discharged, and so on.

When the patient is admitted, she may be asked to fill out a form that assesses her level of safety. Expect your family member's belongings to be briefly searched for any contraband objects (such as pills or sharp objects). You and other visitors may be searched as well.

What happens on the treatment unit varies from hospital to hospital. There may be individual counseling sessions, educational sessions about coping skills, and art or music therapy. The best environment is one that is highly structured.

Get to know the nurses. One on each shift will probably be the primary nurse for your family member. Most important, talk with the admitting psychiatrist, who will visit your family member each day to assess her condition, talk to her about her concerns, and change any medical orders, if necessary.

In general, patients aren't discharged until they fill out the level-of-safety form again and indicate that they're no longer a danger to themselves or others. There should be an aftercare plan that specifies what professionals the patient will see after discharge, what medications they will take, and so forth.

Partial hospitalization, also called day treatment, is when your family member attends educational/support sessions during the day and then returns home in the evening. Typically, inpatient hospitalization is followed by a week or so of day treatment, which provides support, structure, and education without the costs and more confined environment of a hospital.

All this may sound intimidating at first. But it is also a respite for you. Your family member's need for hospitalization is not your fault; you have not failed, and neither has your family member. Remind yourself that your family member is getting cared for by professionals.

BPD Patients Do Get Better!

I don't think that we do people a service by saying that there's only one treatment, and if you can't get it then [your family member] won't get well. People who come to my DBT treatment program say, "This is my last chance, and if I don't get better here I'm not going to ever get better."

We tell them right away that is absolutely not true. We hope our treatment will help you, but we're not your last chance. Sometimes the timing is wrong, or sometimes the mix with the therapist isn't the right match, but that doesn't mean they won't be helped somewhere else. People need to know that there's hope and that people do get better.

Perry Hoffman, president of the National Education Alliance for Borderline Personality Disorder[18]

Chapter 6

Finding Professional Help

*Finding a therapist you can work with can be tough and can take
a few trials and errors before you find the right person. Therapists
are basically human critters like everybody else and come in all
shapes and sizes. Like other people, they sometimes make mistakes, give off attitude, or can at times just seem worthless.
Like other people, some are smarter than others, and some are
smarter at one set of things than they are about another.*
▪ Glenn Johnson, PhD ▪

By far, Welcome to Oz community members' number one complaint is
that finding effective treatment for their borderline family member is
frustrating, expensive, and emotionally trying. The demand for clinicians
experienced with borderline personality disorder—and who are willing
to add someone with this disorder to their client roster—greatly outstrips
the supply.

In an ideal world, someone would give you a few names of possible
therapists so you could look them up, find out that they have much experience treating people with BPD, and hear that they would be delighted to
take on another one—yes, of course they take your insurance—and give
you an appointment for tomorrow, if not yesterday.

Yet, for most people, finding an effective clinician is a process of trial
and error. It's not like picking up the phone and ordering a shirt from a
catalog in a certain color and size. It's more like finding a job that meets

your specific requirements. The good news, though, is that at least this time you're the one who's doing the hiring.

Why It's So Hard to Find a Therapist

If you want to hear a lively and revealing conversation, listen in to a group of mental health professionals talk about patients with BPD. June Peoples, a producer of the *Infinite Mind* radio show, did just that. It happened at a cocktail party attended by social workers, psychologists, and psychiatrists— "smart people and concerned, caring therapists," Peoples says.

> Over hummus and veggies, the group started to talk about patients who, it seemed, were a therapist's worst nightmare. One therapist said that she was careful to make sure she wasn't treating more than one of them at any given time. "I won't treat them at all," said another, and a heated discussion ensued about the importance of a rapid and correct diagnosis of these patients—not for therapeutic reasons, but to make sure you don't get stuck with them.[1]

Therapists develop this negative mind-set for two general reasons. First, BPs are one of the most challenging types of patients to treat—if not *the* most challenging. Second, treating borderline patients can be emotionally draining for the therapist. Each of these factors feeds into the other.

Borderline Patients Are Professionally Challenging

Personality disorders are more tightly woven into the fabric of a person's being than other types of brain disorders. BPD alters the process by which a person thinks, feels, and acts. You can't get any more fundamental than that.

Lower-functioning conventional BPs often come to therapy with a defeatist attitude—understandably, after all the time they've spent in the mental health system without feeling better. Psychiatrist Richard Moskovitz says, "Even during the first therapy sessions, patients make remarks like, 'You can't help me,' 'Why should you be any different from the people in my past who betrayed me,' and 'I am too defective to ever be repaired.'"[2]

What all this comes down to is that borderline patients are probably *the* toughest clients a clinician will ever treat. They test the skills of even the most experienced and well-trained therapists. One common dilemma is finding time to explore deeper issues when the BP is always in crisis. Another is that some therapists (especially those inexperienced in treating borderline clients) have difficulty observing their own limits, such as keeping after-hours phone calls to a reasonable number. Once problems begin, it's tough for the therapist to reverse course without seeming overly critical or abandoning. In situations like these, an untrained therapist can be worse than none at all.

Borderline Patients Are Emotionally Challenging

Mental health professionals are human beings. As such, they have many of the same gut reactions that you do when they're faced with rage and blame—even though they know intellectually it's not personal. "Borderline patients can be hostile or attack," says Marsha M. Linehan. "Therapists can feel so scared, angry, frustrated, or helpless that they pull back. And that is harmful to the patient."[3]

Kathleen, a woman with BPD, agrees. "A lot of the therapists I saw were frightened by my rage and my inability to engage or form an alliance with them. I didn't want really to get better. I just wanted to express rage. I always felt that the people who were treating me were disgusted by me."[4]

On the other side of the spectrum, it can be scary if borderline patients go overboard in the other direction: idealizing their therapists, fantasizing about having a relationship with them, and making them the focus of their lives.

Mental health professionals go into the field because they want to help people. When a client doesn't get better despite the therapist's best efforts, it's tempting to blame the client for the lack of progress and to view their attempts at trying to get what they need as manipulation, rather than to question whether the treatment they're providing is effective.

Of course, all of this is only a problem if your family member is willing to walk through a clinician's door.

How Do I Motivate My Family Member to Seek Help?

Nearly everyone in the WTO community has made numerous attempts to compel their family member to see a therapist. Common methods include

- manipulation
- bribes
- crying
- pointing out the person's flaws
- logic and reasoning
- begging and pleading
- leaving self-help books around the house

What happens next is as predictable as the change of seasons.

Stage 1: The BP says it's the non-BP who needs therapy, not the BP. If the non-BP has unwisely put forth BPD as an explanation for their BP's behavior, the BP accuses the non-BP of being the one with BPD. For good measure, the BP also accuses the non-BP of being abusive, unreasonable, and controlling.

Stage 2: In desperation, often during a crisis, the non-BP finally resorts to an ultimatum such as "Go to a therapist or I'm leaving you," or some other consequence. The non-BP hopes that once the BP is in therapy, the clinician will force their family member to see the light.

Stage 3: Apprehensive that his loved one might actually carry out his threat, the BP agrees to see a therapist, perhaps with the partner or other family members. Therapy, however, goes nowhere. That's because even the best BPD clinicians can't help a patient who doesn't want to be helped.

Stage 4: Once the immediate threat dissipates, the BP finds some reason to drop out of therapy. This is especially true if the therapist is a good one, skilled at bringing the focus to the BP's core issues instead of reinforcing the BP's feelings of victimhood. However, if the therapist takes everything the BP says at face value without probing further—and this is not uncommon—the therapist may inadvertently reinforce the BP's twisted thinking, making things worse.

Stage 5: Eventually, the non-BP realizes that forced therapy is not going to work and that no one can "make" anyone do anything (a good life lesson, by the way). Sometimes the whole process needs to be repeated several times before this truism becomes evident.

Stage 6: Months or years later, the non-BP realizes that her efforts to change the other person simply added a thick second layer of conflict on top of the original issues. She becomes even more disillusioned, depressed, angry, and hopeless. As one WTO member noted, "My attempt to invade his world with facts only caused more pain."

Life-Changing Therapy Requires a Major Commitment

Therapy is hard work. Transforming the way you think, feel, and act while taking responsibility for things you've always blamed on someone else is a tall order. People with BPD who are serious about treatment will pursue it, perhaps with your help, and make a commitment to it. They will make their own appointments, be honest with their therapists, and complete any "homework" the therapists give them. Recovered BP A. J. Mahari says, "The truth is relative, and each person with BPD must come to their own truth in their own time and way."

That said, for the sake of readability, in this chapter the term "you" (as in, "When you call the therapist, leave a voice mail) could mean either you, the family member (parents, especially), or the individual with the disorder.

Rock Bottom as a Motivation to Take Therapy Seriously

Some BPs will only concede that they need help after they have hit rock bottom after someone they love ends the relationship or they wind up in jail or under psychiatric observation.

Rachel Reiland, a woman recovering from BP and the author of the BPD memoir *Get Me Out of Here,* says:

> I believe that there needs to be some kind of major upheaval that serves as a catalyst for a borderline to face the truth. Not want-ing to lose something, perhaps. They can no longer blame the

power-hungry boss or the bitchy spouse or the scores of people who have it in for them.

But denial is a funny thing. What some of us may see as shocking or rock bottom isn't necessarily going to be viewed that way by the BP. So they've destroyed a relationship? They move on to the next one, and so on. They get fired from a job they liked? Blame it on the boss and get another one. Lose custody of the children? It's the damned court system.

The fear of change, the compelling fear of the unknown, is so intrinsic, so vast, so encompassing and overwhelming, that it's greater than the tragic events that would send most people down to their knees. The shock cannot be predicted, nor contrived. It can't be provoked by the greatest of efforts or good intentions on the part of another.[5]

Mahari advises family members to let go of any desire to control what's going on in therapy. "This is *their* journey, not yours," she says. "You can support them, but it can't be your life plan. There are no simple rules here. This is not the rehabilitation of a physical injury. This is the rehabilitation of the entire *self*."[6]

Psychiatrists John G. Gunderson and Cynthia Berkowitz caution that if your family member talks about what goes on during therapy, take a neutral stance, neither agreeing nor disagreeing with their judgments, complaints, anger or devaluation. Gunderson and Berkowitz say, "Be positive, but beware that making *too* much progress can be threatening to your family member. If they enter recovery, the thinking goes, they might lose your intensive support. Plus, if they relapse, you might be disappointed in them. So be encouraging and optimistic, by all means, but be sensitive to this as well."[7]

Preparing for the Search

Whether you're a BP or a non-BP, going into full-throttle search mode for a therapist can help overcome feelings of hopelessness and helplessness.

There are some things that you can't do. But searching for a therapist is one thing you *can* do.

Become an Informed Consumer

Learn everything you can about BPD from recent and reputable resources. Start with "Finding Qualified Professional Help," which is chapter 11 of the *Stop Walking on Eggshells Workbook,* as well as the other material you'll find listed on bpdcentral.com.

You'll come across contradictory information, especially in the area of causes and treatment. So the more research you do, the firmer your foundation will be and the better you'll have a handle on which therapist can best meet your needs. Let a potential therapist know you've done research and the descriptions of BPD symptoms seem to match your family member's symptoms.

Create a Medical History File

Document your own (or your family member's) struggle with the disorder. Write a short medical history that includes the following:

- signs and symptoms by age and any special circumstances, such as self-harm occurring after a bad breakup
- previous treatment (if any), including the name(s) of the clinician(s), diagnoses given, whether the treatment was beneficial, and anything else that strikes you as important. List all medications currently being taken, their dosages, what time of day they're taken, and what they're for. (It will come in handy when you fill out forms.)
- a list of the medications (and dosages) that have been tried and discontinued. Explain why, such as it wasn't effective or produced undesirable side effects. This will help during the trial and error process. Perhaps a different dosage may produce better results or fewer side effects.
- anything else that you think a therapist should know, such as family stressors like a divorce, a move, or the loss of an

important person in your BP's life. You might also talk about
the impact your BP's behavior has had on family members.

Having this information at your fingertips will be useful in many ways.
For example, it will help with continuity of care and remind you of questions you want to ask. Once therapy begins, this record will help the clinician obtain the most information in the shortest amount of time. Many
people find it a validating and healing exercise to see it all laid out in one
place. Feel good about yourself; you've made it this far!

Read Up on Your Health Insurance Benefits

Get up close and personal with your health insurance documentation.
Call the company if you don't understand the plan. Pay special attention
to what the company pays for and what you must pay for. Assess your
finances to determine whether you can pay for co-payments and services
that aren't covered.

Once you do settle on a therapist or treatment program, talk about fees
right away. Bring up matters such as co-payments and how you're supposed to pay them. (Some want payment at each session.) Find out whether
the provider offers a discount for private-pay patients. Some providers will
offer discounts for payment with cash or check because health insurance
has so much red tape. Ask about a monthly payment plan.

Parents, Anticipate Being Blamed

If you are a parent looking for help for your child of any age, mentally
prepare yourself for running into at least one clinician who assumes you
caused your child's disorder.

Some may be explicit about this; others just imply it or treat you in a
disapproving way. This is one reason why it's so important for you to do
your own research, especially on the chemical and genetic risk factors of
developing BPD. The father of a borderline child who is a member of an
online support group for parents says:

> Despite all the new information about what causes BPD, we par-
> ents still come across clinicians who automatically assume that

we've mistreated, abused, neglected, or invalidated our children. This is harder to endure than my daughter's outbursts and even her punching and kicking. It's like screaming for a lifeguard when I see my daughter drowning, then running out to save her, and when the lifeguard gets there he punches me in the gut for deliberately trying to drown my own daughter. And the tragedy is, while he's hitting me, she's still sinking, crying for help.

If you are accused, pretend you have a rubber shield around you so the hurtful words bounce right off you. Do not take them personally. They are no reflection on you, and the next parent who walks through the door will probably get the same treatment.

Make Contact

Here's another way that looking for a good therapist is like searching for a job: networking produces some of the best leads.

- Ask friends and family. Ask them if *their* friends and family might know of anyone.
- For schema therapy, see www.schematherapy.com.
- For dialectical behavior therapy, see www.behavioraltech.com.
- Contact the Borderline Personality Disorder Resource Center (www.bpdresourcecenter.org) or e-mail info@bpdresourcecenter .org. Most referrals are in the major metropolitan areas.
- Check with your primary physician and other health care specialists you see, from your allergist to your dentist.
- If your BP is a child, ask your pediatrician.
- Phone the psychiatric department (often called "behavioral health") of the hospitals in your area and ask the nurse-manager whom she would recommend if someone close to her needed a psychiatrist or a therapist. You don't have much to lose if you also ask her whom she would *not* recommend.
- Consult online "find a therapist" databases. They can contain a great deal of information about the therapist—orientation, interests, philosophy, background—and it's easy to hone in on the

ones who most interest you. You may want to begin your search process by looking at these databases to see the type of information the therapists give.

- If you already have either a psychiatrist or a therapist, the psychiatrist should have names of therapists to recommend, and therapists should be able to recommend psychiatrists.
- Inquire with people you know who are employed at a hospital or clinic, even if they work in a totally different area. The grapevine is long and thick, and they may have a good buddy in a relevant department. If you know a psychiatric nurse or aide, you've hit pay dirt.
- If your family member has a serious co-occurring illness, you may want to start with a specialist in that area. A therapist who treats a co-occurring illness is easier to locate and may know of a peer who works with borderline clients who have that co-occurring disorder.
- Look up local mental health agencies. Some local mental health services are listed in the phone book in the blue government pages. In the "County Government Offices" section for the county where you live, look for a "Health Services (Dept. of)" or "Department of Health Services" section. In that section, look for listings under "Mental Health."
- Call your local state psychological association.
- Find the most respected medical clinics in town that have a behavioral health department. Top clinics like to become associated with top people.
- If you have a local university, call its department of psychiatry. These psychiatrists are often on the cutting edge of research. Also, ask for recommendations of people trained in that university's psychiatry or psychology program.
- Contact the National Alliance on Mental Illness (NAMI), both state and local branches, as well as any other mental health organizations.

- Look in the Yellow Pages. Mental health professionals are listed under "counseling," "psychologists," "social workers," "psycho-therapists," "social and human services," and "mental health." Look for certifications such as Board Certified in Psychiatry or Board Certified in Pediatric Psychiatry.
- Make use of the information and referral services of the United Way—particularly if you are in need of financial assistance. Look into low-cost or sliding fee clinics.
- Check if your company offers an employee assistance program, which may be able to provide the names of psychiatrists.
- Talk with your pastor, minister, priest, rabbi, or other religious leader.
- Take a look at local magazines that may put together lists of top professionals in the area.
- Keep your eyes open for the names of professionals used as sources in the local media.
- After each interview with a potential candidate, ask if he or she can give you any names.

Evaluate the Candidates

Before you contact your candidates, search for them on the Internet. These days, many clinics and practitioners have Web sites that can give you insight into their treatment methods, interests, and philosophy.

Remind yourself that if you were getting your house painted, you would ask for references and check them out. And your loved one's mental health is a lot more important than the color of your house! Call or e-mail the offices of the best candidates. Introduce yourself and explain the reason for the call. Leave a voice mail and suggest good times to call you back.

Once you connect, ask if they have time to chat with you on the phone for a few minutes. The way the therapist answers the questions is also revealing. A good one should encourage you to shop around for the right therapist and not be offended that you're asking questions.

Consider whether you want to use the actual term *borderline personality disorder,* especially if your loved one hasn't been formally diagnosed. If you do, the image of a suicidal, self-harming, lower-functioning conventional BP will most likely come to the clinician's mind. If that doesn't describe your family member, be cautious about using it. Even if you do have a lower-functioning conventional BP family member, you may wish to just describe the traits themselves first to help the therapist keep an open mind. Experiment.

Medical professionals can sometimes loom larger than life. Remember, you're paying them, and, depending on your circumstances, that could run into thousands of dollars. Don't be intimidated by their degrees or the cost of their office furniture. Be open-minded, but trust your instincts. Few people ever say, "I wish I hadn't trusted my instincts."

You'll be evaluating prospective clinicians in three areas: hard factors, soft factors, and attitudes and beliefs about BPD.

Hard Factors

Ask:

- Are you taking new patients?
- How much do you charge? What insurance plans do you accept?
- Do you have a particular focus or interest? (Some therapists work closely with particular populations, such as Christians or ethnic minorities.)
- Are you available after hours for emergencies? (For lower-functioning conventional BPs, this is critical.) Who covers for you when you're unavailable?
- What is your education and training? (The clinician's credentials should be from a nationally recognized, respected organization or an accredited school of higher learning.)
- Do you have a license? (This assures you that the clinician has met at least minimal standards in his education and abilities. Call—or check online—the state licensing board to make sure there's no history of legal or ethical complaints.)

- (If your family member is a child) Have you been specifically trained to treat children and adolescents? (Some clinicians have not been specifically trained; they just prefer working with younger patients. There are fewer therapists who specialize in working with children, so you may have to look harder.)

Soft Factors

Getting answers to a few of the following questions requires at least one visit to the office. Or, the answers may reveal themselves over time. If you're evaluating a clinician who practices within a standardized therapy program, you may find the answers to most of these questions in the program materials.

- How do you see your role in therapy, or what is your style of working? (This is a significant factor that prospective clients often overlook. Some clinicians offer "supportive therapy," which means working on reducing stress and talking about problems in the here and now. Other therapists do deeper work that has the potential to give clients insight into their behavior and effect real change, such as exploring negative patterns in the client's life or ways in which the client may be unconsciously sabotaging herself.)
- Does the clinician have confidence? Clinicians who have confidence in themselves do much better with borderline clients. Being able to say, "I don't know," and answering questions without becoming defensive may be signs that the therapist has confidence.
- Does this person listen, put you at ease, and create a general environment of acceptance while still challenging the client when necessary for his or her own growth? Look for personal qualities such as empathy, flexibility, patience, and a sense of humor.
- How does the clinician view sex role stereotypes? Studies show that sex role stereotypes already play a part in the way BPD is diagnosed. They may also play a hidden role during therapy; watch out for it. For example, women in WTO have said that when

they've expressed deep resentment at their BP husband, they've been dismissed as being overemotional and angry. It works the opposite way, too. Some men find that no matter what's going on in their relationship, they're assumed to be the aggressors or abusers and their female BP is presupposed to be the victim.

BPD-Related Factors

Ask open-ended questions such as the following:

- What are your thoughts about BPD and treating borderline patients? (Don't interrupt, agree, or disagree; rather, jot down anything you want to follow up on later. This will tell you what the therapist considers important. Hesitations and tone of voice can be revealing. Make sure the therapist touches on the definition, causes, and, most important, treatment of BPD.)
- Do you believe that both medications and therapy are necessary in treating someone with BPD? (While meds aren't for everyone, in general the answer should be "yes." A clinician's answer to this question can often clue you in to what she believes are the causes of BPD.)
- Do you have experience in treating borderline clients? (Or, if you're not using the term *borderline)* Do you have experience in treating clients (insert traits or patterns of behavior at issue)? (If "yes") How long have you been doing so? (Naturally, if the BP in your life is a child or adolescent, you'll want someone with experience in that age group.)
- Do you have time to keep up with the latest BPD research? (It's vital that psychiatrists, especially, be aware of the latest studies about medications. BPD is an active area of research, with hundreds of studies published each year. Pick a psychiatrist who stays current. With psychiatrists, you *do* want to use the correct diagnosis.)
- How do you view family members as being affected by their borderline family member? Do you do family therapy as well?

(Whether the therapist involves the family in therapy is not the point; ideally, you at least want someone who understands how the entire family is affected.)

- (If your family member has a co-occurring disorder) Do you have any experience treating someone with this co-occurring disorder? (If not) How would you address both illnesses?

- Do you believe that recovery from BPD is possible, and if so, to what degree? (The clinician's attitudes are influential. Innumerable studies have discovered that people tend to live up—or down—to people's expectations of what they can accomplish. Even those who are optimistic may tell you that a *complete* recovery is unlikely. However they respond, remember that they're probably speaking about lower-functioning conventional BPs, those who are often suicidal and practice self-harm. And if they're negative, don't take this for a fact and lose hope. They don't know you or your family member, and they may not be up-to-date with the latest treatment information.)

The Client-Therapist Relationship

Mental health experts are beginning to realize that only 15 percent of therapy success is related to the orientation of the therapist. The other 85 percent is the therapeutic relationship between the client and a therapist experienced in treating BPD.[8] Data show that even the placebo effect plays a far greater role than the method used. This is probably even truer for patients with BPD, who have major issues with trust, low self-worth, fear of abandonment, and forming close bonds.

In mental health-speak, a good relationship is called a *therapeutic alliance*. A therapeutic alliance is one in which the therapist offers empathy; genuine, unconditional caring; and validation, and who builds a sense of trust. Clients, in turn, feel safe, respected, and understood. Once clients feel safe, they can calmly and noncritically observe their own behavior, which leads to insight and personal growth.[9]

This fact can bring much hope to BPs and non-BPs alike, since it is so difficult to find clinicians as knowledgeable about BPD as you would like them to be, let alone meet the rest of the criteria.

Obtaining a Diagnosis

Why is it so hard to make a psychiatric diagnosis? Widely published psychiatrist Edward Drummond, MD, says it's because unlike some physical illnesses, "Mental illness does not offer up an obvious villain; no rogue bacteria we can scour with an antibiotic or cancer cells we can see under a microscope." This means that while we wish the process of obtaining a definitive diagnosis were more scientific and consistent, we just aren't there yet.

As you go through the process of getting an accurate diagnosis, you'll find that clinicians have different belief systems. Some mental health professionals believe that diagnoses are of minimal value and are too subjective. In therapy, they usually prefer to focus on specific issues and concerns—unless, of course, there are specific treatments (medications or therapies) shown to be effective with this particular problem. In other words, no effective treatment, no diagnosis.

The problem with this point of view is that it doesn't take into account that effective treatments can and do become available, as they have with BPD and a host of other brain disorders. Clinicians who adhere closely to the diagnostic literature find making a proper diagnosis of value because they believe it aids them in developing a deeper understanding of the condition, addressing specific problems, and developing individualized treatment plans.

Treatment Plans

In most cases, the discussions in therapy sessions are somewhat free flowing or flexible. But the patient and therapist should have a plan that outlines the goals of therapy and how they're going to get there. Treatment plans generally include things such as

- the problems that brought the client to therapy, from "stress" to "feelings of emptiness" and how much they interfere with having a normal life (mild, moderate, serious, severe)

- specific goals for treatment and the steps that need to be taken to reach these goals, such as treatment methods, their frequency, and medications
- the role of any other health care providers who may be involved in the patient's care, as well as the intervals when the plan will be reviewed and adjusted if needed.

Diagnosing Children

Because a minor's personality isn't fully formed, clinicians tell parents to defer a formal BPD diagnosis until and unless the traits persist into adulthood. But that can be a long wait, and this reluctance to diagnose can have unintended consequences by depriving the child of help that he or she needs.

Robert Friedel, MD, one of the most influential psychiatrists in the field of BPD, believes that if parents see that their child has BPD-like traits, they should take the child to be evaluated as early as two years old. He also points out that the DSM allows for a BPD diagnosis in childhood if the patient has had symptoms for more than a year.

"If you get them evaluated, you can at least help them through a number of years before a clear diagnosis can be made," he says. "Just as it's possible to taste a spice and then add it to a soup without knowing what it is, it's possible to treat a child who displays BPD-like symptoms without first formally diagnosing BPD."[10]

A major issue is divining what is typical adolescent acting-out behavior and what is indicative of BPD. The answer lies not in the behavior itself, but the *reason* for the behavior.

Blaise Aguirre, MD, the medical director of the Adolescent DBT Center at McLean Hospital in Belmont, Massachusetts, says, "Like typical adolescents, adolescents with BPD may drink, drive recklessly, use drugs, and defy their parents. However, adolescents with BPD often use drugs, self-injure, and rage against their parents as a way of coping with profound misery, emptiness, self-loathing, and abandonment fears."[11]

A comprehensive psychiatric evaluation usually takes several hours and may be spread over more than one visit. The professional interviews the child or adolescent, the parents or guardians, and other professionals involved with the child.

The evaluation frequently includes the following:

- a description of the child's present problems and symptoms
- information about health, illness, and treatment
- parent and family health and psychiatric histories
- information about the child's development, school performance, friends, and family relationships
- if needed, laboratory studies such as blood tests, X-rays, or special assessments (for example, psychological, educational, or speech and language evaluation)

The psychiatrist develops a report that describes the child's problems and provides a diagnosis. This report becomes the foundation for the treatment plan.[12]

Disclosing the Diagnosis

Some mental health professionals don't believe in telling borderline patients their diagnosis. Reasons include

- They might adopt it as a fixed identity.
- They might use it as an excuse not to make difficult changes.
- They believe diagnoses are irrelevant.
- They might become upset and angry, especially because of the stigma.

According to Dr. Aguirre, some clinicians don't divulge a BPD diagnosis to the parents because they don't want to upset the parents and because other diagnoses with some overlapping symptoms, such as bipolar disorder, a conduct disorder, or attention-deficit/hyperactivity disorder, are easier to accept because they're easier to treat. The stigma of BPD is a clinician's issue, not the patients'.[13]

According to psychiatrist John G. Gunderson and others, the advantages of BPs knowing their diagnosis include the following:[14]

- It helps patients feel relieved and less isolated because they now know they're not alone in their misery. Today, dozens of online communities exist where people with BPD share information and support.
- Knowing their diagnosis enables patients to study and investigate BPD. If you walk into any decent-sized bookstore, you'll find several books about BPD (including empathic guides for those diagnosed with the disorder) already stocked on the shelves and many more you can order or find online. (See Resources, page 243.)
- It invites patients to actively participate in treatment planning. BPD psychiatrist Robert L. Trestman, MD, says, "It is important to engage patients in an active discussion and develop a consensus. . . . Unless there is mutual agreement about the significance of the problems, the priority for intervention, and the willingness to participate in treatment to reduce the symptoms and improve functional capacity, little will be accomplished."[15]

What about BPs themselves? Dozens of BPs online say that learning about the diagnosis enabled them to become a critical part of the therapy process. Individuals with BPD all over the world manage their own blogs, Web sites, and message boards about BPD. Several have written books, either autobiographies or books on recovery.

Some BPs *do* become angry—at least at the outset of getting this diagnosis. But that doesn't mean they should be protected from learning why their life has been such an endless struggle. Everyone who learns they're facing a tremendous loss—and having BPD certainly qualifies—can become angry. Even those who felt worse after hearing the news came to view it as a positive turning point in their lives.

Elisabeth Kübler-Ross, MD, a pioneer in understanding the way we face death and dying, identified anger as one of the stages in the grieving process. The others are denial, bargaining, depression, and finally acceptance.

It comes down to this: reconciling yourself to bad news—including being diagnosed with BPD—is a process that can't be hurried. Anger is a perfectly human reaction (although it's sure a lot more intense with BPs). People go back and forth through the stages, and some don't make it all the way through.

There may be good reasons why an individual patient should not be told. There are also good reasons why you might not want the diagnosis written on the patient's chart. It is to be hoped that, as clinicians gain knowledge about new treatment methods, the assumption will be that patients deserve to know.

Be Patient: Therapy Takes Time

Don't underestimate the difficulty of change. It's called a learning curve for a reason. Mental health professionals, no matter how talented, and medications, no matter how effective, can't quickly undo a lifetime investment in the distorted way BPs relate to themselves, those they love, and the world around them.

Mahari explains, "Some with BPD, despite being motivated and committed to the therapy process, will need longer periods of time to take in information, understand things more, and create change. Even when a borderline 'gets it' intellectually, there is still a lot of very ingrained and patterned self-defeating and negatively distorted thinking that they must work through. Recovery from BPD is like thoughtfully peeling away the layers of a giant and complex onion, one layer at a time."[16]

Therapist Andrea Corn echoes what Mahari says. "Clients with BPD take a while to realize what they're feeling. They say, 'The other person made me feel that way, it was her fault, it was his fault, he did it.' It's very hard for them to take the ownership. It can take years to tease this stuff out."[17] So as the BP's therapy progresses, carefully monitor your own hopes and expectations. You should start seeing some progress, but things will go up and down.

Health Insurance

Getting your insurance company to pay for BPD treatment is difficult because of the way the diagnosis is categorized in the DSM.

Axis I versus Axis II

Diagnoses are places in one of five domains, or "axes." Although there are five of them, you need only be concerned with the first two. They are

- Axis I: Clinical disorders, including major mental disorders such as bipolar, clinical depression, and eating disorders, as well as developmental and learning disorders. These are considered "treatable."
- Axis II: Pervasive, persistent, and long-standing personality conditions, as well as mental retardation. These are considered "untreatable."

The purpose of the "multiaxial approach," as they call it, is to assist clinicians in assessing the impact of the disorder and planning treatment. In practice, however, insurance companies are using it to deny treatment for Axis II disorders since they're labeled as lost causes—untreatable—despite the measurable effectiveness of new treatments.

BPD and other personality disorders are Axis II disorders. Because so many BPs also have a co-occurring Axis I disorder, especially clinical depression, they can get some therapy sessions approved. But it's not enough to tackle BPD. Managed care, which tries to limit services wherever it can, intensifies the problem.[18]

Fortunately, a small but growing number of insurers are beginning to consider DBT for borderline patients since DBT research shows that it reduces inpatient stays, as well as visits to the hospital's emergency room.

Experts interviewed by the American Psychological Association's newsletter *Monitor on Psychology* suggest that therapists treating borderline patients do the following:

- Assume that the insurance company will respond to well-thought-out arguments about why they should subsidize longer treatment for borderline patients and then make the best case possible to the company.
- When the insurance is an employer-sponsored plan, there may even be times when it's appropriate to register a complaint

with the employer about the insurance company's handling of a claim.

- Contact the American Psychological Association and their state psychological associations if they encounter egregious insurance company practices, allowing the APA to track the situation and perhaps communicate with the company.[19]

General Health Insurance

Most health insurance plans and HMOs provide some coverage for psychiatric care; many also cover psychological counseling. However, because plans vary considerably, you should check your plans for both outpatient (office visit) and inpatient (in-residence) coverage. Specifically, find out the following:

- What they'll pay for and what you must pay for. This includes the yearly deductible for inpatient care, outpatient care, or both. There may be separate deductibles for each.
- What co-payments are required at each office visit. Depending on your insurance company, this may differ between providers who are in the network versus out of the network. (If the preferred clinician is out of network, it still might be worth paying more.)
- The dollar limits for inpatient and outpatient care that your insurer will pay each calendar year.
- The number of outpatient visits and inpatient days the insurer will pay for. This can make a huge difference in what the therapist can accomplish in the time allowed.
- Whether the insurer has a list of allowable mental health professionals. If they do, obtain the list and make sure it is complete.
- Whether you need a prior authorization from your primary doctor.
- What you're supposed to do in an emergency.[20]

In addition, the National Education Alliance for Borderline Personality Disorder suggests asking the following questions up front:

- What additional charges, if any, will there be for tests, equipment, medications, and so on?
- How often will you be billed? What are the other terms of payment (for example, full payment within thirty days)?
- What forms of insurance or payment do they accept: Medicaid, Medicare, private insurance, credit cards, and so on?
- Is Supplemental Security Income (SSI) affected? If so, how?
- Is a financial counselor available to explain charges and billing procedures?[21]

If your insurance company will only cover services provided by one of the clinicians on its list, talk with your insurance provider and ask if they will make an exception. Point out that the right clinician may keep your family member out of the hospital and emergency room, which will save the company money.

Similarly, if your insurance company doesn't want to cover a certain drug because a lower-cost one is supposed to be just as effective (but isn't), ask your doctor or the pharmacist if you can appeal this. This may be all it takes to get the right medication.

A Therapist's View on Therapy

Byron Bloemer, PhD, is a therapist in Wisconsin who treats borderline patients using an eclectic approach. Here is his view on therapy.[22]

When you're chatting with the potential therapist, you may feel intimidated or nervous and wonder if it's insulting to ask these questions. But do it. If the therapist isn't tolerant of your questions, he's probably not the right one for you.

Good therapists must avoid getting pulled into their borderline patient's misery so they can keep therapy on track. They need a balance between caring about clients and detaching enough to help the patient make progress in therapy. A level of professional detachment protects the relationship; I couldn't continue to work with someone if I took their ups and downs personally. This takes a combination of experience, confidence, and theoretical understanding.

Effective therapists also need to understand that clients are on their own life journey. They're on their own path, and as a therapist they're only going to be a helper in their lives.

Therapist education is a problem. Most psychologists are trained as generalists. The *Diagnostic and Statistical Manual of Mental Disorders* has more than 900 pages, and only a few of them are about BPD. Even during doctoral training or master's training, there is no specific section on BPD. What ends up happening is that after their training is done, some take special courses on BPD to receive continuing education credits.

An experienced therapist can tell intuitively how much time they should spend talking with clients about their past versus their current life and immediate emotional needs. It depends on how sophisticated they are and how quickly they pick things up. Borderline clients are often very, very bright people.

In therapy, the first thing I do is assess how well clients can manage their emotions. Otherwise, we can't go anywhere. If they're unable to do so, I teach them to use relaxation CDs until their medication kicks in. I give them mindfulness exercises and other homework and talk to them about experiences that are really throwing things off. We walk through every step of how this happened and how they might intervene with themselves the next time it happens.

I have had many high-functioning borderline clients who are not suicidal; for some reason they're able to moderate their emotions. It may be that they've found a good psychiatrist and their medications are working well. It may be that they have a lot of intellectual resources and a career that makes them feel good about themselves, or a partner who is reliable and consistent. All those things help. But even these patients may call several times a day, sobbing and in crisis.

It's essential for therapists to have good communication with their client's psychiatrist. That can be hard because psychiatrists are very, very busy. Typically, I send them a letter that explains the client's symptoms and gives them my diagnosis and treatment plan. On occasion, they will reply. Some will leave me a voice mail with lots of information about their perception of the client, how they're going to intervene, what meds they're going to put him on, and what their plan is. It's ideal when we're on the same page in the beginning.

I take a lot of time to accentuate the client's strengths and successes. With one patient, I emphasized a lot of her skills in nurturing and loving instead of talking about the night she fell apart during the week. I will talk with her about the six nights that she kept it together instead of the one night she fell apart. I'll ask, "How did you do that while staying in a good relationship with your husband?" When I do this, clients walk out the door feeling more successful, happier, optimistic, and confident.

I have a lot of compassion for most of my clients, especially those who are willing to work and those who are emotionally vulnerable. When a patient calls me several times a day, I do get frustrated and tired, especially when that call comes at eleven o'clock at night—or later. I think most therapists who treat borderline clients are very compassionate, in particular if the client can put her guard down.

Blaise Aguirre, MD, on Diagnosing Minors with BPD

What follows is an interview with Dr. Blaise Aguirre, medical director of the Adolescent Dialectical Behavioral Therapy Center at McLean Hospital, Belmont, Massachusetts.[23]

Kreger: How does one go about diagnosing a child? Are there any tests?

Dr. Aguirre: Right now, the diagnosis is made using the DSM, although, increasingly, clinicians look for a series of problems in dealing with emotions—especially anger. The adolescents may have chaotic relationships, be confused about their identity and values, practice self-harm, be overly impulsive, or feel empty. They may also present cognitive impairments such as irrational beliefs, paranoia, and dissociation. I don't know of any childhood conditions, other than BPD, where all these symptoms are likely to occur.

Parents often say that their child was diagnosed with another disorder that just doesn't seem to fit and that the medications they were given didn't work.

Also, we know that, in some cases, BPD runs in families. We plan to include genetic testing in our future research. We also want to study the question as to which criteria best help in making the diagnosis of BPD in adolescents. We hope to eventually develop a standardized interview that will help clinicians distinguish BPD from normal adolescent behavior. We also hope advanced imaging techniques can help identify brain differences in these children in the future.

Kreger: How should parents work with clinicians to obtain a diagnosis?

Dr. Aguirre: As with any specific diagnosis, the more a clinician is familiar with the symptoms, the better he or she can recognize the condition. Because kids can't drive or might not be sexually active, I include other impulsive and disruptive behavior such as skipping school, so-called hooking up, and sneaking out at night.

Adolescents who have had more than a year of symptoms often come to us with chronic thoughts of suicide, marked self-loathing, self-injury, relationships characterized with overidealization/devaluation, and stark black-and-white, all-or-nothing-type thinking.

Their abandonment fears are profound. Many recognize that they test their loved ones endlessly to get them to prove their love, although they know these tests can be very destructive to their relationships.

Kreger: How do you tell the difference between BPD and other disorders?

Dr. Aguirre: The main differences lie in the degree of self-destructive behavior, the degree of self-loathing, and the unremitting thoughts of suicide.

Self-loathing is pretty unique to BPD. Self-injury is very rare in oppositional defiant disorder or conduct disorder, although it may be seen in clinical depression. The impulsivity in attention-deficit/hyperactivity disorder is sometimes similar to the impulsivity in BPD.

Although adolescents with BPD can be aggressive, this is not a common presenting symptom at our unit. Often, when BP adolescents are aggressive, they feel ashamed or remorseful after the event. Children with conduct disorder generally do not care at all (or at least do not appear to care) if they have hurt someone.

Two things are absolutely clear. First, adults with BPD almost always recognize that their symptoms and suffering started in childhood or adolescence. Second, adolescents have symptoms that are so consistent with BPD that it would be unethical not to make this diagnosis and treat them accordingly.

Part 2

POWER TOOLS

About Power Tools

In the first half of this book, you learned just how BPD impairs an individual's thoughts and feelings, which in turn triggers behaviors such as raging, perceived manipulation, and excessive blame and criticism. You've also discovered that your reaction to your family member's behaviors sets up negative patterns of behavior that leave both of you feeling frustrated and upset.

In the second half of this book, you'll find out about five powerful tools to help you organize your thinking, learn specific skills, and focus on what you need to do instead of becoming overwhelmed. The power tools are

Power Tool 1: Take good care of yourself.
Power Tool 2: Uncover what keeps you feeling stuck.
Power Tool 3: Communicate to be heard.
Power Tool 4: Set limits with love.
Power Tool 5: Reinforce the right behavior.

Each power tool will build on the previous one, so it's essential that you learn them in order. As with any skill, you will need to practice to become better. Start with something simple and build on the strengths and resources you already have. Remember this is a *process.*

While these power tools are based in research, both formal and informal, it's impossible to predict how any one individual will react to them.

BPD is multifaceted, and BPD behaviors can be wildly unpredictable. Therefore, you'll need to take the information and customize it for your particular situation.

Seek counseling with a mental health professional whose primary concern is *you*. Don't allow yourself to be abused; it will not help your BP, and it will harm you. Always remember that safety—both yours and your family member's—is of paramount concern.

As you increase your mastery of these five basic skills, you will

- feel less stressed and run down
- become more confident and clear about who you are and what you need
- know where to concentrate your efforts
- be able to free yourself from nonproductive, aggressive conversations
- improve your problem-solving skills
- learn how to help your family member without rescuing him
- feel more self-assured about setting limits without backing down

Once you've read through the power tools, the next step is to sort through what you've learned and determine your priorities. If you own this book, highlight as you read. When you're done, look through what you've highlighted and choose just one thing you'd like to learn to do. Make it simple and easy. A great first step is the breathing exercise you're going to learn about in the next chapter.

Then visit the resources section in the back of this book. Resources are divided by power tool so you know how to prioritize your reading. Of course, you don't have to stop there: browse the Internet, go to a bookstore, or take a class in what interests you.

Don't expect to be perfect. You will need to practice using your tools. Some tools will come more easily to you than others; that's normal. There may be habits you need to drop and habits you need to pick up. If you start to feel overwhelmed, you're doing too much. You will find a wealth of resources at www.bpdcentral.com, including links to Web sites, support groups, and other training materials.

If you don't feel like putting all this in motion right now, that's fine, too. Take your time. People go through different stages as they think about changes they might want to make in their lives, from thinking about making changes to tentative exploring, from tentative exploring to preparation, then from preparation to action and maintenance.[1]

People also go through stages in their relationships with people who have BPD: the confusion stage, usually before they learn about BPD; the outer-directed stage, when they try to change their family member; the inner-directed stage, where they look inward; the decision-making stage; and the resolution stage, when they implement their decisions and make changes as needed.

Now, on to the power tools!

Chapter 7

Power Tool 1:
Take Good Care of Yourself

A good night's sleep should be declared a basic human right.
▪ Pierce J. Howard, *The Owner's Manual for the Brain* ▪

The stress of having a family member with borderline personality disorder can lead to a number of physical and mental issues. They can be mild to severe, and include the following:

- irritability or outbursts of anger
- problems falling or staying asleep
- crying spells
- difficulty concentrating
- feeling jumpy and easily startled
- loss of interest in activities and life in general
- feeling detached or emotionally numb
- unintended weight gain or loss
- feeling hopeless or ashamed
- feeling fatigued and weak
- unexplained physical problems (such as headaches, stomach problems)
- loss of interest in sex
- depression, panic attacks, or other psychological problems

As a non-BP, you deal with stressful issues related to having a borderline family member daily. The problems surface in almost every area of life—finances, relationships, work. In addition, if you begin to isolate yourself out of shame, the result is a lack of social support. Each of these difficulties has serious consequences to your mental and physical health.[1]

Power Tool 1 is the foundation for all other power tools. You can't operate power tools safely and effectively if you're too tired, distracted, or otherwise not at your best. That's true whether you're talking about the power tools in this book or those stored in your garage or basement.

You can't help your BP raise her self-esteem if yours is lodged twenty feet underground. Your "I love you's" won't be reassuring if you say them through clenched teeth because you haven't dealt with your anger. And if you're trying so hard to please your borderline partner that you're losing what makes you *you,* then what's the point?

Establish Lines of Support

Just as your family member may need a treatment team, you need a support team. Potential team members include your friends, other family members, your community, and perhaps a therapist.

A Therapist for You

Therapists who practice dialectical behavior therapy in a clinic meet two to four times a month to obtain suggestions and support for their work from their fellow clinicians. When therapists specially trained to work with the borderline population require the assistance of other therapists, you can be sure that family members need help, too.

Because therapists are not emotionally connected to your BP, they see your situation in an unbiased and nonjudgmental light. In addition to listening and validating your feelings, they can guide you in separating the truth from your family member's distortions and help you become aware of your role in the relationship. They offer practical help, too, such as suggesting different courses of action or helping you practice new communication skills.

Some non-BP partners have a pattern of getting into unhealthy relationships. This is something to explore in therapy so it doesn't happen again. If you and your borderline partner have a child together who is a minor, the child may need support, too, depending on the family environment. Be watchful; non-BP partners almost always underestimate the effects of a chaotic and argumentative home environment on children.

If you are a sibling or an adult child of someone with BPD, you probably have two issues: coping with your family member in the here and now, and examining how having a borderline sibling or parent has shaped your own personality.

Friends and Family

If you only get one thing out of this chapter, let it be this: Do not become isolated. Reach out to others. Don't let yourself be embarrassed into isolation or pushed into it by threats, implied or outright. That is no way to live.

One of the best things friends and family members can do is listen. They don't need to have answers. They may not understand everything you're going through—in fact, they probably won't. That's okay. You need a pair of ears to hear you and a pair of arms to hug you. The mouth is optional.

Depend on friends to give you reality checks. When you're in a relationship with someone who has BPD, it's easy to lose sight of what is normal. If two or more friends are giving you the same message, listen carefully, even if you don't want to hear it. (On the other hand, look for aid elsewhere if you're feeling judged or invalidated. Like everything else, it's a balancing act.)

Depending on the situation, it may be helpful if your support people are not too close to the situation. If they also have close relationships with your BP, that could interfere. You should feel safe with whomever you talk to.

A Community

Communities are places where we feel part of a larger social whole. People in communities may share a web of relationships, common values or interests, and a shared history. Whether your community is small or large, right next door, or online, these connections matter.

You may find your community (or communities) in your actual neighborhood. Take the time to learn the names of your mail carrier and pharmacist. Say hi to the older gentleman who's always sitting in the yard when you take your dog for a walk. Churches, workplaces, and schools harbor communities. The Web site www.meetup.com can help you find or start a group for non-BPs.

Today, thousands of communities are a keystroke away on the Internet. Some, like Welcome to Oz, revolve around BPD (see "Resources" on page 243). You can find them by interest, by geography, by faith, by age, by ethnicity, by gender, and by just about anything else. If you're a fan of a celebrity, book, movie, or musical group, you can find groups of people who share your interest. If you like underwater basket weaving under a full moon, there's probably an online community for you.

Take Things Less Personally

When you personalize what someone says, you essentially bring down a hail of guilt, shame, and loss of self-esteem on yourself. You end up running around in circles trying to figure out what is wrong with you, all in a futile effort to control another person's behavior—in this case, someone whose behavior is hardwired into her brain.

Personalization is actually a two-step process. Have you ever seen slow-motion video of a car crash test dummy hitting the windshield? There are actually *two* crashes. The car moves forward, then bang—hits the wall. That's hit number one. In the next second, the dummy (or you, if you don't wear your safety belt) is propelled forward, hitting the windshield. That's crash number two, the crash that does the real damage.

Something similar—but much more subtle—happens when you take things personally. First comes our BP's behavior: an accusation, an insult—whatever. That's crash number one. Half a second later, thoughts like these flash through your mind:

- "I must have done something to provoke her."
- "He's doing this to hurt me."
- "If she says this terrible thing about me, it must be true."

All these thoughts constitute crash number two, personalizing the behavior. You can't stop crash number one, which is whatever your BP says or does. It hurts. But you can stop the useless pain from crash number two because it's going on in your mind, and you have control over your mind.

Elayne Savage, PhD, the author of *Don't Take It Personally!* says, "When we take things personally, we think the world revolves around us. It's all about me-me-me. If we lose sight that there may be something going on with the other person, we'll miss the opportunity to empathize, or put ourselves in their shoes."[2]

Keep reminding yourself that wildly out-of-place and senseless behaviors are the result of a brain disorder that can be explained scientifically. When you feel yourself starting to take something personally, reread the first part of this book. Let those chapters be your safety belt.

Get a Handle on Your Emotions

Is it normal to feel like you're going crazy, like you want to scream in frustration, pummel a punching bag, and lie in bed and sob into the pillow? You bet! Having a loved one with BPD can bring about an amazing number of concerns. Space permits us to look at only four: worry, guilt, low self-esteem, and anger.

Worry and guilt hit parents particularly hard. Adult children of BPs engage in life-long struggles to feel good about themselves. Anger is a predominant emotion of partners, especially those separating from their BP partners. (Parents tend to turn their anger into depression.) Everybody feels helpless.

Don't Worry, Be Happy

The nature of the disorder—unpredictability, lightning-fast triggers, mood changes—makes the future uncertain (here, "future" could mean five minutes from now or fifteen years from now). While all non-BPs worry now and then, family members of lower-functioning conventional BPs worry morning, noon, and night, because they're dealing with life and death issues, including suicide.

Dale Carnegie's *How to Stop Worrying and Start Living* is a classic that has sold millions of copies. The advice it offers is just as good today as it was in the mid-twentieth century when the book was first published. The techniques it describes are the same whether the worrier is a fourth-grader fretting about a math test or a president debating whether the United States should enter a world war.[3]

The Carnegie Problem-Solving Method

Non-BPs feel so helpless in the relationship that they tend to forget they are capable people with fine problem-solving abilities. They often give up on solutions before they've researched them or thought them through. Or, they're too depressed and upset to think straight.

The trick to being a problem-solver instead of a worrier is to compartmentalize your world. When you feel awful, feel awful. Yell, scream, cry, and throw soft objects (or hard if you must) at the wall. Then, take a nap. When you wake up, brew some coffee or tea and put on your problem-solving hat. Focus on what you can do—not on what you can't do. Ask friends and family to help give you a fresh perspective.

These steps will help you become a problem-solver:

Step 1: Choose one problem and lock the other ones in a box, for now. Then, calmly gather the facts for one of your dilemmas. Carnegie believes that half our worries are caused by trying to make decisions before we have all the facts.

Step 2: Calmly analyze the facts. For example, don't just say you can't afford something. Put together a budget. If you cancel cable and brown bag it for lunch, how much will you save? Likewise for time, the other resource generally in short supply. No one has enough time, but *someone's* out there watching reality TV. Weigh what's important to you.

Step 3: Arrive at a decision and act on it. Don't give up too quickly, because there is no quick fix. On the other hand, don't stick with a method that clearly isn't working. (The difference between the two is often a matter of time. If waiting for your BP to change hasn't worked for several years, it's time to try something else.) Rethink or modify your plan as necessary.

Not Guilty!

The purpose of pain is to tell us something is not right. "Good pain" gets our attention so we do something about an injury or illness. Without it, we could bleed to death. Then there's "bad pain," that chronic stuff that does no good, except to those who invest in pharmaceutical stock.

Guilt is like that, too. If you're a writer who has a book deadline coming up but you'd rather surf the Web, "good guilt" can get you back on track so your publisher doesn't have a heart attack. "Bad guilt," on the other hand, benefits no one. Guilt may come from many places:

1. *Hardwired:* The biologically based, irrational parental guilt that insists that if you had just done more of something or less of something else (no one knows what) your child would be on the fast track to the presidency of the United States. Don't expect more from yourself than you do from the professionals.

2. *Cultural:* Society believes that parents (that is, mommy) are *always* responsible for their child's behavioral problems. This pops up everywhere. For example, "refrigerator mothers" were said to have caused autism, and schizophrenia was supposed to come from mothers who appeared to love their children but unconsciously rejected them.

3. *Stereotypes:* As discussed in chapter 4, a long-standing belief is that all BPs have had abusive childhoods. Parents—especially fathers—are seen as suspect.

4. *Your family member:* When non-BPs try to set limits or stick to their guns, BPs often press the "guilt" button. Parents and adult children are particularly vulnerable to this tactic.

Guilt is your enemy for two reasons: First, it feels bad and makes you miserable. Second, it blurs your thinking and can drive you to make the wrong decisions. We'll talk about the second problem in the next chapter. As for the first, when you feel guilty, tell yourself that guilt is a luxury you can't afford. As tempting as it may be not to, you need to put your energy elsewhere. Then, do it.

Self-Esteem: How Low Can You Go?

People who have low self-esteem question their abilities most of the time. They can't think of any good qualities about themselves or take pride in their accomplishments. Their failures loom large, but their opinions about themselves run ten degrees below sea level. They think other people have more worth than they do. When others don't respect them, they figure they've gotten what they deserved.

Some sources of low self-esteem in non-BPs are obvious. In a letter to her ex-girlfriend Terry, a woman with BPD, Chris wrote, "My self-esteem plummeted because of your frequent unpredictable snapping, constant nagging and criticism, and general air of hostility. Even when I was alone, it was like you were constantly there, criticizing me, nagging me, or snapping at me. I began to believe that I really was klutzy, stupid, untidy, careless."[4]

In a post to the Welcome to Oz online family community, another non-BP says, "When the raging and criticism began, I started questioning my reality. He seemed so righteous in his rage. So certain. It made me feel small. Since it was pointless to argue, I sucked it all in. I knew if I weathered it out, it would pass, and we would get back to 'normal' (normal for us, that is). I didn't know it was killing me bit by bit."

Other sources of low self-esteem are more obscure. Carolyn DeRoo, coauthor of *What's Right with Me,* says:

> In this culture we are raised with the notion that if we do the right thing, things will work out for us. But some difficulties have nothing to do with us. We may be doing a whole lot right—even going above and beyond—but we're still struggling. When that happens, we feel bad about ourselves. We question if we did the right thing.

We need to disconnect from the belief that we're doing something wrong just because this struggle exists. We need to bear in mind that this is just a basic part of life, even though it's not reflected out there in the media. And we shouldn't compare ourselves to others, because we don't know how things really are for them.[5]

DeRoo suggests that people in turbulent relationships get a more balanced view of themselves because they may have learned to censor their strengths. Think back to some of the most important people to you, now and in the past. What have they said they appreciate about you? What compliments have you received during your life?

Write down the answers. "You want to *see* the nice things they say about you in black and white," she says. "As you write, consider that these people, as far as you know, do *not* have a brain disorder that affects their perceptions and emotions. Doesn't that make their assessments more persuasive—or at least *as* persuasive as those of your family member?"

The next step is asking the question directly to those you trust the most. Listen to them tell you your good points out loud. The more embarrassing this might seem, the more you probably need to hear it. What about you? What do *you* like about yourself?

If your BP is a parent who disparaged you or put her own needs before yours, you may feel worthless or fundamentally flawed. That's understandable. Tell yourself, "The past is over; I'm not a kid anymore. It's *my* life now to spend with people who love me and make me feel good about myself." Seek professional help and take small steps in the right direction. Self-esteem comes with learning to trust yourself and your own perceptions.

Anger

Anger is often a sign that something needs to change. Who or what are you angry at? What is the reason for the anger? The answers to these questions can alert you if something needs to change. Family members often become angry when people with BPD overstep their boundaries—sometimes, boundaries they didn't know they had. Non-BPs get angry at themselves, at the disorder, at the health care system, and, of course, at their BP.

Some non-BPs don't know that they're angry because they repress it. Unvented, it settles into their bones where it remains as a kind of toxic force that can lead to depression and, over time, resentment and rage. All too often, family members (especially partners) let their anger simmer until they blow up in resentment when they've never really let their wishes be known.

Buried anger has been shown to set off ulcers, heart disease, hypertension, headaches, back pain, depression, and fatigue.[6] Learning from anger is good; managing it is essential. If you get angry at other people for misperceiving who you are or your intentions, keep telling yourself, "I don't have to prove anything to anybody else." Try to separate the disorder—especially the border-lion (see page 58)—from your loved one.

Find a safe and healthy way to release your anger. Find a private place, pretend that you're face-to-face with the person you're angry at (even if it's you), and say anything you want as loud as you want. You'll find that the other person is a great listener. Writing letters you don't send is an alternative, especially if you use a lot of capital letters and exclamation marks.

As you do this exercise, you may be surprised at some of the things that come out of your mouth. You may uncover feelings and thoughts you didn't know you had. The full force of the impact of your situation on you, the tangled mix of emotions, may give you a great sense of compassion for yourself.

Practice Acceptance

When you practice acceptance:

- You acknowledge that things are the way they are at this very moment and that some things are beyond your control. You didn't cause it, you can't control it, and you can't cure it.
- You live in the present, not the past nor future. You don't dwell on negative aspects of the past and try to assess blame.
- There's no place to go but up. Without acceptance, when you look around, all you see is what you *don't* have. After you've accepted the worst, you will see how much you actually have.

Maybe this sounds too "new agey." Actually, it's very *old* agey. We could go back to seventh-century China, but let's take just a short 140-year (or so) jaunt to the American frontier. That's the setting for Laura Ingalls Wilder's "Little House" series of books. The 1970s TV series was an idealized, Walt Disney–type affair; in reality, Laura and her family lived a harsh life fraught by the struggle to survive.

In her book *The Long Winter*, Ingalls Wilder describes how her family holed up in the kitchen during a blizzard season, living on bread and tea. They lost weight and nearly starved to death until Laura's future husband risked his life to get some grain. Laura's hands chafed from twisting hay into sticks to keep the stove going, and Laura and her sisters nearly froze. As they changed into their bedclothes, they could see the breath in front of their faces. Yet they didn't complain. As Wilder wrote, "We knew it couldn't be helped."

Yet most of the time, Laura was joyful. She saw her childhood as a wonderful time; her descriptions have delighted generations. Today, we have lost the ability to say, "It couldn't be helped." Today, we believe things can and should be controlled. And if they're not, then someone's to blame.

Start by accepting the small things. For example, one woman on WTO found she was spending too much time being irritated by everyday problems. Every time she couldn't find an important e-mail or bought a size small when she meant to buy the medium, it put her in a bad mood. One day she decided to change her ways and to expect everything to go wrong. Now it honestly surprises her when she finds the scissors where it's supposed to be or when she actually finds that slip of paper with the important phone number on it.

Once you've accepted that the worst may happen, you have no place to go but up. You reduce the amount of time you spend judging everything. In general, it's not events that cause suffering, but the value judgment we put on them. In other words, the way you view a situation, person, or event has a profound effect on how you feel about it and is quite separate from the problem itself.

Laughter, the Best Medicine

Mona and her husband, Barney, were taking a walk in their subdivision when Mona's cell phone rang. It was Gil, their son who has BPD. He just quit his job again (was fired) and was losing his apartment (evicted). Could he come back home for a while (as long as they would let him) and save up some money (then spend it on drugs) so he could afford first month's rent and security deposit (buy more drugs)?

This was very bad news. Mona told Gil she'd call him back, and she and Barney walked on, silently. Waiting at the light for traffic to pass, they spied the bumper sticker at the same time:

I Child-Proofed My House, But They Still Got In

The couple laughed until they cried. Literally. And lo and behold, when they were done, they felt better.

Smiling and laughing triggers the production of endorphins, morphine-like chemicals that reduce pain and relax the body. Endorphins strengthen the immune system, which fights disease and hastens recovery.

Among themselves, parents often use humor. For example, a group of parents on Welcome to Oz made a list called, "Why Parents and Other Caretakers Do What We Do." Reasons included

- We are a vital force in the economy. The mental health field would suffer a recession if not for us.
- We love the lingo.
- It's only rock and roll, but I like it.
- Whaddya gonna do?

Sometimes, family members use humor among themselves as a way to release tension, defuse anger, and address sensitive issues. This is why professional comedians can get away with saying things that would sound most inappropriate if they were voiced by anyone else. It's okay to use this kind of humor at the appropriate time (away from your BP). If we can joke about Nazis (the film/play *The Producers* and the TV show *Hogan's Heroes*), we can joke about BPD.

Shared humor is a powerful way for people to bond and talk about the illness. A woman with a borderline daughter says, "One day we were at the mall and she said, 'Come here quick, look at this! It's for me!' It was a shirt that said Drama Queen Academy on the front. And I said, 'You're right, that is for you.' She was shocked I would let her have a sense of humor about herself. I said, 'I think that's great that you see that that's for you.' She wore it with pride. I thought, *There's hope for her because she has enough self-awareness to joke about the way she is.*"

Humor can also reduce hostility during a fight—sometimes even stop one or prevent one from happening. But it must be used cautiously, or it can sound sarcastic and backfire. The context, the moods of the people involved, and the subject matter being discussed are of the utmost importance.

Lead a Full Life

You need other people, outside activities, and feelings of accomplishment in your life to stay sane, let alone happy. You also need time alone to rest and think. If you're shaking your head right now and saying, "That may apply to other people reading this, but not me," then that sentence goes double for you.

It isn't always the *amount* of time you have, but what you do *with* the time. You can spend thirty minutes worrying or replaying something negative in your head, or read a novel or nonfiction book on a subject that interests you.

Get involved in projects that make you feel competent and give you a sense of satisfaction. Hobbies that produce a finished product (a handmade cabinet, for example) are especially helpful. If you run out of ideas, review your past activities and accomplishments.

Spending a day or more in another environment with different people can transform your life. As you relate to other people and vice versa, it can help you remember what "normal" is. One overnight trip can power you up for a long time. Spend time alone with your thoughts, too. If you can get outdoors on a beautiful day, do it. Invite your senses along: hear a musical group perform or go to an ethnic restaurant. Whatever you do, just *go.*

In his book *How to Change Anybody,* David J. Lieberman says, "Our identity is very much tied in with where we live, the people we know, and the places we know. By removing individuals from their environment, you shake up their self-concepts and make it easier for them to see themselves differently, and quite often, more objectively. You also get them away from the influences and triggers that snap them back into negative patterns."[7]

Chris, a non-BP, went on a trip alone with her sister Samantha despite her BP girlfriend's objections (she couldn't go for some reason). Chris writes:

> It was so good for my soul to spend a few days away so I could be myself. I could throw all my change, maps, and park guides on the table without you nagging me to be neat. I could mix all my stuff with Samantha's without you getting on my back about keeping our own separate piles. I could eat at a restaurant without you commenting if I dropped a morsel of food on the table. I could relax. And to my sister, my behavior was totally normal.
>
> Those four days in Florida were like a little window to me of how things could be. This blanket of anxiety, which I had gradually come to accept as normal, had been momentarily lifted. I am starting to realize I am okay just like I am!

Breathe Deeply

Our bodies evolved so that when we saw a threat—say, the iconic saber-toothed tiger—our bodies would go into "fight or flight" mode. Our terrified brains tell our adrenal glands to release chemicals that sharpen our senses, tighten our muscles, and make our heart pound faster. Our bloodstream fills with sugars for ready energy. Now we're ready to confront the enemy (fight) or run like heck (flight).[8]

This response is supposed to turn off once the stressor is history. But our modern-day threats are continuing, not acute, and most of the time we can't fight *or* flee. Some of the stress hormones stay high and can weaken the immune system, potentially making cancer and infectious diseases worse.[9] Stress may negatively affect the heart, and two studies appearing in authoritative journals found that first-time heart attack patients who returned to chronically stressful jobs were twice as likely to have a second attack as patients whose occupations were relatively stress-free.[10]

Life itself is stressful enough that stress-reduction strategies such as yoga, meditation, and other relaxation exercises have become popular. When you add in the presence of a personality disorder in someone you love, your stress levels climb even higher.

The degree of your stress depends in part on how BPD presents itself in your loved one. If your BP is at risk of suicide or self-harm, flies into erratic rages, or can easily become threatening to others or self, your stress level may rise to the level of *hypervigilance,* which is a symptom of post-traumatic stress disorder. Hypervigilant people are like the giraffes at a watering hole on page 57. They're always on the alert, looking for danger. Their stress hormone levels rise high and don't go down.

Sometimes complicated predicaments have simple solutions. Abdominal breathing, or deep breathing, counteracts the "fight or flight" stress response. Depending on how long you do it, it can help you feel better, help you sleep better, and improve your concentration. This is a core skill that will be referred to in other chapters. It can slow down racing thoughts and quiet down your emotions.

The first time you do deep abdominal breathing will be a minor production. Once you get the hang of it, you'll be able to do it anywhere. Do the longer version when you have more time or are feeling stressed. Here's how to get started:

Step 1: Lie down on the floor or some other hard surface. Lie on a warm rug or mat, if you can. Try putting a pillow under your knees to support your lower back. Make sure you're comfortable and warm.

Step 2: Relax your body. Just . . . let . . . everything . . . go. Unclench your jaw and hands and let your shoulders flow back. Let everything get soft . . . picture a cat stretched out on a fur rug with butter-yellow sun streaming in from the window overlooking the garden. Put your brain on standby (but don't fall asleep).

Step 3: Put your hands on your stomach. Take a slow, deep breath so that your stomach, not your chest, rises. Your chest shouldn't move. Breathe slowly, deeply. Put a very thick book on your stomach; it should be going up and down. When you do this, you're using a sheath of muscles called the diaphragm. Practice.

It wouldn't hurt to breathe this way all the time. But make sure to do it for at least five minutes when you feel tension coming on.

Get Some Shut-Eye

On average, most people need an additional sixty to ninety minutes more sleep than they get.[11] Late-night arguments and worry top the reasons why non-BPs don't get enough sleep.

As you sleep, your brain organizes the memories of habits, actions, and skills learned during the day. Deprived of sleep, your body cranks up stress hormones that send your blood pressure soaring—putting you at risk for heart attacks or strokes. Lack of sleep can also make it more difficult to master complex tasks and to find creative solutions to life's challenges.[12] In a study in Australia, transportation workers who were deprived of sleep for twenty-eight hours showed the same level of impairment in speed and accuracy as those who had a blood alcohol concentration (BAC) of 0.05 percent. After longer periods without sleep, the workers' performance was as impaired as those who had a BAC of 0.1 percent. (In the United States, it is illegal to drive with a BAC of 0.08 percent or above.)[13]

Pick Up the Pace

You've always known that moving around improves your physical health. The equivalent of thirty minutes of brisk walking also provides an immediate boost to your brainpower and mental health, too. Psychiatrist John

Ratey, MD, says that a bout of exercise increases the level of the mood-enhancing neurotransmitters dopamine, serotonin, and norepinephrine in your brain.[14]

Jim Phelps, MD, is the author of the book *Why Am I Still Depressed?* The book, which is about bipolar disorder, has a brilliant chapter called "Exercise and Mood: Not the Usual Rap."[15] The chapter discusses the barriers to exercise (to begin with, it's giving to yourself, it takes time, and the benefits don't happen right away) and how to overcome them and make movement a part of your life. You can read the chapter for free at psycheducation.org/hormones/Insulin/exercise.htm.

Making Changes the Easy Way

Are you in love with immediate gratification? Most everybody is, not just people with BPD. In fact, the need for instant satisfaction is an epidemic. The cure for this "disease" is to take things slowly. Go ridiculously slow—say, a 5 percent change each day. If you're spending five minutes walking on Monday, try increasing that by 5 percent on Tuesday. You can do it!

Looking back on this chapter, what speaks the most to you? What is the easiest change you can make that has the most impact? Pick one. Do something. Then increase it by 5 percent tomorrow, or in a week, or whatever time frame you choose. For example, after you are finished reading this sentence, put the book down, take a deep breath, and think of something you like about yourself. Go ahead—try it!

You're probably wondering how much good 5 percent of anything can do. The answer is "a whole heck of a lot." First, small steps add up in a hurry. We age a tiny bit each day. And as we age, our metabolism gradually slows. Sure enough, we get old and put on pounds before we know it.

There's another reason why small moves lead to big results: as long as you're moving forward—no matter how slowly—you won't be going backward. You'll also find that success breeds success. Progress is its own reward, especially if you measure and track it. If you're having a bad day and 5 percent seems too much, then temporarily scale it back to 1 percent.

You might think that this power tool would be the easiest one to learn how to use. It isn't. It's too easy to overlook or dismiss. Self-care is like food. Three times a day (plus snacks) you eat and drink to replenish the calories you have expended working, studying, taking care of your family, and so forth. Just like running uses up a lot of calories, having a borderline loved one takes a great deal of mental and emotional energy. Self-care replenishes that energy.

Chapter 8

Power Tool 2:
Uncover What Keeps You Feeling Stuck

*Insanity is doing the same thing over and over again
and expecting different results.*
▪ Albert Einstein ▪

What you avoid controls you.
▪ Elizabeth B. Brown ▪

Consider the following questions:

- Do you feel unable to move because danger lies in every choice, yet you feel compelled to do *something*?
- Do you and your BP have an unspoken agreement that his needs are more important than yours?
- Does your satisfaction with this relationship depend on your BP making significant changes—yet he hasn't demonstrated a lasting desire to do so?
- Have you made compromises you realize you can't live with in the long term, but have no idea how to go back and change things?
- Is this relationship too good to leave but too bad to stay in?

If you answered "yes" to most of these questions, chances are you're stuck.

Psychotherapist Barbara Cowan Berg, author of *How to Escape the No-Win Trap,* says, "Double-bind situations often build up slowly and catch you off guard. They can be subtle and insidious, wrapping you up in a web of confusion. Most often, you don't recognize situations that have the ability to make you crazy until you're deeply involved."[1]

Non-BPs hold their borderline family member responsible for their entrapment. But after spending some time in Welcome to Oz, many come to realize that some inner need of theirs keeps them tied to the turbulence. This is mostly true of non-BPs who choose to be in a relationship with someone who has BPD; in fact, their inner needs may be one reason why they chose their partner or friend.

Berg says that interpersonal double binds can appear to be about what is going on with the other party. But when you look more closely at the underpinnings of the conflict, the story is more about you.[2] The longer you have been stuck in a chosen relationship, she says, the more likely it is that the solution to the problem lies within you.[3]

Uncovering and resolving the source of your feelings of entrapment is the most essential element that determines not only the course of your relationship, but the degree of distress you will experience from having a borderline family member. This is because feelings of helplessness and lack of control can cause just as much suffering as the presence of the personality disorder itself.

Study after study has found that in different types of situations—at work, in relationships, in nursing homes, when facing terminal illness, while playing sports—the urge to feel in control of your own destiny is a universal motive. With it, we gain an inner sense of mastery and feelings of satisfaction. Without it, we are at risk for hopelessness, stress, and depression.[4]

What Keeps You Stuck?

Most non-BPs feel stuck for one or more of the following six reasons:

- unhealthy bonds forged by emotional abuse
- feelings of fear
- obligation, roles, and duty
- guilt mingled with shame

- low self-esteem
- the need to "rescue"

Unhealthy Bonds Forged by Emotional Abuse

Emotional abuse, according to therapist and author Beverly Engel, is non-physical behaviors or attitudes used to control, intimidate, subjugate, demean, punish, or isolate another. Abusers tend to degrade, humiliate, or instill fear in their victims. Emotional abuse includes *symbolic violence,* such as slamming doors, kicking walls, and throwing objects.

The behavior and attitudes Engel refers to include classic BPD traits such as accusing, blaming, unpredictable responses, unreasonable demands, the "silent treatment," criticizing, and constant chaos and drama. The effects can include a lack of motivation, confusion, and difficulty making decisions—all of which can keep people stuck.[5]

Engel says that people who are emotionally abused wonder, *Am I as bad as she makes me out to be, or is she just impossible to please? Should I stay in the relationship or should I go? If I am as incompetent as he says I am, maybe I can't make it on my own. Maybe no one will ever love me again.*

You might think that the obvious choice for the abused person would be to simply avoid the abuser and try to rebuild self-esteem. Instead, the opposite occurs: people who feel abused and controlled develop strong, unhealthy bonds that keep them in a dysfunctional dance with the person who is bullying them.

This dynamic is so well known it even has a name: the *Stockholm Syndrome.* The name comes from a 1973 incident in Stockholm, Sweden, in which hostages became emotionally attached to the criminals who held them hostage during a bank robbery.

The syndrome includes these key elements:

- the belief that the abuser/controller is an imminent threat to one's physical or psychological survival
- the presence of a perceived small kindness from the abuser/controller to the sufferer

- isolation from perspectives other than those of the abuser/
controller
- the belief that one is unable to escape from the situation

The following are signs that the Stockholm Syndrome might be at work:

- thinking, *I know she hurts me all the time and does terrible
things to me, but I love her anyway!* (Extremely common.)
- receiving warnings from others about the relationship and dis-
missing them because others "just don't understand." Eventually, the sufferer avoids those who don't approve of the abuser/
controller.
- giving the abuser/controller positive credit for small tokens
of kindness (a birthday card) or for *not* being abusive when
abusiveness was expected (such as not getting jealous when
an opposite-sex co-worker waves in a crowd).
- making excuses for the abuser/controller's behavior (such as,
"He couldn't help it because he was abused as a kid").
- becoming preoccupied with the needs, desires, and habits of the
abuser/controller in an effort to prevent the abuser/controller
from having an outburst.[6]

Feelings of Fear

"Fear is at the root of every human struggle," say Bill Klatte and Kate
Thompson in their book *It's So Hard to Love You.* "It is experienced in
many guises and to varying degrees. Fear can take hold of your mind
and twist your insides into knots."[7] The following fears are common for
non-BPs:

- fear for the BP's health and welfare (common with lower-
functioning conventional BPs). Suicide threats are the most
potent fear.[8]
- fear of conflict, for example, "I can't say that. He might get
upset."
- fear of being alone (abandonment). (BPs aren't the only ones.)

- fear of failing or being perceived as a failure (for example, with having a failed marriage).
- fear of financial problems (common in partners).
- fear of the unknown.
- fear of the BP's threats coming true.

If fear is keeping you stuck, be specific about your fears so you can address them. Instead of saying, "I fear conflict," zone in on what that really means to you. "I am afraid he will start an argument" is more specific. Keep asking yourself, "Then what?" "Then he will yell." (Then what?) "Then I will become uncomfortable." (Then what?) "Then I might have to leave the house. Then I would wait until he calmed down before I came home." The answers to "then what?" may not be as scary as you think.

Feel the Fear and Do It Anyway is a classic book that helps people face all kinds of fears. Author Susan Jeffers says that all we need to do to diminish fear is develop more trust in our ability to handle whatever comes our way. She writes:

> You know that you don't like the fact that lack of trust in yourself is stopping you from getting what you want out of life. Knowing this creates a very clear, even laserlike, focus on what needs to be changed.
>
> You don't have to scatter your energy wondering why [you're afraid of something]. It doesn't matter. What matters is that you begin now to develop your trust in yourself, until you reach a point where you will be able to say, "WHATEVER HAPPENS TO ME, GIVEN ANY SITUATION, I CAN HANDLE IT." [9]

For those in chosen love relationships, the definitive fear is losing the relationship. Because of unhealthy bonds, the more dysfunctional the relationship, the worse the fear. We'll come back to fear of losing the relationship in chapter 10, Power Tool 4: Set Limits with Love.

Obligation, Roles, and Duty

Dana has an abusive borderline/narcissistic mother, Gloria. Dana's husband and friends keep telling her to cut all ties with her mom, and Dana would love to. But she can't—it would feel too disloyal. If she doesn't call her mother twice a week, she feels guilty. What kind of daughter would she be if she deserted her mother?

Our concepts about roles and obligations are supposed to keep life predictable and create an orderly, stable society, say Klatte and Thompson.[10] The family unit provides for the needs of each member in a grand attempt to perpetuate the species and perhaps the family name. Then, myths and ideals evolve around what the perfect parent, child, sibling, or grandparent should be like.

The sad truth is that while families may have evolved to ensure the survival of its members, sometimes survival is dependent on giving up the myths of the ideal parent, sister, or other family member, and accepting reality, no matter how much we wish it were otherwise.

Take a close look at your beliefs and decide which ones are based on myths and which are based on reality. This consists of asking questions such as "What do I do out of a sense of obligation? What feelings rise up when I ask myself that question? Which of my obligations feel good to me? Which ones do not?" Your situation is different in ways that may be hard to explain to others. But you don't necessarily owe anyone an explanation.

Guilt and Shame

Shame is a global feeling: I *am* bad. Guilt is a more limited feeling: I have *done* something bad.

Guilt drives parents to lose their sense of judgment and go to ridiculous lengths to assuage their guilt. A typical story is that of a couple who let their adult daughter live with them for free while the daughter ordered them to clean her clothes, feed her, and pay her bills.

Perry Hoffman says,

> I have a cartoon I show at my presentations to families. It's a picture of a duck walking down the hall to the living room, where the parents are sitting on the couch. And the mother says to the father, "We are absolutely, positively not driving Earl to Florida this winter."

That depicts what happens to families. Family members often lose their good intuition. They need to step back and say, "Let's try to be objective about what we're willing to do and not do." It helps to have someone outside the situation give some perspective.[11]

Clinical psychologist Debra Resnick says that about 25 to 33 percent of the parents of her dialectical behavior therapy clients overinsert themselves in their child's life.

They take on too much responsibility for their child's behavior and don't allow their child to succeed or fail on his or her own terms.

Society says that parents who have a child who isn't functioning well are not up to snuff. People feel embarrassed when they have to go to family functions and say that one of their children isn't doing well. Parents need to acknowledge the shame, put it on the table, and formulate a plan to overcome it so it doesn't act as a barrier.[12]

Siblings feel guilty for having feelings they're not "supposed" to have or for not having emotions they think they "should" have. Like other family members, they put themselves on trial in a kangaroo court and mete out punishment before the judge has banged the gavel.

If you feel guilty, ask yourself, "What am I feeling guilty for?" Be specific. If you think you should have known something, what is it, and how would you have known? If there is something you regret, learn from it. Make amends if necessary, put a plan together to prevent it from happening again, and try to turn any aspect of what happened into something positive.

Low Self-Esteem

Barbara Cowan Berg, author of *How to Escape the No-Win Trap,* says that low self-esteem is a big reason why people feel stuck. The key to getting unstuck, she says, is knowing beyond a shadow of a doubt that *we* have a right to be heard and to get our needs met, too. Without self-esteem, she argues, life is only one double bind after another. The longer we have been

the target of emotional abuse, the more likely it is that we need professional help.[13]

Self-esteem is what gives us that strength to keep our head about us
when others are losing theirs and blaming it on us. Some non-BPs, such as
parents, have normal to high self-esteem. It plummets, however, when they
can't "fix" their child. Like guilt, low self-esteem can cause parents to feel
less competent and lose faith in their parenting abilities. When children
sense that their parents lack confidence in themselves, it becomes easier to
act out to get their own needs met. Parents become even less self-assured,
and the cycle continues.

Many partners already have low self-esteem by the time they meet
their borderline mate. If the BP is emotionally abusive, the partner's self-
esteem falls even lower. Feeling insignificant, they let their limits slide and
their BP's behavior becomes worse. As before, the cycle continues.

A combination of invalidation, inconsistency, and unpredictability fills adult children of BPs with shame and feelings of inferiority that
can haunt them for life. These feelings, ironically, keep them emotionally
tied to their abusive parent, still searching for that ever-elusive approval.

You may know on an intellectual level that your family member's attacks on your character are unjust. But on an emotional level (which is
stronger), you may believe you deserve the treatment you're getting. Criticism is a corrosive acid that eats away feelings of self-worth and fractures
the bonds that keep people together.

People with low self-esteem often try to relieve their shame by being
good. "Goodness" comes from sacrificing themselves and what they want
out of life to make up for their perceived inadequacies. It may mean making
excuses for abusive behavior, ignoring advice from people who care, and
being blind to actions they could take to improve their lives. Being perfect
relieves shame—but only temporarily. The BP gets used to it and requires
higher doses. Both BP and non-BP get hooked. These insidiously toxic behaviors can be reinforced by others, especially if the result is fewer demands
on them.

Your BP is right about one thing for sure: you are imperfect—just like
the rest of humankind. All human beings have the delicious and inalien-

able right to be imperfect. Not only that, you get the right to want and need things for yourself, too. Compromises are supposed to be mutual.

Keep reminding yourself that while your family member may be smart, intuitive, and an expert about many things, he is *not* an objective authority on your character. The disorder creates a powerful need in its victims to maintain a facade of flawlessness. This requires projecting everything "bad" onto other people—especially those nearest and dearest.

Starting today, it's time to trust your inner voice. No one but you has the power to define you. As you start to become more confident and trust your own judgment, you will stop giving other people control of how you feel and what you do. Trusting yourself enables you to set limits that work because you finally, truly, believe you have a right to set them.

The Need to Rescue

Phil says he should have known better than to hook up with Jon. "Everybody in my circle told me not to—including his ex-boyfriend Kelsey," says Phil. "Kelsey told me a lot of horror stories. Looking back, the indisputable red flags were there. But I was *positive* I was going to be the one guy in his godforsaken life who didn't let him down.

"I stopped going out with my friends on Friday night because he was jealous. I told him it was okay to call me eight times a day at work so I could assure him I still loved him. I stayed with him even after I caught him lying to me again and again. I did make him feel better—for a little while. Eventually he reverted back into his misery, and took me right along with him."

Hugh and Emma Simpson, like most parents, are desperate to see their borderline son, Tom, succeed. When it looks as though he's getting himself together, they give him money to help him get on his feet again. His credit card bills are out of sight because every penny is going toward his new car and credit card bills—they *told* him not to buy the big-screen TV, but he did anyway. So when he yells at his boss and loses his job and begs for money again, what are they supposed to do?

Like Phil and the Simpsons, rescuers start out with the best of intentions. They love their family member and want to help. So they "help," often by doing things they don't want to do or by giving up things they don't want to give up. When things don't improve (or get even worse), they "help" some more—even though they resent it and think it's unfair.

Rescuers are ruled by their emotions, especially guilt, worry, fear, and, most of all, helplessness. Rarely do they take stock of their methods, see that their efforts aren't working, and try something else.

Why Rescuing Doesn't Work

Rescuers protect people from the consequences of their own behavior, thereby enabling/encouraging them to act irresponsibly. For example, Phil's boyfriend Jon experienced no consequences for lying. So he kept doing it. The Simpsons keep paying for their son's spending sprees. So he buys whatever he wants.

Rescuers do things for people they could do for themselves, thereby enabling/encouraging their dependence. Phil rescued Jon from having to deal with his feelings of jealousy and the need to make his own set of friends to hang out with on Friday nights. Tom could learn ways to manage his anger but has no incentive to do so. It doesn't matter that he can't keep a job, because his parents will pay his bills.

The Portrait of a Rescuer

A rescuer is usually a compassionate, kind person who wants to alleviate the suffering of others. The person with BPD idolizes and adores the object of his affection, who can't help but enjoy the special attention and the feeling that she, and she alone, can make the other person feel loved.

Rescuers can be male or female, and they may share similar characteristics. They

- gain self-worth from being needed and making sacrifices.
- overfocus on the problems of others, often trying to fix the problems.
- place a great deal of value on being "good" and define themselves by what others think of them. They constantly seek approval.
- have a low sense of self-worth. They feel insecure and doubt their ideas and needs.

- strive to meet others' expectations of them without questioning whether the expectations are reasonable.
- take too much responsibility for the feelings of others.
- will do anything to keep the peace and avoid conflict, including taking the blame for things that are not their fault.
- quickly dive into relationships based on intuition rather than real shared interests, values, or goals.
- believe they can make relationships happen by force of will; believe they can make others love them through sheer tenacity.

Sometimes rescuers act the way they do because they need to be needed; it provides them with an identity and self-esteem. They may feel lost on their own. These "saviors" are repeatedly drawn to people with massive problems that only the savior can solve.

The Effects of Rescuing on the Non-BP

Rescuers unknowingly relinquish control of their lives to their borderline family member, whose impaired thoughts, feelings, and actions now determine their own. The consequences of doing this are pervasive and severe. According to psychologist James J. Messina, rescuers

- feel manipulated, intimidated, powerless, irritated, angry, and frustrated. They give everything they have, but it's never good enough. They try to please and end up criticized and humiliated. Bliss turns into despair.
- waver back and forth about their situation because their ability to make good decisions has been diminished.
- have slowed personal growth because all their attention is focused on others.
- have lower self-esteem and may be driven by feelings of fear, guilt, and emotional dependence.[14]

The Effect of Rescuing on the Person with BPD

- BPs who don't learn that behaviors have corresponding consequences may be hobbled in many areas of life. They may not realize that their positive actions can lead to good feelings, too, such as feelings of accomplishment and pride.

- BPs may become more dependent on others for a variety of things, from financial support to emotional regulation. There is no way of knowing what they might have done on their own.

- Enabling behaviors can reinforce borderline traits such as impulsiveness and intolerance to distress.

- People who are dependent on others resent them for it. This resentment adds to the problems in the relationship.

- When non-BPs suddenly become angry because they don't feel appreciated, BPs get mixed messages and think the non-BP family member is being unfair (which is understandable). This can spark another series of arguments.

The Effect on the Relationship

Relationships become *enmeshed* when each person needs the other one to feel whole. In his song "Codependent With You," John Forster describes enmeshment with the lines "You hold your breath, dear, and I turn blue . . . when I die the life that flashes before me will be yours."[15]

Angelyn Miller, who wrote about enmeshed relationships in her book *The Enabler,* says, "Over the years, the dependent and the enabler have cultivated a very deeply rooted way of relating to each other and other people. Any change in this pattern threatens the very idea of who they are, whether the change is forced by circumstance or initiated to achieve health."[16]

In other words, both people become stuck.

Getting Unstuck

Albert Einstein once said you can't solve a problem with the same level of thinking that created the problem. In other words, you may be able to find solutions to feeling afraid, guilty, obligated, controlling, and bad about yourself—all of which contribute to feeling stuck—if you approach them in a different way.

Become More Authentic

Becoming authentic is another way to get unstuck. The authentic self has nothing to do with your job, family role, or function in society. It's what makes you unique: your genetic ancestry comingled with your distinctive skills, beliefs, experiences, and opinions. It's everything that makes you *you*.

You can determine how authentic you are by examining your core beliefs and attitudes and asking yourself questions like these:

- Are these beliefs verifiably true?
- Do these beliefs serve my best interest? Do they make me happy, healthy, and safe?
- Do these beliefs get me more of what I want and deserve, or less of it?

During the day, pay attention to how you feel and react to things. Listen to the thoughts floating in your head and the feelings they bring on without censoring them. It's essential that you not judge these thoughts and feelings. Just listen to them. Listen to what your body is telling you, too. How does it feel when you think or do certain things?

Look at your life the way it is right now. Are you living in accordance with your values or at odds with them? What are you passionate about, and what role does that play in your life? Do you know, in vivid detail, who is the real you, or do you live a compromised existence? Where will you end up if things keep going in the same direction?

Own Your Choices

Non-BPs in similar situations make wildly different decisions about living situations, amount of contact, types of limits, and so forth. For example, some adult children see their borderline parent often. Others will only talk on the phone. Some have no contact with their parent at all. Then there's everything in between, such as seeing the parent under some circumstances, but not others.

Recognize that you decide how to respond to the people, actions, and events in your life. You have *choices*—not necessarily fun ones, but choices nonetheless—choices that could lead to better times. Banish phrases like "He made me . . ." or "She forced me to . . ." from your vocabulary unless they refer to a legal document. Rather than say, "I *have* to," say, "Right now, I *choose* to." Then, open yourself up to new ideas.

Learn from the Past

If your current methods aren't working or are making things worse, *and* you've given them a fair test, cease and desist—even if you've been using these techniques for a long time. We hate to acknowledge that something's not working when we've invested a lot of time and energy into it. But the alternative—sticking with what you know *doesn't* work—is worse.

Also, look back on past relationships. Are these feelings familiar? Have you ever been in a situation like this before? Rescuers usually have a history of one-sided relationships, where they do all the giving and the other person does all the taking. They may not know what a healthy romantic relationship looks like because they've never had one.

Help Others without Rescuing

Allow people to be who they really are instead of who you want them to be. Provide assistance in ways that encourage—not discourage—responsibility and independence.

Author Elizabeth B. Brown says that healthy help comes from the heart, not as a maneuver to gain, but as a gift. She says:

> It's tough to stand by and watch when you know the negative consequences of a decision, but sometimes there is no other option. Criticism turns off hearing. Threats fall on deaf ears. Love and encouragement offer the strongest hope.
>
> We cling to the belief that if we hold someone up long enough, he will get strong. But strength develops as one stands on his own. There is no magic formula. Your help may make a significant difference; it may not. But don't forget that the wrong kind of help may be worse than no kind of help at all.

Brown says that simple comments and questions that can aid in loved ones seeing the truth may be the best help of all. She says that healthy support includes messages like these:

- I'm here if you need me.
- I'm here if you choose unwisely.
- I'm here, but there are limits and boundaries.
- I'm here to encourage you.
- I'm here to be an objective sounding board.
- I'm here, but I know your choices—and their consequences— belong to you.
- I'm here but I'm willing to lose the relationship if we become twisted together.[17]

Other ways to offer assistance include the following:

- Listen to your family member and empathize with her feelings (see the next chapter).
- Express confidence in her ability to find solutions for herself by pointing out a time when she did so (even if it's small) or reminding her of her strengths ("You're so good at such-and-such").
- Ask, "What do you think your options are?"
- Ask, "Would it help you if I did such-and-such?"
- Ask, "Have you thought of . . . ?"

Staying Motivated

When you find yourself thinking in old patterns, come up with alternative messages to yourself, such as

- "I wish I could fix her problems for her. But I can't. Only she can do that. I can only offer my love and support."
- "It's not up to me to fix his problems, either, even if he expects me to. My job is to take care of myself."
- "Even people who are disabled, chronically ill, or have more severe forms of mental illness are still expected to do whatever they can."[18]

Chapter 9

Power Tool 3:
Communicate to Be Heard

My emotions consume me. The only way to release my anger is to lash out at others. I don't care about their feelings, only my anger. I become paranoid and believe they want to hurt me. My wrath is my effort to get some control. In the end, I drive people away.

▪ Janna, recovering BP ▪

Mac Calhoun was doing dishes when his adult son, Zak, came through the kitchen door. Mac was going to nag Zak for leaving the back door unlocked all day—again—when he got a look at Zak's glum face and heard the lackluster tone in his half-grunted, "Hi, Dad."

He shifted gears. "What happened?" he asked.

As it turned out, Zak had resigned from work that day because he learned his employer was going to release a deeply flawed product that could ruin the company's reputation. Mac strenuously objected to Zak quitting, saying he should have stayed on anyway because he needed the money. Zak shook his head and calmly responded, "I can see other people doing that, but I just couldn't."

Zak's cousin, Alma Kebron, had an equally bad day. She had spent the day—her birthday—fighting her health insurance company. Then her husband, Kurt, forgot her birthday and neglected to pick up her prescriptions as promised. After Kurt got home—no pharmacy bag in hand—they argued a bit. Alma's voice rose and shook, and she tried not to cry. Kurt apologized profusely and said he would make it up to her.

She replied with a few unfavorable comments about his memory and organizational abilities. He allowed he *should* have some sort of calendar and to-do list, took her hand, and gently reminded her that on her last birthday they had taken a trip to Mexico. She gave him a morose smile. After he took her out for Mexican food (and stopped at the pharmacy on the way back), all was forgiven.

Across town, Kurt's younger brother Jake was complaining about his girlfriend, Jenny, to his friend Cliff. Jake and Jenny, evidently, were having issues. About sex. As Cliff and Jake walked from their biology class to the dorm room they shared, Jake caught a glimpse of Cliff's screwed-up face. He knew the look—"too much information, dude." So instead of going into detail, Jake lifted one eyebrow and made a gesture. Cliff gave him a knowing nod.

BP Communication Deficits

These conversations between the Kebron and Calhoun clans are much more sophisticated than they seem. Each person is displaying advanced interpersonal skills that allow him or her to manage conflict, problem solve, and further the interests of the relationship—*all in real time*. Their skills include

- accurately monitoring their thoughts and feelings
- making correct conclusions about thoughts and feelings of others—sometimes with very small clues (Cliff's facial expression, Zak's inflection)
- actively listening to the other person instead of thinking about their own response
- putting aside their own immediate desires to take care of some-

one else's (Mac had originally wanted to talk about the door; Jake changed his conversational tactics)

- thinking things through instead of acting impulsively (Mac and Alma)
- putting things into perspective and giving others the benefit of the doubt (Alma realized Kurt was forgetful, not unloving)
- feeling unthreatened when others have a different opinion (Zak)
- calming themselves down quickly when it would have been more satisfying to vent (Mac, Alma)

As you've learned, people with BPD are lacking in many, if not most, of these interpersonal skills. The disorder garbles both incoming and outgoing messages, causing massive chaos and confusion. As an analogy, think of BPs as having "aural dyslexia," in which they hear words and sentences backward, inside out, sideways, and devoid of context.

Of all the limitations imposed by borderline personality disorder, those involving communication are the most brutal because they can lead to impulsive aggression that can harm—even destroy—the close relationships people with BPD crave. Discord is inevitable; the way we manage it determines, in large part, the health of the relationship.

Even in the absence of aggression, poor communication can hinder BPs from making solid connections essential to authentic closeness and intimacy. As psychologist Bennett Pologe says, "A relationship is only as strong as the verbal and nonverbal communication between the partners. Everything else is secondary."[1]

The Splitting-Shame-Fear Spiral

People with BPD process information differently than you do. Never forget that. When people with BPD see a threat—and threats lurk everywhere—their intense emotions hijack their brain, holding the logical parts hostage. Next, impulsivity growls, *"Do something NOW!"* like a drill sergeant hyped up on two pots of coffee. The splitting-shame-fear spiral instantly switches on to do the drill sergeant's bidding and shapes

BPs' responses like Play-Doh being pressed through a mold into a star-shaped ribbon.

Shame crafts insults from general remarks, whips negative intent out of thin air, and twists innocent phrases into daggers. Fear of abandonment emerges like the black-robed Ghost of Christmas Yet to Come, pointing a gaunt finger to a desolate future. Splitting turns shades of gray into stark black and white. Then impulsive aggression (the "border-lion," pages 58–59) rakes its claws inward, outward, or both.

The key thing to keep in mind about the splitting-shame-fear spiral is that it usually comes out of nowhere, swirls you up, and flings you into the Land of Oz without so much as a forecast of bad weather. Untrained, you can't see it. But with training and experience, you'll be better prepared to sense it coming on and use the strategies in this chapter to keep it from forming, defuse it while it's still small, obtain outside help, or get out of the way altogether.

Here's what might have happened if Zak, Alma, and Jake had had BPD.

Splitting-Shame-Fear Spiral		
THREAT OR EVENT triggers an emotional hijacking	SPLITTING, SHAME, and FEAR	IMPULSIVE AGGRESSION (the "border-lion")
Zak's dad says Zak made a big mistake.	"He thinks I'm stupid, probably always has. He thinks I can't make my own decisions. Well, if that's what he thinks, then I don't need him. Screw him!"	Yells; avoids father for a few months (rejects him first).
Alma's husband slights her.	"I thought he loved me. All this time he said he did, and he was lying! Why does this always happen to me? He's going to leave me just like all the others. Maybe he's in love with somebody else."	Depending on which way the border-lion turns, Alma accuses him of an affair, tears into him some more for his disorganization, threatens suicide, or practices self-harm.
Jake sees a negative facial expression.	"He thinks I'm weird. Crap. He probably doesn't want to be my friend anymore. This hurts! I can't stand it!"	Drinks a six-pack of beer when he gets home (self-medication). Goes to get more beer and has a car crash.

This model is simplified and doesn't cover all interactions. Interactions vary considerably depending on the situation, the BP's mood, and a variety of other factors. A "threat" may not be visible to the non-BP (Alma's example) or experienced consciously by the BP (thoughts and emotions can be fleeting). Other BPD traits are in play, too, such as emptiness and lack of identity.

Fear Becomes Interpreted as Anger

Both anger and fear arouse the central nervous system in the same way—it's that sinking feeling in the stomach and a quick beating of the heart. Normally, we rely on our thoughts to tell us whether we're angry at someone or if we're afraid of something they might say or do. But that takes logic, and logic has been beaten into submission by the powerful, pulsating amygdala.[2]

Also, some BPs—the higher-functioning invisible type, mostly—find it unnerving to acknowledge their fears, especially fear of abandonment. Fear brings up all kinds of uncomfortable doubts, questions, and memories. The focus turns to blame and past failures, which triggers more shame and splitting. Anger is a much easier out.

Fights Over "Nothing"

Have you and your family member ever had a major row over something insignificant or just plain stupid? This happens from time to time in all relationships, but it's the norm when your loved one has BPD. Non-BPs frequently feel hounded about small trifles, and all-out fights can erupt over nothing—at least, nothing the non-BP can see.

On her Web site, Chris, a non-BP, lists fifty-five "acceptable reasons" her girlfriend had for yelling at her, including Chris using too much water in the tub, paying too much at the store, going through a yellow light, not shuffling cards right, objecting to a racist remark, and putting the wrong kind of olives on her salad.[3]

The *real* issues, of course, are much deeper. They aren't new, though: they're the same ones we've been discussing all along; things like splitting, control, shame, feeling invalidated and worthless, and lack of identity. They're just disguised.

Control, for example, comes into play because people with BPD feel so wildly out of control of themselves. Therefore, they maintain a tight grip on their environment—and "the environment" includes you. When one non-BP visited his BP mother for a few days, she tried to control what he wore, what he ate, how he ate, when he exercised, and when he went to bed. He was fifty-two years old; she, seventy-three.

"Control is really about regulation. Emotional regulation, personal regulation, thought regulation and the ability to be centered and grounded within one's self," says recovered BP A. J. Mahari in her essay "BPD: The Power and Control Struggle."[4]

Actions that come across as "intimidating, invalidating, self-absorbed and often abusive" (as Mahari puts it) are rooted in the belief that others are judging them in a negative way. The alternative to feeling helpless and out of control is to assert power over others. For the BP, the decision to control is subconscious.

Another issue is a combination of shame and lack of identity. With no solid sense of self, people with BPD live in outline, like a figure in a coloring book. And you wield the crayons and have the power to color them black (evil), totally black, or for-all-time black. With no way to hold a good image of themselves to counter what they see as your "all-bad" opinion of them, they resist with everything they have.

Psychotherapist Philip Chard says, "People without a solid sense of self are easily threatened by any competing versions of 'the truth,' and they often experience differences of opinion as a personal affront."[5]

Many fights come about because of the phenomenon of *feelings equal facts,* which you read about in the chart on page 34. Additionally, your emotional edges may be quite tattered by walking on sharp eggshells with bare feet. It may not take much to push *you* over the edge, either.

Compensating for BPD Limitations

In the rest of this chapter, you will learn several approaches to improving communication with your family member. The approaches fall into three groups: (1) lay the groundwork, (2) prepare to communicate, and (3) use intentional communications. Of all the tools in your toolbox, this one will see the most use.

Higher-functioning invisible BPs may present wildly different communication challenges from lower-functioning conventional BPs. Some techniques are appropriate for both types; other techniques may be best reserved for one or the other. Keep in mind that no communication technique, no matter how good or how well executed, can completely overcome BPD "dyslexia."

If you and your family member are in therapy, consider working on communication skills during your sessions. This setting is a great place to do so because therapists are well versed in these methods and might be able to persuade your family member into trying them, too. The therapist can also give you feedback and help keep conversations on track.

You need time, too, to make these techniques automatic. It's hard to quell the urge to be defensive and respond in kind. Practice with friends in low-stress situations until you feel comfortable. Memorize phrases you like. When you're conversing with others, pay close attention to the words they use, their body language, and the tone of their voice. Notice the feelings their communication evokes in you.

When you use these methods, track what seems to work and what doesn't. Give things time. There are many variables, including your loved one's mood, the topic at hand, and what's going on in your relationship. You'll find that other family members will pick up on what you're doing—even the children. Give yourself plenty of praise and congratulate yourself for your efforts. You're amazing!

Lay the Groundwork

Your state of mind and that of your family member impact the effectiveness of your communication.

Create a Climate of Cooperation

A climate of cooperation is one in which working for the common good—the relationship itself—is more important than who is right and who is wrong. This is the foundation upon which everything else lies. It is fundamental to finding win-win solutions and makes the relationship worth having in the first place.

Convincing your family member that her beliefs and perceptions are wrong may trigger the splitting-shame-fear spiral. Instead, advocate for the relationship itself, holding the position that the relationship will become stronger—and each of you is more likely to be ultimately satisfied with it—when you resolve to reduce conflict as a team. (Note that this is a climate of cooperation; in other words, the environment surrounding your discussions. In the next chapter, Power Tool 4: Set Limits with Love, we'll build on this concept as it applies to specific limits.)

Remind yourself and your BP that you are experiencing these difficulties because you both *care*. The two of you want to find a way to get along, to be a team, and to be supportive of each other. At most, you want love and intimacy. At the very least, you want to be able to be in the same room without overt hostility.

Creating a climate of cooperation is challenging when each person is entrenched in his or her position and egos are at stake. This new climate doesn't develop overnight. Yet, your work toward such a climate is powerful: you are demonstrating your commitment to the relationship and modeling behaviors you want your family member to emulate.

Reconsider Your Family Member's "Authority"

The more authority someone has, the more likely his criticism and/or blame can hurt us. So it's worthwhile to examine who has authority over us, and where they're getting it from.

The word *authority* is defined as "The power to influence or command thought, opinion, or behavior."[6] Some people have authority because of their position, such as a supervisor or an elected official. Others have authority because of their expertise, such as a doctor or professor. Some have both.

Our family members, partners, and friends have a different kind of authority: "authority by relationship." They may not *know* more than we do. Very few can control us against our will (unless the non-BP is a minor). Rather, we *give* them authority because we love them, respect them, and want to please them. Consider these examples:

- Miranda wants to please her parents. So she chooses a mate and career based on what they would like. Miranda thinks her parents have authority over her behavior, when in fact, she has unconsciously given the authority to them (perhaps because it was easier than going against their wishes).
- Henry thinks his wife, June, has no talent for financial matters. So he pays the bills, does the checkbook, and calculates their

taxes. June always thought she was good at fiscal matters, but she defers to Henry. June has given Henry the authority to determine her feelings about her financial skills—perhaps because she's not confident.

Reconsidering a family member's authority means taking a close look at the way she influences your thoughts, opinions, and behavior and asking yourself some pointed questions:

- Where does the authority come from? If your parent has BPD, remind your adult self that she no longer has power over you unless you give it to her.
- Does your BP have the expertise to determine your qualities and traits? Could some of his perceptions about you be influenced by his disorder? (Hint: The answer to the second question is "You bet!")
- Are you trying to please someone who just will not be pleased?
- Is it possible to show you care about someone without giving that person the authority to determine what you think, how you feel, and what you do?

Letting others determine your worth is always a dicey proposition. Letting someone determine your worth who has a disorder that, by definition, causes distorted perceptions of self and others, makes no more sense than some of your family member's strangest accusations.

It's key to sort this out in your mind before an interaction and then to come up with a way to remind yourself of this during the interaction. Following are some of the methods you might try:

- Beforehand, seek a higher authority (or more authorities). If .your family member thinks you're selfish, ask others if they hold the same opinion. If your self-esteem has taken a beating, or if you are an adult child, consider therapy.
- As you converse with your BP, use affirming self-talk to remind yourself that your family member is not as authoritative as he might seem. Think, *She's talking like this because she's scared.*

This isn't really about me. *He may have a problem with such-and-such, but no one else seems to. She may have a high IQ, but her emotional intelligence is low.* Give the authority to your inner voice, and it will become stronger.

- If you feel intimidated, picture the childlike aspects of your BP's personality by imagining him dressed like a child, perhaps holding a toy. Right now, is he acting the part of the abandoned or abused child, or the angry and impulsive child (pages 53–54)? Humor works wonders. If picturing your loved one with a lollipop or baby bottle works for you, go ahead, feel free. There is a lot at stake.

Prepare to Communicate

In the rest of this chapter, you will learn a powerful communication system called the "Row Your Boat" system, so called because you can recall each segment by learning the following little ditty, which is sung to the tune of "Row, Row, Row Your Boat."

Breathe, breathe, safety first,
Acknowledge what you hear.
Don't defend, delay instead,
Distract, defuse, or DEAR.

When you're driving your car or waiting in the checkout lane at the grocery store, go through the lyrics until the song—and the system it refers to—are imprinted on to your brain.

Breathe, Breathe

When things start to get tense, your body releases chemicals that turn it into a "fight or flight" machine. Your breaths get short and shallow. When neither fighting nor flighting is a viable option, this biological stress response wreaks havoc on your body and mind. It becomes even more difficult to think straight.[7]

To counter this process, take long, deep breaths, as described on pages 142–144. Deep breathing will calm you down, help you concentrate, and give you a few extra seconds to think. To better understand how this works, close your eyes and visualize yourself in the middle of a typical crisis. Then take a slow, deep breath so that your stomach rises, not your chest.

You might even create your own "breathing room"—an imaginary place that's safe and offers support. You can make the walls of your breathing room out of anything you want—thick brick if your family member is a rager, perhaps, and thin Plexiglas when you want to be close but also need to feel secure. You can build your room on the treetops of the jungle or underground in a bunker. You can invite your family member in for coffee or put a "do not disturb" sign on the door. Build as many rooms as you want—they're free!

Safety First

The first rule for communicating with your family member is to know when it's safe to communicate and when it's not. According to *Stop Walking on Eggshells,* the greatest safety concerns are rage/verbal abuse, physical abuse, and threats of suicide.[8]

RAGE

One of the toughest challenges of having a family member with BPD is the annihilating raging. Jack says, "When my wife, Loreen, raged at me, I would rage back. She called me names, so I called her names, too. We were both out of control. I hated who I was becoming because I'm actually a pretty even-tempered guy. It took awhile for me to learn how to stop getting caught up in her anger." (See pages 196–197 for more of Jack and Loreen's story.)

Inappropriate, frequent displays of temper can appear out of nowhere, which is what makes them so fearsome. Whether you spot the border-lion with your binoculars (preferred) or you're staring at the jagged teeth close up (not preferred), gauge the intensity of your family member's anger on a scale of one to ten, with ten being the highest. According to Christopher Bojrab, MD, people with BPD may be able to calm themselves down when the emotional level ranges from one to five. At six and above, without treatment, they may not be able to calm themselves down.[9]

If your family member is at a six or higher, visualize the emotional centers of his brain going ka-ching! ka-ching! ka-ching! like a slot machine spewing forth tokens. Your family member's thoughts and feelings are warped, and what he's saying makes about as much sense as throwing away your hard-earned money in games you know are designed to put your cash into the casino's pocket.

Don't listen to your family member berate you and call you names. Right now, he can't see your point of view or think through the effects of his interactions with others. It's not that he won't; it's that he can't. Verbal abuse harms you: ongoing, repeated verbal assaults can be every bit as emotionally devastating as physical battering—especially when it is meted out by an intimate partner or by someone in a position of authority. Anxiety, low self-esteem, and depression are all tied to verbal abuse.[10]

Instead, bring the interaction to a temporary close. Say, "I will not discuss this any more if you continue to yell. I am willing to be supportive and listen if you can tell me what it is you want and need." If the rage continues, leave immediately (or ask your family member to leave).

Repeat any of the following statements. Don't argue or try to have the last word. Notice that these statements don't point fingers at your family member directly:

- "I want to hear about it, but it's hard for me when things get too emotional" (instead of "you get too emotional").
- "We'll talk later, when things calm down. I want to give you my full attention, and that's too hard for me to do right now."
- "I can't listen right now. Not until things are calmer."
- "Let me have a little while to calm down and then we can talk."

Say to yourself:

- "I am not going to take this personally. This is the border-lion talking."
- "If I stay here and argue, things are going to escalate. If I stay and get beaten down, it's going to hurt me and the relationship."
- "My family member can't grasp all that right now, but I can.

I am deciding to do what's best, even if it doesn't feel comfortable right now. It will get more comfortable as I keep doing it."

PHYSICAL ABUSE AND SUICIDE

About 30 percent of men who batter have BPD, and about 50 percent of women who batter have BPD.[11] If either physical abuse or threats of suicide are even a remote concern, you will need a safety plan.

Physical abuse of parents by their adolescent children is a growing national problem, as is physical abuse of men by their female partners. Both are underreported and stigmatized. If your BP has a problem, break the silence and seek help right away. If your family member becomes violent in other ways—for example, breaks things when she's angry—be on the alert.

The risk of suicide in borderline individuals is discussed at great length in other books about BPD and elsewhere, so it won't be repeated here because of lack of space. Briefly, if threats of suicide are an issue, read as much as possible on the subject. If your family member is suicidal and making imminent threats, call 911 or take him to the emergency room. Keep the following phone numbers handy: a local suicide hotline, the nearest emergency room, a nearby psychiatric facility, and the person's therapist and family doctor.

Psychiatrists John G. Gunderson and Cynthia Berkowitz say:

When families see the signs of trouble, they may be reluctant to address them. Sometimes the person with BPD will insist that her family "butt out." She may appeal to her right to privacy. Other times, family members dread speaking directly about a problem because the discussion may be difficult. They may fear that they would cause a problem where there might not be one by "putting ideas into someone's head." In fact, families fear for their daughter's safety because they know the warning signs of trouble from experience. Problems are not created by asking questions. By addressing provocative behaviors and triggers in advance, family members can help avert further trouble. People with BPD often have difficulty talking about their feelings and instead tend to act on them in destructive ways. Therefore, addressing a problem

openly by inquiring with one's daughter or speaking to her therapist helps her to deal with her feelings using words rather than
actions.[12]

Use Intentional Communication

People don't enter into heated discussions intending to make things worse,
yet it happens all the time. We vent our anger, defend ourselves, and try
to convince the other person that we're right and he's wrong (and possibly
ignorant, mean, and unreasonable). The trouble is that even if we get what
we want, the cost to the relationship and our own psyche can be high.

Compared to the "average" person, people with BPD can be much
more provoking—and more easily provoked. The costs are higher. The
automatic conversational tactics that non-BPs slip into—including defensiveness, finger pointing, blaming, and telling the BP that she's wrong—
trigger splitting-shame-fear spirals that set up family members to be the
border-lion's scratching post.

Intentional communication is a good alternative to the spout-off-at-the-
mouth-and-fight-to-win approach. Instead of talking off the top of your
head, guided by intense emotions, you have an underlying intent in mind,
such as "calm this person down," "obtain their cooperation," or even "build
closeness and have fun."

Intentional communication gives you an advantage for these reasons:

- You're much more likely to reach your objective when you know
  what that objective is.
- Even if you don't reach your objective, you're heading in the
  right direction.
- You feel more in control of the situation because you can better
  manage your own responses.
- You're less likely to say something you regret, something that
  might make things worse.

The techniques that follow come under the umbrella of intentional
communication.

Acknowledge What You Hear

Acknowledging, or more properly *empathic acknowledging,* is the most powerful communication technique in this chapter; it is similar to the term *validation.* Lawrence J. Bookbinder coined the phrase on his Web site, "Touch Another Heart."[13] It is a blend of empathy, listening skills, and acknowledging.

During conflicts, your family member experiences a loss of connection with you. Untethered, she becomes caught up in the splitting-shame-fear spiral. Family members use empathic acknowledging to grab hold of that spiral, to slow it down, and to start to rebuild the emotional connection.

There are two steps to empathic acknowledging:

- *Step 1:* Actively listen to your family member with 100 percent of your attention without interrupting, asking questions, offering solutions, or thinking about what you're going to say next.
- *Step 2:* Separate your BP's distorted *thinking* from the intense, overwhelming *feelings,* and then empathically acknowledge those emotions to your family member *without necessarily agreeing with the thoughts that link the two.*

Because empathic acknowledgment does not require agreeing with the thoughts connected with the feelings, it can be used with anyone, from small children who are scared of the bogey monster to veterans who are having a flashback and think they're in the middle of a battle.

Also, there is no such thing as too much empathic acknowledging, or validation. Repeat your main message—I care about how you feel—often and in different ways. The border-lion is a little deaf.

Let's take a closer look at the three components of empathic acknowledgment: empathy, listening, and acknowledgment.

EMPATHY

Empathy is different from sympathy. *Sympathy* has to do with compassion and commiseration; for example, "I'm so sorry your mother passed away." Metaphorically, people who express sympathy are like people who drive by the scene of an accident, slow down, give an encouraging expression to the driver of the banged-up car, then speed up and go along their merry way.

Empathy is emotionally putting yourself in someone else's place to the point when you can almost vicariously experience the other person's thoughts and feelings. Metaphorically speaking, people who express empathy pull over, get out of their car, clasp the shoulder of the driver, and say, "Oh wow, I bet this is the *last* thing you needed to happen right now," in a way that implies, "I've been there, too" (whether or not they actually have).

Think back to the times when someone has expressed empathy to you. Have you ever been really, really excited about something and rushed to tell a friend, who then gives an enthusiastic "whoop!" and hops up and down a few times? Or, have you ever had a surprising upset, called a friend, explained what happened, and heard the person gasp, "Oh no! How terrible!" almost as if it were happening to him, too? Empathy feels great!

ACTIVE LISTENING

Most of the time we listen on automatic. We hear "blah, blah, blah" and other thoughts float in and out of our head. Mostly, we think about how we want to respond. When the topic has stirred up conflict in the past, we may say something and wait, with steam coming out of our ears, for the person to shut up so we can talk again. We filter out what we disagree with or don't want to hear and focus on whatever affirms our own beliefs.

When we listen on automatic, we miss out on the subtleties of what is being said—or unsaid. We may miss an emotional tone in the voice or a gesture that could have clued us in to a problem. This creates frustrations, misunderstandings, and predictable, predetermined interactions with predictable outcomes.[14]

Active listening is powerful because it says, "You and what you say is so important that I'm giving you my undivided time and attention. I am willing to listen to you with an open mind." This helps you achieve a climate of cooperation, which, hopefully, eventually, the BP will try to create for you.

Suspend your judgments, opinions, and history with the person speaking. Push everything out of your mind except your family member—you're about to enter his world. Focus on what he's feeling as well as saying, with his words, tone of voice, facial expressions, and body language. Resist the urge to make faces if you don't agree with what he's saying.

Sometimes, the splitting-shame-fear spiral is covered by a cloak of invisibility. It's hard to know what the *real* issue is. As you listen, be a detective. Just what is going on here? Take note of her feelings—not just the obvious ones, but the ones that might lie deeper. (In the next step, you'll be rephrasing what your BP is saying, so pay attention.)

Don't interrupt. In fact, don't talk at all unless safety is an issue or you're confused and need clarification. Bookbinder says, "Advising, comforting, encouraging, and other help-oriented verbalizations interfere with more than the other person's talking because these verbalizations stem from our thinking about how to help, which interferes with an essential activity of empathic acknowledging—thinking about what the talker's words mean to *her*" [italics mine].[15] If you're male, watch your tendency to want to jump in and solve problems.

Verbal Acknowledgment

According to validation enthusiasts Gary and Joy Lundberg, the authors of *I Don't Have to Make Everything All Better,* responses should be kind, gentle, and respectful with the intent of understanding the other person.[16] For example:

- Use verbal encouragers: "Oh," "Hmm," "Really," "Wow," "That's interesting," "Cool," or "I see." These responses show you're listening.
- Reflect their feelings: "That sounds (frustrating, sad, scary, wonderful, difficult, exciting)." "I bet that was (difficult, etc.)."
- Show involvement: "I'm (happy, sad, glad) for you." "I would feel (confused, lonely, happy), too."
- Punctuate intense emotions: "I can't believe that!" "Oh no!" "How wonderful!" "I'm so sorry that happened to you."

Asking validating questions is another form of acknowledgment. The Lundbergs say:

Asking the right question is vitally important in helping someone discover the solutions to their own problems. Without these questions, they will fall back on, "What should I do?" Remember you don't have to solve their problem. In fact, you don't even have the power to solve it.

You can help, however, by asking the kind of validating questions that will lead them to the exploration of their own feelings and desires, and to their own best solutions."[17]

The Lundbergs, the group NUTS (parents Needing Understanding, Tenderness, and Support to help their child with borderline personality disorder), and others suggest phrases such as the following:

- What did you do the last time this happened? How did that turn out?
- What are your options? What are the pros and cons of each one? How does each one make you feel?
- Would you like me to listen, or are you looking for specific suggestions? How can I help you?
- Do you have a plan for solving this?
- What might the first step be in solving this?
- What does your gut tell you?
- Is there somewhere you can go or someone you can call to find out more information?
- What about using a map? The Internet? Going to the library? (and so on)
- How did you feel the last time this happened?
- Do you think there could be another way to look at this?
- You've come up with some good solutions in the past. Could something similar work?
- How would you suggest a friend handle something like this?

"Why" questions, such as "Why did you do it that way instead of this way?" may bring on defensiveness. Avoid them if you can. *Clarifying questions* may help you and your family member sift through the splitting-shame-fear spiral to uncover the real issue.

Ask your family member to be specific, but don't grill her. You must be genuinely interested, not provoking. Otherwise, you can make things worse. Your sincere willingness to understand her rather than fight her is incredibly validating. It works because it addresses what is most likely the *real* issue—your family member's emotional vulnerability. Here are some examples of clarifying questions (put them in your own words):

- "When you said I sounded angry, what did you mean? Was it the tone of voice or the words?"
- (When things are vague and you're just getting raw emotions) "Is there anything I could say or do that would make you feel better?" "What do you think we might do to have less conflict?"
- (When your BP is making mountains out of molehills) "I really want to understand you, but I'm having trouble appreciating the depth of your feelings about this. Can you try explaining this in another way? I care, I just need to understand better."
- (When your BP has been using vague words or phrases such as "You're selfish" or "You don't care about me") "What did you mean when you said that?" "It's impossible to talk about these in a meaningful way in the abstract. What exactly did I do that showed selfishness? How often did I do it?" "What makes you think I don't care about you?"

NONVERBAL ACKNOWLEDGMENT

Back in the 1970s and 1980s, pioneering professor Albert Mehrabian conducted research that would forever change the way we look at inter-personal communication. He discovered that we overwhelmingly deduce our feelings, attitudes, and beliefs about what someone says not by the words spoken but by body language and tone of voice.

His research showed that we convey a puny 7 percent of our attitudes and beliefs through the actual words we speak. The rest—a whopping 93 percent—comes from our tone of voice (38 percent) and our facial expressions (55 percent). Furthermore, if our words and body language disagree, listeners will believe the nonverbal communication, not our words.[18]

Without nonverbal cues, all we're left with, essentially, is e-mail—a method so fraught with the possibility of miscommunication that we had to invent the "language" of emoticons to make sure we're not misunderstood. (For example, typing a sly wink ;) shows we're just kidding.)

Research is starting to suggest that people with BPD are better able to read subtle changes in the facial expressions of others.[19] Adolescent psychiatrist Blaise Aguirre says, "People with BPD can appear to be incredibly attuned to nonverbal communication to the point where others remark on their intuitiveness."[20]

Nonverbal communication is one of the most powerful—and simplest—ways to communicate with your family member. You can use it by itself to reinforce your verbal message or to correct a mistaken impression. Remember that when it comes to attitudes and beliefs, your body speaks louder than words. Be aware that your body is always communicating something. Make sure you're "saying" what you mean to.

Following are some do's and don'ts for empathetic acknowledging and listening:

Do's:

- Use direct, but unthreatening eye contact that shifts between each eye and the mouth. Your eyes should be soft and steady and show interest.
- Relax your facial expression (no tightening or scrunching up) with a neutral expression or genuine half-smile—no false smiles that don't reach the eyes.
- Uncross your arms.
- Tilt your head slightly.
- Nod your head slowly to show you're listening (unless you disagree with what your family member is saying).
- Relax your body (seated or standing).
- Keep your arms loose by your sides.
- If seated, lean slightly forward to show interest. Don't slouch.

- Avoid using your legs or feet as a barrier.
- Be close (avoid having furniture between you), but not too close.
- When it is your turn to speak, wait a full second and talk at a normal pace.
- To make your BP feel more comfortable, mirror his body position in a subtle way. (If he's sitting, you sit. If he's crossing his leg, cross yours, too.)
- Touch is the ultimate nonverbal connection. Where and how depends on the type of relationship and the specific situation. Even quick touches are powerful. Take stock of the situation to make sure touching is okay. Be cautious, because it can be misconstrued.

Don'ts:

- grit your teeth
- stare, glare, or look away
- close your eyes
- grimace
- frown or scowl
- furrow or arch your eyebrows
- yawn
- fidget
- put your leg over the chair
- tense up your body
- lean backward
- look at your watch or the exit
- tap your foot
- watch TV, do bills, and so on[21]

Don't Defend

John G. Gunderson, MD, and Cynthia Berkowitz, MD, say that defensive responses provoke people with BPD because essentially the message is, "Your feelings are wrong." It is not a good strategy to add feelings of invalidation on top of whatever caused the original upset. They say:

The natural response to criticism that feels unfair is to defend one-self. But, as anyone who has ever tried to defend oneself in such a situation knows, defending yourself doesn't work. A person who is enraged is not able to think through an alternative perspective in a cool, rational fashion. Attempts to defend oneself only fuel the fire.

What that individual wants most is to be heard. Of course, listening without arguing means getting hurt because it is very painful to recognize that someone you love could feel so wronged by you. Sometimes the accusations hurt because they seem to be so frankly false and unfair. Other times, they may hurt because they contain some kernel of truth.[22]

Gunderson and Berkowitz say that if you feel that there is some truth in what you're hearing, admit it with a statement such as, "I think you're on to something. I can see that I've hurt you, and I'm sorry." However, they say, be careful not to reward the yelling. Instead, say something like, "You have a point I want to talk about when things are calmer." (As you gain more experience, you'll get better at sensing what to do on the fly.)[23]

This *doesn't* mean it's okay or that you should *accept* the anger, criticism, or blaming (as in, "I can't help it—I have BPD!"). Your loved one is still responsible for recognizing she has a problem and managing her illness. What it *does* mean is that people with anorexia don't eat enough, people with depression cry, people with rapid-cycling bipolar disorder are moody, and people with BPD yell.

But you can take back some of your own power if you can recognize deep in your gut that your family member has a brain disorder defined, in part, by impulsive, excessive, and inappropriate anger. Let the words pass *through* you without doing damage to you by recognizing the splitting-shame-fear spiral for what it is, thereby robbing the border-lion of its power.

Delay, Distract, Defuse, DEAR

When you use these methods, avoid phrases that "point fingers" because they can trigger splitting, shame, and fear. While avoiding these phrases may not accurately describe what is happening, it helps you achieve your goal (remember, we're using intentional communication).

Finger Pointing	Neutral Description
You started a fight.	Then we ended up fighting.
You couldn't stop screaming, so I had to leave.	I needed to leave because the fight got to be too intense.
You didn't do this.	This wasn't done.
You did this.	This happened.
You yelled.	Voices were raised.

DELAY AND DISTRACT

When emotions are high, the emotional part of your family member's brain is planning a major coup. The border-lion is pacing in its cage, looking for a way out. If you can delay the proceedings in an empathic way—in other words, not come across as if you're brushing your family member aside—there's a chance you can help your BP rein in the impulsivity and emotionality. Distraction is especially helpful when you're in the car and you can't physically remove yourself from the situation. Here are some examples:

- "I can see you're upset and really want to talk about this right now. I want to be able to give you my full attention. But right now I'm so caught up in such-and-such. Can you wait (time interval here—even a few minutes can help)? Then I can listen to you without being distracted." (This response is the gold standard.)
- "I can't talk about this now. Let's chat after dinner."
- "I need to think about this. There's a lot here, and I want to consider everything we've talked about up until now."
- "I know you want an answer right now, but I need time to think."
- (Come up with something the two of you need to do together so your loved one doesn't feel abandoned.) "Let's talk about it after we (go grocery shopping before it gets crowded, see a movie, take a walk, etc.)."
- "Why don't we sit down and talk about this? First, let me (get us a cup of coffee, change into my sweats, make a quick phone call)."

- "Oh no! I just remembered I've got to (turn my cell phone on/off, pick up your child from school, put the soap in the dishwasher that's just begun the cycle, put the shirt you're wearing in the washing machine that's already started)." (If it turns out you forgot to turn the dishwasher or washing machine on in the first place, it may not matter.)
- "Hold on a minute while I (go to the bathroom, take an aspirin, put on a sweater, set up TiVo to record something, make a sandwich, or let the dog out)." Make it urgent so your BP doesn't feel brushed aside: your headache is pounding, your TV show is about to start, you're starving, and the dog is looking mighty anxious.
- (If you can't think of anything) "Hold on a minute." (Then go somewhere and think of something to say when you get back. Needing to go to the bathroom is something no one can usually argue with—unless you're already *in* the bathroom.)

DEFUSE

Use these noncombative statements that help you reach your goal and inject some reality into the situation. It's critical that your tone of voice and body language be calm, reassuring, and open without being patronizing. Otherwise, some of these phrases could incite more conflict.

You are the expert on yourself:

- "I appreciate what you said, but what I mean is . . ."
- "At the time my motivation was . . ."
- "Actually, what I really feel/think is . . ."
- "Maybe I'm not making myself clear. What I'm saying is . . ."
- "Perhaps you misunderstood me."

Manage the conversation:

- "Could we get back on the subject?"
- "So-and-so doesn't really have anything to do with this. Let's talk about you and me."

- "Let's discuss that at a later time. I'd like to keep the focus on . . ."
- "I was hoping we could talk about this. I don't see how we can resolve the situation if you won't talk with me."
- "I'm willing to see if we can find a compromise and focus on . . . I'm *not* willing to bring up the entire issue of . . ."
- "I'm not going to get in the middle of that. Now about you and me . . ."
- Don't let yourself be rushed into replying. If you're not sure what to say, listen with an empathetic stance.

Create a climate of cooperation:

- "Maybe we can find a way to . . ."
- "Maybe we can work together to . . ."
- "What we *do* agree on is that . . ."
- "Since we both care about each other . . ."
- "We have a lot in common, like . . ."
- "I hope we can . . ."
- "I don't think there are any villains here. We just have an honest disagreement."

Respond to unwarranted criticism or abusive statements. Assume the assertive nonverbal stance, discussed on pages 220–222. Use phrases like the ones below in a neutral tone of voice. Don't preach. Calmly explain what you're going to do if your BP keeps bullying you.

- "I respect myself too much to listen to this, so I'm going to leave if this continues."
- "I won't stand here and listen to you abuse/yell/attack me, so I'm going to leave if this continues."
- "No, I won't tolerate that kind of language, so I'm going to leave if it continues."
- "No, I won't allow you to speak to me in this way, so I'm going to leave if this continues."
- (Recognize that your family member has an opinion—and that

you do, too.) "I'm hearing you say that . . . My own opinion is
that . . ." (This phrase is especially useful.)

- (State a limit) "Name-calling isn't going to get us anywhere. If
  it continues, we're going to have to talk at another time." (More
  on this in the next chapter. The best-case scenario is that you've
  already set this limit when things are calm and told the person
  that you will leave the room if it happens again.)
- Leave (see the discussion on safety on pages 174–177).

DEAR

DEAR is an acronym that stands for Describe, Express, Assert, and Reinforce. It's mostly used to set limits, so you'll be learning about it in the
next chapter.

Prepare and Practice

Previously, you took your family member's hurtful comments at face value,
as if she were unaffected by a serious disorder. Recognizing this tendency
in yourself as you read this book is easy. It's harder to keep it in mind during an actual conversation.

Previously is the keyword. Now, you're going to do things differently,
starting by anticipating conversations and preparing for them. As author
Elizabeth B. Brown puts it, the secret to not being caught by dysfunctional
behavior is to expect it.[24] Here are some ways you can prepare.

Desensitize Yourself

Think back to previous conversations you and your family member have
had. It's likely that your BP will say the same kinds of things he's said one
hundred times before and you've heard one hundred times before. When
you're feeling safe, picture your family member saying them until the words
become almost meaningless and lose the power they once had over you.

Visualize

Ice skaters going in to competitions never think about the last time they
fell on the ice. They do the opposite: picture the routine just as they want

it to go. Picture the conversation just as you want it to go, saying the right thing and using the right nonverbal communication techniques. Get a mental picture of how you're going to feel once you've accomplished your communication goals.

Practice

Eventually, the techniques in this chapter will come to you automatically. In fact, family members see so many benefits to these methods that they start to use them with everyone. This can only happen with learning and practice.

Read this chapter many times and investigate the other communication resources listed in the back of this book. Make flash cards and memorize phrases you like. Then, start using them in low-stress situations with other people. Role-play with a friend or use an empty chair to substitute for your BP.

If you ever feel ambushed and forget what to do and say, remember these four key points:

- Breathe deeply.
- Stay safe. Leave or call for help if necessary.
- Keep your eyes soft and steady. Relax your face and mirror your BP's body position. Keep your arms uncrossed.
- Actively listen and empathically acknowledge the person's *feelings,* even if you don't agree with his or her *words.* Keep your tone of voice neutral.

What NOT to Say	
Avoid saying anything that is *invalidating*, meaning phrases that say outright that your family member's thoughts and feelings are wrong. Avoid phrases like the following:[25]	
Ordering them to think or feel differently	"Stop being so emotional." "You should be happy about it."
Denying their perceptions	"You've got it all wrong." "This is a stupid thing to fight about."
Minimizing their feelings	"It's not worth getting upset over." "It can't be that bad."
Judging and labeling	"You are too emotional." "You are such an angry person."
Belittling questions	"What's the matter with you?" "Why are you making such a big deal out of this?"
"Always" or "never"	"You always ruin things." "You never give me compliments."

One Mother's Communication Method

Sharon, who maintains the online group NUTS (parents Needing Understanding, Tenderness, and Support to help their child with borderline personality disorder) has a twenty-nine-year-old daughter, Amanda. Amanda was diagnosed with BPD at age thirteen, when she was hospitalized for hiring gang members to kill Sharon and her husband.

Over the years, Sharon and Amanda have developed a communication system that compensates for the deficits caused by the disorder. It helps avoid emotional outbursts, allows for better problem solving, and even deepens their relationship.

Sharon says, "When I have to bring up a serious topic, the first thing I do is ask Amanda what kind of mood she is in. If it's a good time to talk, I prepare her by saying something like, 'Amanda, I need to talk to you about something. It may be upsetting to you.' That also helps her identify her feelings."

Other introductory phrases Sharon uses include

- "This might sound invalidating, but it isn't meant to be."
- "This might hurt your feelings, and I'm sorry. But it's best in the long term if we keep the lines of communication open."
- "Something didn't feel right the other day, and I'd like to talk about it so that we aren't misunderstanding each other."
- "I know this is bad news, but in the long run, things are going to work out okay."

Next, Sharon uses "I" statements when describing the problem:

- "I'm feeling overwhelmed by this conversation. I'm going to take a walk and calm myself down."
- "If I understand right, I feel like I'm being blamed for something I feel I didn't do."

- "I can somewhat understand what you're feeling, but it isn't something I am able to change."

When Amanda describes her feelings, Sharon makes empathetic statements:

- "I can see why you might have thought that. (Pause to let the validation sink in.) However . . ."
- "I probably would have felt the same if I were in your shoes. (Pause.) Yet from the outside looking in, I saw . . ."
- "I remember feeling hurt when that happened to me. How does it make you feel?"

Sharon says, "If I see Amanda losing control of her emotions, I'll say something like, 'Let's do something else for a while so that we can let this all settle in. Then we'll talk some more.' This gives Amanda a chance to try to calm down her emotions, time to think the situation through, and hopefully not act impulsively.

"Sometimes it works better if we talk while we're busy with something else. That takes some of the pressure out of the picture. Or, if possible, we'll talk more about the subject another day."

Amanda, like most BPs, needs a lot of reassurance and soothing statements. Even after Sharon thinks a problem is resolved, it often is still not settled for Amanda. "With all her emotions swirling around, sometimes she isn't able to listen carefully enough."

It has taken many years for Sharon and her daughter to develop this system. Amanda has also learned some communication techniques from dialectical behavior therapy.

As a leader of a support group, though, Sharon believes these techniques could work well for others. "It just probably wouldn't go as smoothly until both parties learn how to do it and it becomes a natural way of communicating," she says. "Eventually, though, it will be. That is how it happened with us."[26]

Chapter 10

Power Tool 4:
Set Limits with Love

*Our lives begin to end the day we become silent
about things that matter.*
▪ Martin Luther King Jr. ▪

When members of the Facing the Facts message board (BPDFamily.com) were asked, "What happened the last time you tried to set limits with your family member?" the majority told tales such as these:

- "I told my borderline boyfriend he didn't understand my perspective; he told me I didn't understand his. It went in circles endlessly. He weaves magical webs with his words. Nobody is exempt from his super powers."
- "She accused me of being controlling and telling her what to do."
- "She has a sometimes subtle and sometimes blatant way of making me feel guilty."
- "He made it seem as though he was being my savior through all this, and at the end I apologized."

Some non-BP partners reported that they ended their relationship with their loved one when, after many years, they were forced to acknowledge their partner was never going to respect their boundaries.

But another group of respondents said that after a long period of testing, their BPs began to observe their limits. Message board members who thought they would have to break off contact were able to start re-building trust and intimacy.

Take Jack and his borderline wife, Loreen, for example. Loreen is an alcoholic with a history of suicide attempts. At the time Jack decided to start setting limits, she was under the care of a psychiatrist and taking medications. Jack was also seeing a therapist, who helped him put some limits in place after not having any for many years. Jack says:

> Loreen's rages were uncontrollable. She would go from zero to ten over almost anything. Once I went on a business trip and she shouted, "I hope you come back in a body bag." She called me names and said things like, "You've destroyed my confidence in myself," and "You're making me drink because being drunk is the only way I can deal with you."
>
> She threatened suicide all the time, yelling, "You probably want me to kill myself. So maybe I'll just do it, and it will be your fault." I was always on edge, afraid of saying the wrong thing. Things got worse and worse.
>
> After I started talking to other family members online, I real-ized two things: First, I was going to have to get strong and stay strong because this was really tearing me apart. And second, I had to start re-establishing boundaries.
>
> One day I found her on the floor after another suicide attempt. The ambulance came, and they were trying to revive her. It hit me that even though I had been trying not to offend her for years, she was still suicidal and drinking. Whatever I was doing wasn't working. I was scared.
>
> My therapist explained that her actions were out of my con-trol. That was a harsh thing to hear. Living like this was going to kill me. So I decided to try boundaries. I had nothing to lose.
>
> I told her, "What we're doing isn't working, and things are going to have to change around here." I said if she started raging and calling me names, I was going to leave and pick up the con-

versation at a different time. That sounds simple, but it wasn't. It just fired her up, made things ten times worse. She screamed that I was a control freak and that's why she was so sick.

But I was prepared. I had convinced myself ahead of time that leaving was the best course of action. It helped that members of her family had told me I had been giving in to her for years and I needed to be firm.

I ended up leaving the house several times. I just said, "I just can't be here with you," and walked out the door. Sometimes I stayed away for a day or two. She called me, asked when I was coming home. I said, "I honestly don't know. I've assessed my life and decided that things have to get better because this is destroying me." She knows I am loyal and I would never walk away if there had been any other choice.

Eventually, it started to sink in to her that I was serious. Finally, one day she called me and apologized. This was the first time she had ever said she was sorry for anything. I just about fell off the chair. That's when I started to realize this boundary thing was working. And it did. It took time, but it got better.

She even started apologizing more, saying things like, "I'm sorry, I didn't mean to say that," or "I know I reacted badly to that." She was starting to feel responsible for her actions.

Finally, we got to a place where we could have a real heart-to-heart talk, and I could say, "This bothers me a lot." I had been afraid to do that because she was so volatile. She really started listening to me.

I learned you have to take care of yourself, because BPD is like an incredibly powerful vacuum that will just suck you in, whoever you are. Setting boundaries was a way of saying, "I care about our relationship. If this keeps happening, I can't stay, and I want our relationship to continue."

You have to be willing to accept that things will get worse before they get better. But it may be the only chance you have.[1]

Anecdotal evidence from Welcome to Oz and BPDFamily.com over the past eighteen years, representing some 100,000 members, has shown again and again that setting limits and *following through with them* is a powerful thing a family member can do to help people with BPD gain control over their behavior, as Loreen did, thereby repairing and improving the relationship. Just as limits help save *lives* in some therapy programs (such as clients in DBT who have to rate the intensity of suicidal thoughts, if any, on daily diary cards), limits save *relationships*—especially chosen relationships (such as partners or friends).

What Is a Limit?

When you hear the words *boundaries* or *limits*, the first thing that probably comes to mind is what you will and will not "allow people to do." For example, you might tell your friends not to call you after 9 p.m. These kinds of limits are like traffic signs or borders around states or countries. Most of this chapter is dedicated to these types of "observable" limits.

Other limits have to do with our mental and emotional selves and are less observable. We're programmed with the general drive to be close and connected to others and to please them. This helps us function in families and societies. But at the same time, we yearn to be who *we* are, not what other people want us to be. We need space and independence.

A healthy equilibrium between pleasing ourselves and pleasing others, and being who we are versus what other people want us to be, is fundamental to the health of any relationship. The following chart by sociologist Donna R. Bellafiore illustrates the difference between healthy, balanced relationships and unhealthy, unbalanced relationships.[2]

Healthy Relationships	Unhealthy Relationships
• Feeling like your own person	• Feeling incomplete without your partner
• Feeling responsible for your own happiness	• Relying on your partner for your happiness
• Togetherness and separateness are balanced	• Too much or too little togetherness
• Friendships exist outside of the relationship	• Inability to establish and maintain friendships with others
• Focuses on the best qualities of both people	• Focuses on the worst qualities of the partners
• Open, honest, and assertive communication	• Game-playing, unwillingness to listen, manipulation
• Commitment to the partner	• Jealousy, relationship addiction, or lack of commitment
• Respecting the differences in the partner	• Blaming the partner for his or her own unique qualities
• Accepting changes in the relationship	• Feeling that the relationship should always be the same
• Asking honestly for what is wanted	• Feeling unable to express what is wanted

Why Limits Are Important

Limits are a necessary ingredient to your relationship for three reasons—the health of you, of the relationship, and of your family member.

To You

In their book *Better Boundaries,* authors Jan Black and Greg Enns explain that establishing limits in relationships can very quickly raise our life experiences to a new level of competency and joy. Limits, they say, protect us from being or feeling "controlled, manipulated, 'fixed,' misunderstood, abused, discounted, demeaned, or wrongly judged."

According to the authors, limits form an identifiable shape around our beliefs and preferences. They bring order to our lives: without them, we become overwhelmed with the demands of others and are tempted by "sirens of opportunity" to do things that steer us off course. In this way, limits are our values in action, free from anyone else's control or influence.[3]

Jack's limits kept him safe from the border-lion—not by caging or controlling it, but by putting a protective circle around him that his wife's border-lion couldn't penetrate. Jack took care of Jack, and he let Loreen take care of Loreen. She could decide to gain control of herself and have her husband around, or she could call him names and be by herself.

To the Relationship

Limits are an important element of a relationship's foundation. Limits ensure mutual respect and create safety. When limits are honored, each party becomes more willing to share his or her genuine self, giving acceptance and trust the chance to take root. Trust leads to comfortableness, intimacy, joy, and feelings of connection—all those things that people with BPD want so badly.

Without limits, relationships can become chaotic, unstable, and hostile. People close up and develop walls and defenses—all things that thwart trusting connections. In other words, as much as BPs dislike limits, limits lead to the close connections they crave.

To Your Borderline Family Member

Limits also help your family member because the outside world—bosses, the court system, schools, the IRS—will set limits for her, whether she's ready or not. It's unlikely that others will have the patience and understanding of the disorder that close family members have.

Second, according to DBT psychologist Dr. Debra Resnick, people with BPD do better in structured environments. "Borderline individuals don't have well-established boundaries," she says. "They may rail against limits, but usually they benefit from them. This is one reason why most people with BPD benefit from hospitalization." Jack sensed something similar about his wife, Loreen. "She reacted vehemently to limits, but I got the feeling that deep down she knew she needed them."

Some people with the disorder feel shame and remorse when they hurt someone they love. "Many of my patients know they've lost control and feel very bad about it," Resnick says. "If their [non-BP] family member can avoid fueling the rage, there is a chance the borderline individual may be more mindful that their anger is likely disproportionate to the situation. That may allow them to regain control of their emotions."[4]

Properties of Limits

The best way to get a good grasp on limits is to discuss them concretely, not in the abstract. Therefore, we will be referring to the following exercise throughout this chapter. Please work through the exercise as you read it to achieve the maximum benefits.

The "Gnome Home" Exercise

For the purposes of this exercise, we'll assume that you and your BP live together, merge your incomes, and jointly pay expenses. (If you live separately, pick one of your abodes and come up with a pretend income. The specifics don't matter; just make a choice and stick to it.)

One day, your BP decides to start collecting garden gnomes. He buys gnomes of all types and in a variety of sizes and styles, including Santa gnomes, bearded gnomes, clean-shaven gnomes, reclining gnomes, and nearly naked gnomes.

Gradually, the hobby becomes problematic. It's becoming expensive, and you need the money for other things. There's a space problem, too: The gnomes are sprawling out into the yard, leaving no room for other uses (such as an actual garden). If you live in an apartment, you've run out of places to display and store them.

Your neighbors are angry about the traffic generated by people driving in to gawk at the "Gnome Home." Finally, each time you mow the lawn, many of the gnomes need to be moved. (Or, your landlord and neighbors are complaining because your BP is using someone else's storage compartment in the basement.)

Now, using the home and income you decided on at the beginning of this exercise, answer the following questions:

- What do you believe is a reasonable amount of money to spend on the gnomes per year?
- What do you believe is a reasonable amount of space to dedicate to gnomes, keeping in mind the pressure from the neighbors?
- Who should move the gnomes when it's time to mow, clean them, or otherwise maintain their cheery little faces?

Have a good idea of what you really *want* and what you *need* because your answers will become the limits you will be setting. When you finish this exercise, please come back to this book.

Limit Property #1

Most likely, you found it difficult to come up with your answers because there are so many variables, including obvious ones like income and living space. Chances are that if you were doing this exercise with a roomful of people, each of you would come up with a different set of limits. And *that* is the point of limit property #1:

Your limits emerge from a variety of factors unique to you. You own them just like you own your feelings, thoughts, and beliefs.

While this may seem obvious, it's not. Most people believe that there is one standard that should apply to everyone, and most arguments are about divining what that standard is. Take a look at your local newspaper. You probably have an advice column that goes something like this:

Dear Advice Columnist:
My son's best friend, who is sixteen, eats over at our house all the time. But he's big—he plays football—and it's getting expensive. My husband says just "eat" the cost, so to speak. I think it's too much to have us fill in where the high school cafeteria stops. Who is right? Me or my husband?
Signed,
Fed Up

Fed Up assumes that advice columnist sits atop the Temple of Truth, who has the special ability to divine who is "right" and who is "wrong." If the anointed columnist says that Fed Up is wrong, Fed Up should back down and cook for four instead of three.

But will that fix the problem? Will Fed Up immediately go out and buy steaks for the grill, bake fresh homemade biscuits, and make chocolate-covered strawberries for dessert? Will Fed Up feel less resentful toward her husband and possibly her son and the son's friend?

No!

Emily Post and the Ten Commandments aside, there is no Temple of Truth, no anointed standard bearer. This family dispute is, essentially, another garden gnome exercise. How much does the food cost? Does Fed Up have enough space in the refrigerator for the extra food? And who is doing the dirty work—shopping, cooking, and dishes? (Most likely, the answer to question number 3 is Fed Up, which, over time, could develop into bitterness.)

Likewise, if your family member says that your limits are wrong or unreasonable, he is speaking about what is right and true for *him*, not you. You are your own Temple of Truth. You live and deal with the difficulty every day, be it dirty gnomes or dirty dishes. Your limits are your own. And your very first limit is that you have the inalienable right to set limits.

Limit Property #2

Now think about the *process* you went through to come up with your limits in the gnome home exercise.

- Did you develop them based on what one person wanted, or did you try to balance everyone's needs and desires?
- Was your intention to hurt, punish, or control or to develop a plan that made the most sense based on all the competing factors?

Most non-BPs err on the side of trying to take care of everyone but themselves. It never occurs to them that they can say "no" or that their wants and needs are just as significant as those of everyone else.

This leads us to limit property #2:

> Your limits are *for* you and *about* you, not against others. They are
> about respect: respect for yourself, respect for others, and respect
> for the relationship.

People with BPD sometimes see other people's limits as a personal affront, something designed to punish or control them. That's because they
feel punished and controlled, and for them, feelings equal facts. Naturally,
you'll have discussions and try to come up with solutions that benefit everyone. But compromise because you *want* to, not because your feelings
are "wrong" or unimportant. (This is why you need to know what you
want and what you need.)

Limit Property #3

Some people completing the exercise feel strongly about some of their limits, but not others. Perhaps cost is a major issue, but mowing isn't a big
deal. Some people highly value a fashionably decorated home in their own
personal style (French country, traditional); others are quite happy with
college freshman décor (with or without empty pizza boxes).

This leads us to limit property #3:

> Different people have different boundary styles, and boundaries
> have different aspects.

According to Jane Adams, author of *Boundary Issues,* boundaries vary
in three ways:

1. Their permeability, or how thick or thin they are.
2. Their flexibility, or how variable they are.
3. Their complexity, or how intricate and interconnected they are.

These qualities may vary from situation to situation. But in general, we
each have our own boundary style, which is an interplay between these
three factors. Some individuals have rigid boundaries. One gnome over the
line and they're biting their nails. Other folks are more flexible; the gnomes
need to be falling into the cat's litter box before they take much notice.

Not surprisingly, some higher-functioning invisible BPs are quite rigid about their limits, while some non-BPs (particularly friends or those in intimate relationships with BPs) tend to fall on the weak, flexible side—sometimes too-flexible side. Non-BPs' limits also have a tendency to be too permeable (thin), meaning they let everything in. As a result, they feel inundated and overwhelmed.

When people with large boundary style differences are paired, conflict is nearly inevitable. Adams says, "Boundary differences are often the cause of friction, discontent, or problems in relationships, although they often masquerade as something else—fights over money, the kids, the in-laws, the deadline, the broken promise, or forgotten occasion."[5]

Three Keys to Setting Limits

Most books discuss limit setting as if it were an event instead of a process. Setting limits has to do with mental preparation and planning. The three keys to mental preparation are

- steering clear of FOG: fear, obligation, and guilt (an acronym coined by Susan Forward in her excellent book *Emotional Blackmail*)
- trusting your own perceptions, feelings, and opinions—most significantly, those about yourself
- refusing to rescue your family member from your limits, which gives mixed messages

Steering Clear of the FOG

In chapter 8, Power Tool 2: Uncover What Keeps You Feeling Stuck, we discussed FOG in the context of the relationship. FOG also comes up like little wisps of smoke during limit-setting conversations. If you don't prepare for it, it can blur your vision and make it hard to see and remember what you want and need. The next few pages will show you how to prevent FOG from sabotaging your convictions about the limits you must set to make this relationship work (or make your situation bearable).

Fear of Losing the Relationship

There are many different kinds of fears. Most of them can be approached using the Carnegie problem-solving methods described on pages 134–135. The fear we will deal with here is fear of losing the relationship.

Family members say that underneath the disorder, their loved one is a great person. Common adjectives members use to describe their BP include *bright, funny, compassionate, loving,* and *beautiful.* It's very hard to accept that their loved one's borderline behaviors aren't isolated anomalies, but a central part of who he is.

To keep themselves safe from their loved one's erratic and often abusive behaviors, family members give in on issues they actually feel strongly about. The BP's emotional blow-up acts as a punishment; the non-BP giving in to prevent the punishment acts as a powerful reward. Over time, non-BPs have let their limits slide so far they can no longer be seen with the naked eye.

Psychotherapist Beverly Engel explains how limits disappear. She says:

> Most of us begin a relationship thinking we have certain limits as to what we will and will not tolerate from a partner. But as the relationship progresses, we tend to move our boundaries back, tolerating more and more intrusion or going along with things we are really opposed to. . . . [Individuals] begin tolerating unacceptable and even abusive behavior, and then convince themselves that these behaviors are normal, acceptable, [and deserved].[6]

Maura, like many non-BPs, is boxed in. She knows just what will happen if she makes any demands on her boyfriend, Fred. When she says she needs time alone or time with her friends, he says he'll leave her. Not only leave her, but make her life miserable by spreading rumors and lies about her to their friends.

Her family and friends tell her the relationship isn't healthy and that Fred has problems. But she is terribly afraid of losing Fred and wishes that others could see what a wonderful person he is underneath it all. If she can just settle Fred down and not make waves, things will be fine.

Signs of abuse include dictating how others should live; isolating them from family and friends; controlling money or other resources; blaming those they mistreat for the mistreatment; being overly jealous and possessive; or pushing, grabbing, hitting, kicking, punching, or throwing objects.

If this describes your family member, you may think that by remaining silent, you are "helping" this person or "saving" the relationship. This is untrue. Both of you need help immediately from experienced mental health professionals. Reread the section on the Stockholm Syndrome on pages 149–150. Call someone who cares about you or a domestic violence hotline. Men and parents can be abused, too. If you don't seek help, the consequences could be tragic.

Obligation and Guilt

Yeardley just *knows* that her borderline sister is going to ruin her wedding. "You have to ask your sister to be your maid of honor," their mother insisted. Yeardley had wanted her best friend in that role, but she gave in to her mother's wishes. It's been like this her whole life—she always receives love and praise from her parents when she "does her duty" by her sister.

Suzanne Roberts, author of *Coping in New Territory: The Handbook for Adult Children of Aging Parents,* says, "We rarely, if ever, set boundaries with our families, yet we're confounded when they seem to have the ability to turn our lives around on a dime. We appear to be perfectly happy to gift wrap our lives and give them to the first family member who asks."

Roberts says we don't set adequate boundaries with family members for two reasons: self-induced guilt and the fear of what people will think. She says:

> I don't believe we even consider that we have a right to set boundaries with family—after all they're *family.* In actuality, we not only have the right, we have the *responsibility* to allow our family members to be subject to the same criteria as anyone else on the planet.
>
> To the people who stomp on our boundaries, demanding more of us than we can give, we may appear to be selfish. But

it's not selfish to take care of yourself. Not only that, people with no boundaries, who function with knee-jerk reactions to every demand, are too tired, angry, and resentful to be kind and loving.[7]

Feelings of guilt and obligation are common when they set limits, say members of BPDFamily.com. Here are some examples:

- "She said my limits about having my own money meant I didn't love her or take our marriage seriously."
- "She said, 'How can you do this to your own mother? What kind of a son are you?'"
- "She accused me of being like her terrible ex-husbands."

FOG is "penetrating, disorienting, and obscures everything but the pounding discomfort it produces," says Susan Forward, author of *Emotional Blackmail*. The pressure is so uncomfortable, we give in as quickly and as automatically as we would put our hands over our ears when a siren shrieks past.[8]

Once the FOG button works, BPs will press it again and again. One family member summed up this dynamic beautifully: "When I try to set limits, my BP keeps at me until I give up, even if it takes hours. It is much easier to give in within the first thirty seconds."

Forward says that one of the most powerful techniques people can use to cut through the FOG is to say, "I CAN STAND IT" repeatedly. This puts a new message into the conscious and unconscious mind. When thinking about taking steps to end the blackmail, breathe deeply and say, "I can stand it," at least ten times. The rewards are worth enduring someone getting upset. At a minimum, the rewards are increased self-confidence and a sense of mastery over life.[9]

Trust Your Perceptions, Feelings, and Opinions

Does wanting to go on a vacation with just your husband, and not his extended family, qualify as abuse? It does according to Ralph, says his non-BP wife, Ann. She says:

When I asked him if we could go somewhere by ourselves, he got upset and said, "You know how much my family means to me. Why do you do this to me? I can't believe that you're abusing me like this!"

After a while of him saying this again and again, I began to question myself. It took such a toll on me I started going to counseling. I told the counselor, "Either I'm living with somebody who is very out of control, or I just don't see myself correctly. I need to figure out which of those it is."

In *Stop Walking on Eggshells,* therapist Elyce Benham explains that when someone constantly undermines what we know or believe about ourselves, the faith we have in ourselves starts to shake. A type of "brainwashing" takes place.

"The techniques of brainwashing are simple," she says. "Isolate the victim, expose them to consistent messages, mix with sleep deprivation, add some form of abuse, get the person to doubt what they know and feel, keep them on their toes, wear them down, and stir well."[10]

To get its way, the border-lion will goad your family member into making negative and inaccurate judgments about who you are, what you value, what your motivations are, and what kind of personality you have. Nearly every family member on Welcome to Oz and BPDFamily.com have been called selfish and controlling when they set limits. Many have been called worse.

The word *selfish* is loathsome for most non-BPs. They gain self-worth from being needed and making sacrifices, and being called "selfish" is the worst crime imaginable. They've learned, "When in doubt, don't disagree, don't have needs, don't have opinions, and, above all, never say 'no.'"

Before you can comfortably express your needs, you must believe you have a legitimate right to have those needs. You have the right to your own beliefs, even if they are different from your family member's. You have the right to make mistakes, to act illogically, and to not have to explain yourself. You also have the right to like yourself even though you're not perfect.

In *I Don't Have to Make Everything All Better,* authors Gary and Joy Lundberg say, "Who you are is who you choose to be. When you have a strong belief system based on what you've learned, studied, and experienced, then you have developed a model of life that is used to evaluate everything you come into contact with. You can hear another viewpoint and evaluate it on its merits and ask the question, 'Is this right for me?' Because you are comfortable with yourself and your own value system, you can listen and learn, and accept or reject what other people say or do."[11]

Stop Rescuing Your BP from Your Limits

Recall the Karpman Triangle on page 63 (you may wish to reread this page before going further). It is an explanation of the patterns that family members get into again and again. During disputes, different family members alternate playing the roles of victim, persecutor (who bullies the victim), and rescuer (who saves the victim). Two people can play, too, switching off roles.

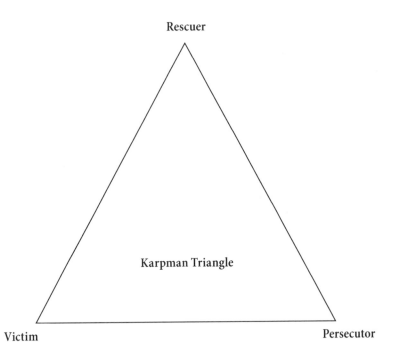

Rescuer

Karpman Triangle

Victim   Persecutor

When non-BPs set limits, BPs put themselves in the role of victim and their family member in the role of persecutor, saying something like, "I can't believe you're doing this to me. You are so selfish and controlling!" Then, under pressure, the family member rescinds the limit or acts in a way that makes it meaningless (for example, doesn't establish consequences for stepping over the line).

Once a family member becomes rescuer, a major shift occurs. He moves on the triangle from the lower right position (the persecutor) to the top of the triangle (the rescuer). Unknowingly, he has sabotaged his own limit. Now he's the victim, and his BP is the persecutor.

Dr. Blaise Aguirre, medical director of the Adolescent DBT Center at McLean Hospital in Belmont, Massachusetts, says:

> For parents, the guilt swings back and forth between two poles. First, they get frustrated and angry at their child's behavior. They feel invalidated and manipulated—especially if they haven't been taking care of themselves like they should.
>
> Then, when the child is desperate, feeling worthless, suicidal, and self-injurious, they become terrified. They go into caretaking mode and place their child in the hospital. After a short while, the child apologizes and says she's learned her lesson. The parents then rescue their child by taking her out of treatment. Their guilt diminishes. Then three months later, the child is acting out again, and the cycle keeps repeating.[12]

Limit Property #4

This next limit property is one of the most important concepts in this entire book:

> You stop being a victim by taking responsibility for your limits. You avoid being a persecutor by letting your borderline family member take responsibility for how he reacts to your limits. By eliminating yourself as victim and persecutor, you give your family member the opportunity to be accountable for his own emotions and actions—in other words, to rescue himself.

The concept of owning your decisions is so powerful it can transform not only your relationship but your life as a whole. While you may not be able to change some circumstances you find yourself in, you can begin to appreciate that you have a variety of choices about how to react, emotionally and otherwise.

Allowing your BP to take responsibility for her choices is easier said than done, especially for family members of lower-functioning conventional BPs. They must try to sort out what their family member *can't* do and what he *can* do (but wishes he didn't have to do).

Psychiatrist John G. Gunderson, one of the foremost experts on BPD, says that people who set limits can help motivate their borderline family member to take on greater responsibility and have appropriate limits within herself. He and coauthor Cynthia Berkowitz say:

> [Although BPD can take] an emotional and financial toll to the individual and the family . . . do not protect [borderline individuals] from the natural consequences of their actions. Allow them to learn about reality. Bumping into a few walls is usually necessary.
>
> [When family members rescue the borderline individual from his or her own behavior], the results . . . are complex. First and foremost, the troublesome behavior is likely to persist because it has cost no price or has brought the individual some kind of reward. Second, the family members are likely to become enraged because they resent having sacrificed integrity, money, and good will in their efforts to be protective. In this case, tensions in the home mount even though the hope of the protective measures was to prevent tension.
>
> Meanwhile, the anger may be rewarding on some level to the individual because it makes her the focus of attention, even if that attention is negative. Third, the individual may begin to show these behaviors outside of the family and face greater harm and loss in the real world than she would have faced in the family setting. Thus, the attempt to protect leaves the individual unprepared for the real world.[13]

Planning for Limit-Setting Discussions

Setting limits will very likely stir up the splitting-shame-fear spiral. Therefore, it's imperative that you create a plan that will act as a road map and safety net. Each of the following five "Cs" is a component of the plan:

- Clarify.
- Calculate costs.
- Come up with consequences.
- Create a consensus.
- Consider possible outcomes.

Clarify Your Limits

Think about the limits you would like to set. Although you will pick something small to begin with, try brainstorming with others and get everything out on the table. (Other people frequently see options that non-BPs don't.) Look through this book or others like it to give you ideas. If you have a higher-functioning invisible BP, questions like these can get you started:

- What subjects do I try to avoid?
- What is best for my life, long and short term?
- What is best for those in my care?
- What do I *want* in this relationship?
- What do I *need* in this relationship?
- What makes me feel safe?
- What makes me feel angry?

If you have a lower-functioning conventional BP, you may wish to take the problem-solving approach discussed in the sidebar "Limits and Your Borderline Child" on pages 224–225 in this chapter.

Perry Hoffman says, "Your limits may be less about what you expect the other person to do and more about what you are willing to accept. Decide what you're willing to tolerate and then put it in a plan. For example, a mother who was attacked by her daughter required that the daughter be in treatment to keep receiving rent money. Or, if her daughter destroyed something, then the mother would not be willing to drive her daughter to her friend's house."[14]

Some parents report that they have a tendency to do too much for their children. Trial and error can help you determine what lower-functioning conventional BPs can and can't do for themselves.

One parent says, "My wife and I did a lot of soul searching about whether we should swoop in and insert ourselves into her business. We decided that some areas were off limits, like school, job hunting, and making doctor appointments. As a result, she started exhibiting more independence in those areas. We learned that when we did meddle, if something went wrong it was going to be all our fault."

As you plan, leave room for negotiation. Freda Friedman, PhD, a therapist whose primary focus is BPD, says, "Sometimes two people have to negotiate their differing limits. This may mean that each one has to give a little at times and try to validate where the other is coming from."[15]

Calculate the Costs

We are so busy living our day-to-day lives that we don't keep very good track of the things that gnaw at us. When faced with a problem we can't solve, we ignore it and hope it will go away. Or, we use problem-solving methods that never worked before, just in case of a miracle.

Then, a crisis occurs, or our situation deteriorates to a point where old coping techniques don't work anymore. Ruefully, we conclude, "Uh-oh, I shouldn't have ignored this. This cost me more than I thought it would. I wish I had been paying more attention, or really thought this through earlier. Perhaps I would have made different choices."

The gnome home exercise forced you to look at a problem that needed limits and to make some decisions. But in real life, we tend to let things go on. We wait for the proverbial last straw or a cataclysmic event to make us focus. Non-BPs seem to delay limit setting until their very survival is at stake.

Jack, whom you met earlier in the chapter, waited to set limits until he was in survival mode. He says, "Because of Loreen's name-calling, I started to feel totally incompetent at work. This was disheartening because it had always been the one thing I was confident about. I started to realize I didn't like myself anymore. I wasn't the person I wanted to be."

This leads us to another limit property that involves time.

Limit Property #5

To maintain your limits over the long haul, you need to have conviction that the limit is necessary and appropriate. Conviction comes when you know how much it costs *not* to have the limit in place. The longer you wait, the more it costs.

Jack waited to set limits until his survival was at stake. But you don't have to! Ask yourself how much *not* having limits in central areas of your life is costing you right now. What about in the future? You might look at actual costs, say, of giving money to a child, or the costs in stress, amount of time spent, pleasures you've had to forgo, opportunity costs, and so on.

Come Up with Consequences

Virginia, a member of BPDFamily.com, says, "Boundaries don't work. I mean, what can I do? Am I supposed to leave the house each time my husband breaks the boundary? Well, I tried that. It didn't work. I suppose I *could* have left the house and stayed with a friend each time he broke one. But then, I would have ended up living with my friend most of the time!"

Limits without consequences is known as nagging. This means that yes, Virginia *does* have to leave the house (or have some other consequence) when her husband doesn't observe her limits. The fact that limits have consequences is not a value judgment. It is not even a statement about people with BPD. It is about human nature and the fact that human beings tend to repeat actions that are rewarding and avoid actions that are unpleasant. (More about that in the next chapter.)

Earlier, you learned that in healthy relationships limits are in balance between our drive to be connected (please others) and our drive to be independent (please ourselves). You also found out that non-BPs tend to have boundaries that are too weak and too thin. Modifying your boundary style, or "changing the baseline" of what you will and won't accept, can bring a healthier balance to the relationship.

Sheila could tolerate many things. But not everything. She says, "In the fourteen years we were married, my husband, Ryan, crossed most of my boundaries. But I had two laid in stone—he couldn't be unfaithful, and he couldn't try to hit me or do anything physical. To my knowledge, he never did either."

Is it coincidental that Ryan crossed everything but those two limits? What would have happened had Sheila had a third, fourth, or fifth limit he dare not cross? And what if the consequences of those additional limits were not so drastic, all or nothing, but graduated?

Changing your baseline means changing the parameters of what you will or will not tolerate or accept. Even if these are unstated, the people who know you best know just how far to push before you push back. Sheila's baseline is set at "Do anything *but* hit me or be unfaithful," and there's a good chance Ryan was able to refrain from doing these two things because of it, whether on a conscious or unconscious level.

Another example: Bert and Nan love to play right before dinner. Their mother calls them in to supper every night at 5:30. But Bert and Nan are no fools. They know that Mom will yell again in another five minutes with a note of irritation in her voice. A couple of minutes after the second call, she'll call one last time threatening them with no TV that night. That's when they head home, looking forward to their favorite TV programs.

Mary, their mother, is sick to death of this hassle. It frustrates and irritates her. If Mary sat down and thought about it, she might realize that she doesn't take TV privileges away because the kids would complain and aggravate her even further. She doesn't realize her baseline is set at 5:45 p.m.

Changing your baseline will require some soul searching and decision making. Make sure you're being realistic. You might even keep a daily journal to remind yourself of the costs to keep you motivated. Keep in mind you're coming up with consequences *for* you and the relationship, not *against* your family member. And finally, remember that these limits are unique to you. You don't need to justify them to anyone.

Create a Consensus

Everyone in the house needs to be on the same page—including siblings. An experienced parent on BPDFamily.com observes, "This division between the parents is as big as the Grand Canyon when a child plays on the sympathies of the softer parent to get his or her way. Parents who are not united *will* have marriage problems. It also exacerbates the splitting behavior."

Consider Possible Outcomes

Universally, family members who set limits find that their BP's actions get worse before they get better. These actions are designed to restore things back to the way they were. They can start small, with mild disagreement, and work up to threats and enlisting allies to pressure you. This is a normal response to limits; we all do it. With people who have BPD, however, it is more intense.

In *Stop Walking on Eggshells*, the authors explain, "When you assertively redirect the pain back to the BP so they can begin to deal with it, you are breaking a contract you didn't know you signed. Naturally, the BP will find this distressing . . . Your ability to withstand these countermoves will determine the future course of your relationship."

In the past, you probably weren't expecting this. Now, you can plan for it. Your first step is to get out of deer-in-the-headlights mode. Untangle any threats and fears and consider each one in a logical manner using the Carnegie problem-solving process outlined on pages 134–135.

Consider all the possible outcomes and prepare for them. Ask friends to help you think things through and give you support. Signs that you may need help from a mental health professional include the following:

- The BP's actions are unsafe to either you or her, for example, major rages or threats of suicide.
- The relationship has been dysfunctional for many years.
- The person with BPD is in a position of some authority, such as a parent.
- You depend on your family member for practical matters, such as financial support or a place to live.

- Your family member has made threats in the past, especially scary ones.
- Your BP has enlisted allies to pressure you.

Discussing Limits

In this chapter, you've done an amazing amount of work. Now, it is time to start talking to your family member about your decisions. Most likely, you will have many discussions over days, weeks, and even months. Think of this as a process, not an event. Again, start small and go slowly with a limit or two—don't suddenly give your BP a laundry list of everything you want.

Safety First

When Ken wrote a letter about limits to his wife, Andrea, she called him up at work. As Ken puts it, "She attacked me for twenty minutes, questioned me like a police interrogator. I felt as if I was in front of a firing squad." Ken stayed on the phone and tried to reason with his wife—a bad idea, as you now know.

Safety comes first, as always. Remember, once someone with BPD reaches a six on a one-to-ten measurement of emotional intensity, he may not be able to calm himself down. You can say, "Let's take a time-out," or, "I'm not at my best now." Gunderson and Berkowitz, who are experienced in treating lower-functioning conventional BPs, say:

> Do not tolerate abusive treatment such as tantrums, threats, hitting and spitting. There is a range of ways to set limits on them. A mild gesture would be to walk out of the room to avoid rewarding the tantrum with attention. A more aggressive gesture would be to call an ambulance. Many families fear taking the latter step because they do not want an ambulance in front of their home, or they do not want to incur the wrath of the person having the tantrum.
>
> When torn by such feelings, one must consider the opposing issues. Safety may be a concern when someone is violent

and out of control. Most people would agree that safety takes priority over privacy. Furthermore, by neglecting to get proper medical attention for out-of-control behavior, one may turn a silent ear to it. This only leads to further escalation. The acting out is a cry for help. If a cry for help is not heard, it only becomes louder.[16]

Use the DEAR Technique

Researcher Marsha M. Linehan has developed a set of skills for communication between people with borderline personality disorder and those who care about them. The acronym is DEAR, which stands for Describe, Express, Assert, and Reinforce.

As you go through these steps, use empathetic acknowledgment and the other communication techniques from the last chapter. It's vital to keep everything you've learned in mind: the biological reasons for the disorder, the shame and fear the BP feels, and so on. You may wish to reread the empathy exercise on pages 50–52.

If you have been wishy-washy in the past, you may wish to acknowledge that and say something like, "We've spoken about this before, but I've come to realize I've been giving you mixed messages about this. That wasn't fair to either of us." Acknowledge that everyone in the family has a right to identify their own limits and needs.

Describe the situation as you see it in a factual, unemotional manner. "You call me more than a dozen times at work each day. It distracts me and makes it hard to focus. I share an office, so other people can hear, and I'm not supposed to take personal calls at work."

Express your feelings or opinions about the situation clearly. "I am feeling really frustrated because I've told you before that this can't continue. When I am at work, I have to stay on task."

Assert your limits, making them simple. The limit should be small, attainable, and realistic. "I can take two or three calls a day. I can't take any more calls than that unless there is an emergency." Keep repeating this limit until your family member hears you. Come back to it again and again.

Reinforce the benefits of your limits, if appropriate. This will work much better if you have been able to create a climate of cooperation. "We can talk when I get home. I won't feel so frustrated because I'll be able to work, and you will feel less frustrated because I won't have to tell you I can't talk."

Don't Ask Permission or Overexplain

What you *don't* say is just as important as what you *do* say. If, after previous discussions, you felt as though you had been agitated through a washing machine, unsure about why things got off track, you probably made the mistake of asking permission to set the limit instead of stating your expectations. This is by far the most common mistake that people make. It may take some effort and a change in attitude to eliminate the urge to overexplain.

To avoid being pulled into an argument about your limits, you must let go of your compelling need to make your family member agree with you. Don't overexplain or defend. To that end, minimize the word *because,* especially if it seems as though your family member is likely asking questions so she can refute or poke holes into any explanation you give. Don't get pulled off topic. You can return to discussions about the relationship itself at another time, if you wish.

You don't have to answer questions right away. Don't let yourself be rushed. You can say, "I don't know," or "I need time to think about that." Don't take insults as an indication of the person's deepest feelings. If you were as bad a person as she says you are, she wouldn't want to be around you.

Be Assertive, Yet Gentle

Use everything you learned in the last chapter about empathy and validation. Freda Friedman, coauthor of *Surviving a Borderline Parent,* says, "When the interaction is just focused on limit setting without any validation of the other person's wishes and needs, then usually neither person feels heard or understood or acknowledged. It might feel like the person with BPD is outrageous or manipulative, but he or she feels misunderstood and invalidated."[17]

Remember that your tone of voice, facial expressions, and other body language communicate much more about your attitudes and beliefs than what you say. At times, you may want to emphasize the gentle side; at other times, the assertive. Body language is an excellent tool, and you can adjust it moment by moment.

Do's:

- Use eye contact; be sincere, but firm and level.
- If standing, stand straight with feet planted on the ground. Wider stances and bigger mannerisms show more assertiveness.
- Use a gentle tone that is calm and soothing. Lower (alto, bass) rather than higher (tenor, soprano).
- Speak at a normal pace, not too fast.
- Don't raise your voice—in fact, you may want to lower it a bit to show you're not in competition and so your family member needs to keep his low to hear you. Make your voice gentle, calm, and soothing.
- Stay close, but not too close, which can be threatening.

Don'ts:

- finger point or jab
- increase the volume of your voice
- glare or narrow your eyes
- snort
- tighten your jaw muscles
- press your lips together
- look down submissively
- thrust out your chin
- clench your fingers into a fist with white knuckles
- run your fingers through your hair
- cross your arms
- place your hands on hips
- stomp

- sit on the edge of your chair
- kick the ground
- invade the person's intimate space
- bite your nails
- pick your cuticles
- sigh
- strain your voice
- wring your hands[18]

Make Sure Your Family Member Feels Heard

Acknowledge the other person's needs and wishes and how important those feel, while at the same time establishing or reiterating the limits that have been set. Use phrases such as

- "I'm not trying for one of us to be right or wrong, but for the relationship to be the best it can possibly be. I need . . ."
- "I've given this a lot of thought. I am learning more about myself and what I can and can't do and what I need. And I need . . ."
- "I understand you think it means I'm selfish. Still, I need . . ."
- "I am not trying to be controlling. I am trying to be open and honest about how I feel. I need . . ."
- "I'm not sure how to answer that. But what I do know is that things can't go on this way. I need . . ."
- "It is true that we don't see things the same way. I wish we did, because this isn't easy for me either. What I need is . . ."

Practice, Practice, Practice

Practice the conversation as much as you can. Pretend your BP is in an empty chair and run through what you're going to say. Better yet, role-play with a friend, with your friend playing the role of the BP. If you are not usually assertive, start off by being more assertive in low-stakes situations, for example, telling a server in a restaurant if something is wrong with the food.

Try Positive Self-Talk

One way to drown out the roar of the border-lion is to have a steady stream of positive self-talk. Self-talk is the chit-chat within our heads that goes on nearly all the time. Try positive, reassuring thoughts like these:

- "Setting and observing my limits may feel strange or unfamiliar right now. That's okay. All things are strange and unfamiliar until you get used to them."
- "I'm feeling afraid—but what am I afraid *of* exactly? Wait—I've thought this through. I've made it safe for myself. I'm going to be okay."
- "I'm working on this because I love my family member so much. She can't see this, but it's okay. I will see it for both of us."
- "I need to meet my own limits right now so I can meet his needs in the long run."

Setting Limits for Children

Sarah and Joe, who has BPD, have two children. Sarah sets limits for her children as well as herself. She says:

In the past, my husband used to rage at our teenage boys at the drop of a hat for no good reason (God forbid they should hold their knife the wrong way at the table). At first, I got angry back at him. But that only escalated tensions and led to more problems. Now, either I will leave or ignore him.

When my husband starts raging at one of the boys, I calmly ask my child to go up to his room for five to ten minutes. I've talked with the children separately to let them know that they are not in trouble but that their father needs some time to calm down and deal with his emotions. At that point, he seems able to get himself under control.

Alternatively, I've told the children not to acknowledge or speak to him when he is using his raging voice. They are to ignore him during these times, but only when I am physically present so that they are not endangered. If I'm not going to be home evenings and my husband and children will be alone together, I try to make arrangements for the boys to be elsewhere, or I take them to school with me.

You can find more information about setting limits for children in *Stop Walking on Eggshells*.

Limits and Your Borderline Child

Parents set limits for their children for practical reasons and to help them learn how to function in the real world. Unfortunately, the kind of limit setting that works for normally functioning children may not have much effect on those who have borderline personality disorder.

Sharon from NUTS believes the following:

- Some borderline minors are unable to grasp the concept that their actions have consequences. For example, a child will take a risk and crash the car, unable to visualize that without the car he can't go places. (Of course, this is true of teens who don't have BPD, but with BPD children, it's exaggerated.)
- When they *can* visualize consequences, there may be too much of a lag between the act and the consequence.
- The consequences don't have the impact the parents wish they would.
- Because of impulsivity, the child ignores the consequences and does whatever she wants anyway.[19]

Although often the limits might not have the effect you intended, it is still important that the limits be set and there be consequences. In addition to limit setting, take a problem-solving approach. Gunderson and Berkowitz say:

> People with BPD have many obvious strengths such as intelligence, ambition, good looks, and artistic talent. Pleased with their progress, they may shoot for grand plans they aren't ready for. A setback can result in a crashing swing in the opposite direction. Help your child set smaller, more realistic goals where the chances of success are greater. Break goals into steps and be sure to take one step at a time. Ask your child if they want help; don't just jump in.
>
> Problems are best tackled through open discussion in the family. People are most likely to do their part when they are asked to participate and their views are respected. Recognize the difficulty of what you are asking and ask if they feel capable of the task before them.
>
> Family members may have sharply contrasting views about how to handle any given problem behavior in their relative with BPD. Parental inconsistencies fuel severe family conflicts, and siblings also have their opinions on what should be done. Communicate openly about your contrasting views on a problem, hear each other's perspectives, and then develop a plan that everyone can stick to.[20]

Let Your Light Shine

In her book *A Return to Love: Reflections on the Principles of A Course in Miracles,* Marianne Williamson says, "Our deepest fear is not that we are inadequate. Our deepest fear is that we are powerful beyond measure." Many people have heard that part of the quote. However, Williamson then goes on to say, "And as we let our own light shine, we unconsciously give other people permission to do the same."

That's what this chapter has helped you to do. Limits are a powerful tool in restoring balance to a relationship. Now that you have taken responsibility for yourself—the only person you control—it's up to your family member to do the same: to make her own decisions and to take responsibility for herself.

In the next chapter, you'll learn how to respond to your BP's choices.

Chapter 11

Power Tool 5:
Reinforce the Right Behavior

The people in my WTO group have found that BPs tend to see
the line we draw, touch their toes to it, and if nothing happens,
place their foot over the line repeatedly until it gets cut off.
▪ Welcome to Oz member ▪

Now that you've set your limits and communicated them to your family member, the next step is learning how to maintain them. Welcome to Oz and BPDFamily.com members need to develop skills in this area. Here are some typical comments from them:

- "When I set my boundaries, I had all kinds of newfound resolve. But when he tried to dismantle them, I went soft. Just when I thought I'd reached the end of my rope, the rope got longer."
- "When I set limits, he always has some sneaky way of getting around them—even if the purpose of the limits was to help him."
- "After I set a boundary, he would improve his behavior for a while—even long periods. But then all hell would break loose. Boundaries set, boundaries broken. The cycle just keeps going."

Your family member will test your limits many times to see how seriously you are taking them. This is human nature: We learn as young children that even if Dad wants to spend the day in a hammock, we can get him to take us to Mount Splashmore if we ask enough times in a high, whining tone and refuse to give up.

When your family member starts testing your limits, all the communication tools you've learned take a backseat to your actions. What counts now is what you do, not what you say. To make limits work, reinforce the behavior you want—observance of your limits. Do not inadvertently reinforce breaches of your limits. Most non-BPs do just that, which compromises the limits they've tried so hard to set.

Reinforcement

Reinforcers are behaviors that, occurring in conjunction with some kind of action, either increase the probability that a person will act that way again or decrease the same.

Positive and Negative Reinforcers

Behaviors that increase the likelihood of a repeat performance are called *positive reinforcers.* Those that decrease the chances are termed *negative reinforcers.* Here are some examples:

A one-year-old baby cries.

Positive reinforcers: Getting picked up and hugged, being given a bottle, or having her diaper changed. These actions make it more likely that when the baby is lonely, hungry, or wet, she will cry again.

Negative reinforcers: Being ignored. A television news program once showed children in an orphanage in a foreign country who received little adult supervision. When one of the toddlers accidentally banged her head on something, she didn't cry because she knew from experience it would not bring help.

Jane is upset and calls her friend Amy.

Positive reinforcers: Amy listens, makes her laugh, and offers to buy her a cup of coffee the next day. Jane is likely to call her again.

Negative reinforcers: Amy points out that Jane's problems aren't so bad compared to hers, then goes on to tell Jane all her problems. Jane is less likely to call again.

Reinforcers and Limits

Whatever you do, do not positively reinforce your family member for not observing ("violating") your limits. In this example, a mother unknowingly positively reinforces telephone-calling behavior.

Tacy and Betsy

Tacy has told her adult daughter Betsy that she cannot call her at work more than three times a day unless there is an emergency. Betsy is living at home and is supposed to be looking for work. This scenario happens the day after Tacy set the limit; Tacy is at work and Betsy is home, not feeling well.

8 a.m. to 12 p.m.	Betsy calls Tacy twice for various reasons.
1 p.m.	Betsy makes her third phone call of the day. Tacy reminds her of the new rule.
3 p.m.	Betsy calls again. In an irritated voice, Tacy reminds her that she wasn't supposed to call again. Betsy said it *was* an emergency because she needed to know when Tacy would be home (something Tacy had already told her). The conversation gets a bit heated, and Betsy hangs up on her mom.
3:05 p.m.	Betsy calls to demand an apology for the way Tacy spoke with her. Tacy does, figuring that now she'll get some peace.
4 p.m.	Betsy calls because she can't figure out how to work the DVR and watch a program she recorded. She's feeling upset and needs something to do, and she's frustrated because she can't get it to work. Tacy sighs and explains how it works, resolving to have another discussion about her limits.
That night	Betsy accuses her mother of being abusive because she's home alone, and Tacy doesn't even care. Tacy tries to explain and thinks, *Limits just aren't worth it!*

Find the Positive and Negative Reinforcers

Now, let's take away the words and look at the behavior.

8 a.m. to 12 p.m.	Betsy calls Tacy twice.
1 p.m.	Betsy calls again, and Tacy talks to her. Betsy uses up her allotment.
3 p.m.	Betsy calls again, and Tacy talks to her.
3:05 p.m.	Betsy calls again, and Tacy talks to her.
4 p.m.	Betsy calls again, and Tacy talks to her.
That night	Tacy believes that limits don't work.

Wow, that is a different way of looking at it! Tacy's limit was ineffective not because *Betsy* wasn't observing it, but because *Tacy* wasn't observing her *own* limit. Always keep in mind that it's what you *do* that matters, not what you *say*. Here is a slow-motion instant replay.

The 3 p.m. call was The Test. Tacy took the bait and spoke with her daughter, not observing her own limit. She jumped the triangle (see page 210), moving from "persecutor" to "rescuer." You might think that speaking with Betsy in an annoyed fashion might be negative reinforcement. But here, it's just the opposite.

At home, alone, Betsy was feeling lonely, unloved, and invisible. When she called, Tacy spoke with her and gave Betsy her full attention. Even though it was in a negative way, it was reinforcing and made Betsy more likely to call Tacy again.

Always remember, arguing can be reinforcing. Tacy was paying attention to what Betsy was *saying* (the talk about when she was coming home) and ignoring what Betsy was *doing,* which was calling again. Writer Amy Sutherland says, "When couples argue, what they say steals the show rather than what they are doing—fighting."[1] Author Karen Pryor agrees: "[Y]ou argue each point into the ground, and you can be dead right about the words being said . . . but you are still not dealing with the [fighting]."[2]

So, what should Tacy have done when Betsy called? She should have determined the answer to that question during her planning process (pages 213–218). If Tacy doesn't have voice mail or a secretary, once she hears Betsy's voice, she could say in a neutral tone, "We'll talk when I get home tonight" and then gently put the phone down each time Tacy calls until the behavior is extinguished (see pages 232–233).

Some limits need to be spelled out in detail to include specific definitions, such as what constitutes an "emergency."

Sarah and Joe

You met Sarah and her borderline husband Joe on page 223. The couple have two sons. Sarah says:

> When my husband, Joe, thinks he's being "ignored," he frequently says, "That's it. We're done. I'm not living like this!" He threatens divorce, throws a temper tantrum (which nobody acknowledges), and then sulks.
>
> The very moment he stops sulking and starts acting "normally" and under control, my two children and I come back into the room. We speak kindly to him, offer to get him a glass of water, and so on. As a parent, I have to work to minimize any confusion for the children and to repair any hurt feelings. But things are much calmer at home now. If the relationship ends at some point, I'll survive, and I've made my peace with that. But I will no longer tolerate abuse.

Intermittent Reinforcement

If Tacy had hung up gently (or screened her voice mail) the first few times Betsy called, would that cement her limit for all time? No. Tacy will need to keep up her end of the bargain. *If* Tacy acts consistently, not taking more than three calls each day without fail, Betsy will learn. When the problematic behavior stops, it has been "extinguished."

However, let's suppose that that one day Tacy takes one more call than she said she would. Betsy calls for a fourth time and blurts out,

"Bloomingdale's is having a 50 percent off sale on shoes!" before Tacy says anything. Startled, Tacy starts thinking about shoes and says, "Thanks, I'll stop by on my way home." Tacy has just reinforced Betsy's phone calling behavior in an inconsistent way. This is called "intermittent reinforcement," and it paves the way for Betsy to call Tacy several times a day to alert her that the local grocery store has a fifteen-cents-off coupon on a box of eggs.

Intermittent reinforcement makes behavior nearly impossible to extinguish (or, put the opposite way, motivates a subject to keep repeating a behavior even if it is only rewarded every so often). The best example is playing slots: it pays out sometimes, but you can't predict when that will be. Other examples:

- Your TV doesn't work right. When you hit it in just the right place, though, sometimes you can get it working again. You will hit the TV for a long time before you finally concede it's time to buy a new one.
- You and your girlfriend fight all the time. But every once in a while, you have a great time together. That keeps you hanging on.

Once you set a limit, it is *critical* that you observe it every time a broach occurs. Old habits are hard to break. Being mindful of observing your limits takes a lot of energy at the beginning, which is another reason why you start small. Your BP may even test you a year or two later.

Extinction Bursts

In the last chapter, Jack said, "You have to be willing to accept that things will get worse before they get better." This means that the "testing the limits" phase will be long and hard, as your family member acts out even more in an effort to put things back the way they were before. This phenomenon is called an *extinction burst*. Keep reminding yourself that it will take even *more* energy to keep dealing with the problematic behavior.

Extinction bursts occur when the behavior stops eliciting rewards. The subject wonders what happened and raises the level of the behavior. Still no deal. So the subject takes the behavior to new heights. This happened to

Jack when he told Loreen that if she called him names, he would leave and pick up the conversation later. Jack said, at first, "It just fired her up, made things ten times worse."

An oft-used example is the elevator button. Every workday, you take the elevator to the fourth floor, where your office is located. Let's say you ride the same elevator. You get in, you push the button for your floor, and you're rewarded by the doors closing and the elevator taking you to your destination.

One day you get in and push the button, and the elevator doesn't budge. Irritated, you push the button again. Nothing. So you jab it a few times, harder and faster. Finally, you realize the elevator must be broken and decide to walk up. Pressing the buttons several times was the extinction burst.

The key is to anticipate this heightened activity and to let it run its course. If you rigorously withhold the reinforcement, the actions should then begin to lessen—slowly at first, and then more rapidly. Beware, though. If you let your limit go unobserved sometimes, you will be giving intermittent reinforcement.

Your planning journal from the last chapter comes in handy at this point. You can read it to remind yourself what *not* having this limit has cost you in the past and what it could cost you in the future. Keep in mind that the first few weeks or months are going to be the most difficult.

Sharon and Amanda

Sharon, mother of Amanda who has BPD, says, "Folks with BPD are used to things happening a certain way. When new limits change old, familiar ways, they will often use stronger or other inappropriate behaviors to get what they need and want thinking, *It worked before. If I just do it harder, it'll work again.*" This happened to Sharon when she set a limit on Amanda's verbal abuse. Sharon explains:

> At first, when Amanda said hurtful things I either argued back or just kept quiet. Then I learned that a better response was, "I'm uncomfortable with this conversation. It is painful to me, so I'm going to my room. If and when you are ready to treat me with respect, let me know and we can talk." Then I left.

Amanda would continue to scream at me, sometimes through the closed door to my room. When this didn't get my attention, she tried to involve me by throwing objects at the door and by threatening to hurt herself.

After quite a few instances of my going to my room and Amanda acting out, the acting out periods started to get shorter and less intense. Eventually she learned to go to her room (occasionally at my suggestion), calm herself down, and then come out to talk to me. Or, as she would start to escalate, she would see it happening and turn it around on her own.

It took many years and lots of practice to get to this point, but now Amanda knows herself well enough to warn me about her moods ahead of time. She will say things like, "Mom, I'm really upset and trying my best to control my behavior, but I want to apologize in advance if I say something cruel."[3]

Behavior Communicates

Several years ago, *New York Times* writer Amy Sutherland was researching behavioral techniques for a book about animal trainers. After watching the trainers using techniques based on positive reinforcement to demonstrate how they taught baboons to skateboard and hyenas to pirouette on command, she resolved to use some of these methods to deal with her husband's idiosyncrasies—small things like forgetfulness and hovering over her in the kitchen.

She wrote an article in the *New York Times* about it, and it was so well received she turned her findings into the 2008 book *What Shamu Taught Me about Love, Life, and Marriage.*[4] In the book, she describes how understanding the science of behavior changed her views about the way people interact and try to alter each other's behavior.

She says, "My outlook is more optimistic. I'm less judgmental. I have vastly more patience and self-control . . . I have peace of mind that comes from the world making so much more sense to me."[5]

A few decades earlier, in 1984, scientist Karen Pryor wrote the book

Don't Shoot the Dog: The New Art of Teaching and Training, which is about how "shaping," or reinforcing, behavior that is already occurring can make the behavior happen more frequently.[6] The principles in the book are being used in a program called TAGteach, which is drawing interest from professionals in the areas of sports, special education, autism, physical education, physical rehabilitation, general classroom, and business management.[7]

At first glance, using reinforcement and other behavioral science methods may seem unethical or manipulative. However, in any interaction, we are training others, as is evident from the examples at the beginning of this chapter. Training, Sutherland says, is a form of communication—a more direct method of communication than talk.

Following are some of the highlights of these women's work as it applies to nudging behavior in ways that produce more harmonious relationships.

Untraining Unwanted Behavior

Interactions between BPs and non-BPs are usually "patterned"; that is, they have been going on for so long that they're now a reflex. Give yourself time to unlearn these habits.

The "Least Reinforcing Scenario"

Animal trainers use the least reinforcing scenario (LRS) when an animal has done something wrong—for example, if a trainer is teaching a dolphin to wave a pectoral fin and the dolphin squirts water, the trainer stands still and remains expressionless because any response might provoke a behavior. Sutherland says to think of it not as the cold shoulder, but a head-to-toe poker face.

You can use this technique if you're being provoked by an unpleasant comment that is supposed to grab your attention but not really communicate. Don't use it with behavior that is abusive or otherwise unsafe.

LRS is not pointedly ignoring behavior you don't want; rather, it's overlooking it, as if it's too much to even bother with. During the pause, collect yourself and take a deep breath. Ask yourself what might be going on in your loved one's life or mind that sparked the comment.

Sutherland gives these examples:

- When a postal clerk snapped at her for putting a label on incorrectly, Sutherland blankly fixed the label on her package. The clerk backpedaled, wishing her a nice day.
- When her friends kept trying to get her to try acupuncture after she had made it clear she wasn't going to do so, she tried using an LRS rather than protesting. Sutherland says, "Their lobbying efforts did not cease but lost their typical zeal and breadth. And the pregnant pause of my LRS usually provided a chance to change the subject."[8]

The urge to respond runs deep, so you will need to muster self-control.

Incompatible Behavior

The *incompatible behavior* technique is based on the premise that when people are doing something you don't want them to do, it's easier to redirect them into something else than stop them. Gently steer your BP into another activity that is incompatible with the undesirable behavior. In other words, you can't do them both at the same time. "Go and play outside" is probably the mother of all incompatible behaviors.

Sutherland was irritated when her husband crowded her as she cooked on the stove. To lure him away, she set up another area in the kitchen for him to chop vegetables and grate cheese. Other examples might be

- You notice your borderline mother doesn't insult you when other people are around. Therefore, when you visit you always bring a friend.
- Your BP has a hard time being alone on Sunday because you have a part-time job as a church organist. So you invite him to come with you or suggest that he visit friends that morning.

Rita, whose mother had both narcissistic personality disorder and BPD, used the incompatible behavior technique starting when she was only nine years old.

I noticed my mother couldn't rage and laugh at the same time. So when she was in the middle of a rage, as hard as it was, I would compliment her on something that was really important to her. She could go from a red-hot volcanic rage to a discussion about herself in a moment.

One day she was raging at me outside in her garden. I told her the garden looked like it was orchestrated by God himself. All the flowers were planted to bloom at different times of the year. The colors were chosen to coordinate with each other, and I told her I hoped she at least took some pictures. I asked her to tell me more about her garden and what I could do to get one of mine to look like that and to grow.[9]

Reward the Absence of Problematic Behavior

With this technique, you reinforce anything that isn't the behavior you don't want. Karen Pryor used this on her mother, who called her and complained and made accusations that angered Pryor. When her mother was complaining and so on, Pryor used the least reinforcing scenario.

But when her problematic mother asked questions about her grandchildren or spoke of other things, Pryor chatted enthusiastically. Pryor says, "After twenty years of conflict, within two months, the proportion of tears and distress to chat and laughter in our weekly phone calls became reversed."[10]

One of the most confusing aspects of BPD is that many of those who have it act perfectly normally at times. But from a behavioral standpoint, this gives you plenty of opportunities to reinforce other behaviors. Consider all the things you love about your family member and your relationship.

It's great to do it anytime, of course, but research shows that timely reinforcement is more powerful. If you're in a chosen relationship, remember the compelling reasons you chose to be together. The key to success with this is to provide a reinforcer at the time the behavior is happening. You can say things like

- "I love it when you . . ."
- "I'm having a great time with you . . ."

- "I feel so close to you when we . . ."
- "Thanks for doing that . . ."
- "You really tried hard to . . ."

You can also reinforce behavior nonverbally by touching, moving closer, and so on. Sutherland has a technique she called the Jackpot, which is a "big fat, juicy serving of positive reinforcement" used when things are going particularly well or the person really needs it. Once when her husband had to do a very unpleasant task, she gave him an early Christmas present.

General Praise

Whenever you can, build on your family member's strengths rather than dwelling on the negative. Give your family member attention when things are going well; don't wait until there is a problem. If you can't give it now, schedule some time in the future she can look forward to. Structure is always good. Spend time in nature together, enjoying the silence. Take walks or do other kinds of exercise together.

You can also reward positive healthy coping mechanisms; for example, "The other day when you were upset, you took a walk instead of throwing something at the wall" or "It's great that you can tell me you're angry in this way because I understand what's going on." When people express an interest in doing something positive, immediately show your support to help build momentum.

However, John G. Gunderson, MD, and Cynthia Berkowitz, MD, warn parents not to compliment their child *too* much. They say:

> Countless parents say their child went into crisis just as that person was beginning to function better. When people make progress, they fear that loved ones will pull away, thinking all is well. Messages like "You've worked so hard. I'm pleased that you were able to do it, but I'm worried that this is all too stressful for you" are empathic and less risky.
>
> You also want to be sure you're not implying that your love is dependent on their behavior (unless it is). You might say something like, "I know you are doing great. I am proud of you. But

if you decide to go back to your old ways, I will still love you, no matter what. You have my unconditional support."[11]

Other Methods

There is much more to behavioral science than positive and negative reinforcement. Following are a few more techniques:

Watch for Cues

Sutherland writes that, before a trainer walks into a cage with a wild animal like a cougar, she looks for signs that the animal is having a bad day. If it is, she may decide to work with a different animal. With cougars, she looks for a head hung low and a slight crouch.

Human animals also show signs that they best not be disturbed. Certain events may be provoking, as can times of day or days of the week. When you're caught up in your own little world, it's easy to forget to consider what's going on in someone else's.

You may also be able to look for physical clues; the earlier, the better. Think nonverbal. If you see any of the following signs of emotional distress, you may be able to distract the person if you catch these signs early enough:

- a rigid, tense facial expression
- hand-wringing
- fidgeting
- crossed arms
- overall body and facial tenseness
- clenching of fists or jaw
- trembling lips
- slouching
- tension in the brow

Positively Reinforce Yourself

You can even use positive reinforcement on yourself by noticing and praising yourself when you do something right instead of criticizing yourself when you fall short of your own expectations. Pryor tells the story of a squash-playing lawyer who decided to praise his good shots instead of cursing his errors.

He told her, "At first I felt like a damned fool . . . [but now I am] four rungs higher on the club ladder than I've ever been. I'm whipping people I could hardly take a point from before. And I'm having more fun."[12]

Watch for your own cues, too, to stay in touch with your feelings. Stress tends to pile on, and stress from one area of your life can exacerbate stress in another. If you're prone to physical and/or emotional problems, know what sets them off. If you're not at your best, try to avoid challenging situations with your family member.

To learn more about these techniques and find out about other ones, see "Resources" on page 243.

TIPS about Praise

Praise is the opposite of the least reinforcing scenario. Reward in small steps; things don't have to be perfect. The acronym TIPS will help you make your praise most effective. Make it

T: True. People can see through underserved praise, or it may make them expect praise without having to work for it.

I: Immediate. Give the praise as the behavior occurs, if possible.

P: Positive. This makes the behavior more likely to occur again.

S: Specific. What, exactly, went right? How is it helpful? Say what you observed rather than making judgments. For example, "When you counted to ten before you got mad, you avoided a fight" is better than "I liked the way you counted to ten." The first helps build self-esteem, while the second makes them depend on your opinion.

Start Today

*What saves a man is to take a step. Then another step. It is always
the same step, but you have to take it.*

▪ Antoine de Saint-Exupery ▪

There is an oft-told story about a man of faith who found himself in a massive flood. He climbed to the roof of his house and watched as people got into boats and evacuated the town.

The water rose and rose. As the rescuers passed him, they kept urging him to get in the boat, where they would take him to a safe place. "No," he said. "God will take care of me. This is a test of my faith."

Three boats came by. Three times he refused.

Finally, the water rose to his neck and he cried, "Where are you, Lord? Why haven't you rescued me?"

To his surprise, the clouds parted and sunlight streamed down on his face. In a booming voice, God said, "What are you talking about? I sent you three boats!"

Hope and miracles are around you, if you take a closer look. Your life may not be what you envisioned at the start of your journey. But unlike our unfortunate friend on the roof, you have realized that you make your own hope and make your own choices. You can't change your loved one, but you can change yourself. And you have the power to make a difference for those to follow. It only takes three things:

1. A long, deep breath.

2. A "leap of faith." A leap of faith means going to the edge of your blindness—then a little more ways. The leap of faith for those who have BPD is to trust in the love of others, however imperfect it may be. The leap of faith for those who care about someone with BPD is not to take the behavior personally, however hurtful it may be.

3. Now, go find your boat.

Resources

This list is only a beginning, and it primarily represents those resources used while writing this book. Many worthy ones are not included because of space. To see a fuller list with links to purchase the materials, visit www.bpdcentral.com.

Materials with one or two stars are either exceptionally good and/or were the most significant in formulating the content of this book and its predecessors. Materials with a plus sign speak frankly about the effect of BPD behaviors on family members. They may be triggering for individuals with BPD. Some books may appear in more than one category. Some authors have Web sites, which are also listed.

Materials About Borderline Personality Disorder

Materials about BPD Not Available in Bookstores

Back from the Edge, DVD (White Plains, NY: Borderline Personality Disorder Resource Center, 2007), www.bpdresourcecenter.org.

Border-Lines. Newsletter subscription available at www.bpdcentral.com.

Eddy, W. A., *High Conflict Personalities: Understanding and Resolving Their Costly Disputes* (San Diego, CA: High Conflict Institute, 2003), www.highconflictinstitute.com.

———, *Splitting: Protecting Yourself While Divorcing a Borderline or Narcissist* (Milwaukee, WI: Eggshells Press, 2003), www.bpdcentral.com, 888-357-4355. A companion CD is also available.

Kreger, R., and E. Gunn, *The ABC's of BPD: The Basics of Borderline Personality*

Disorder for Beginners (Milwaukee, WI: Eggshells Press, 2007), www .bpdcentral.com, 888-357-4355.

Kreger, R., and K. A. Williams-Justesen, *Love and Loathing: Protecting Your Mental Health and Legal Rights When Your Partner Has Borderline Personality Disorder* (Milwaukee, WI: Eggshells Press, 2000), www.bpdcentral.com, 888-357-4355.

Lewis, K., and P. Shirley, *You're My World: A Non-BP's Guide to Custody* (Milwaukee, WI: Eggshells Press, 2001), www.bpdcentral.com, 888-357-4355.

Rashkin, R., *An Umbrella for Alex* (Roswell, GA: PDAN Press, 2006), www.pdan.org. This is a book for children about a parent with mood swings.

Winkler, K., and R. Kreger, *Hope for Parents: Helping Your Borderline Son or Daughter Without Sacrificing Your Family or Yourself* (Milwaukee, WI: Eggshells Press, 2000), www.bpdcentral.com, 888-357-4355.

Materials About BPD Available Wherever Books Are Sold

**Aguirre, B. A., *Borderline Personality Disorder in Adolescents: A Complete Guide to Understanding and Coping When Your Adolescent Has BPD* (Beverly, MA: Fair Winds Press, 2007).

**Chapman, A. L., and K. L. Gratz, *The Borderline Personality Disorder Survival Guide: Everything You Need to Know About Living with BPD* (Oakland, CA: New Harbinger Publications, 2007).

**Friedel, R. O., *Borderline Personality Disorder Demystified: An Essential Guide for Understanding and Living with BPD* (New York: Marlowe & Company, 2004), www.bpddemystified.com.

Gunderson, J. G., and P. D. Hoffman, eds., *Understanding and Treating Borderline Personality Disorder: A Guide for Professionals and Families* (Washington, DC: American Psychiatric Publishing, 2005).

**+Kreger, R., with J. P. Shirley, *The Stop Walking on Eggshells Workbook: Practical Strategies for Living with Someone Who Has Borderline Personality Disorder* (Oakland, CA: New Harbinger Publications, 2002), www.bpdcentral.com

Kreisman, J. J., and H. Straus, *Sometimes I Act Crazy: Living with Borderline Personality Disorder* (Hoboken, NJ: John Wiley & Sons, 2004).

**+Lawson, C. A., *Understanding the Borderline Mother: Helping Her Children Transcend the Intense, Unpredictable, and Volatile Relationship* (Northvale, NJ: Jason Aronson, 2002).

Linehan, M. M., *Skills Training Manual for Treating Borderline Personality Disorder* (New York: Guilford Press, 1993), behavioraltech.org. This manual is written for clinicians who use dialectical behavior therapy (DBT), but it has useful worksheets for those with BPD.

**+Mason, P. T., and R. Kreger, *Stop Walking on Eggshells: Taking Your Life Back*

When Someone You Care About Has Borderline Personality Disorder (Oakland, CA: New Harbinger Publications, 1998), www.bpdcentral.com.

Moskovitz, R., *Lost in the Mirror: An Inside Look at Borderline Personality Disorder,* 2nd ed. (Lanham, MD: Taylor Trade Publishing, 2001).

**Reiland, R., *Get Me Out of Here: My Recovery from Borderline Personality Disorder* (Center City, MN: Hazelden, 2004). Warning: This book may be too emotionally intense for some borderline individuals.

+Roth, K., and F. B. Friedman, *Surviving a Borderline Parent: How to Heal Your Childhood Wounds and Build Trust, Boundaries, and Self-Esteem* (Oakland, CA: New Harbinger Publications, 2003), www.survivingaborderlineparent.com.

Resources by Power Tools (Skills Training)

Power Tool 1: Take Good Care of Yourself

Carnegie, D., *How to Stop Worrying and Start Living* (New York: Pocket Books, 2004).

Hamilton, M., *Serenity to Go: Calming Techniques for Your Hectic Life* (Oakland, CA: New Harbinger Publications, 2001).

McKay, M., and D. Harp, *Neural Path Therapy: How to Change Your Brain's Response to Anger, Fear, Pain, and Desire* (Oakland, CA: New Harbinger Publications, 2005).

Tartell, G., and T. Kavanau, *Get Fit in Bed: Tone Your Body and Calm Your Mind from the Comfort of Your Bed* (Oakland, CA: New Harbinger Publications, 2006).

Power Tool 2: Uncover What Keeps You Feeling Stuck

Beattie, M., *Codependent No More: How to Stop Controlling Others and Start Caring for Yourself,* 2nd ed. (Center City, MN: Hazelden, 1992).

**Berg, B. C., *How to Escape the No-Win Trap* (New York: McGraw-Hill, 2004).

**Black, J., and G. Enns, *Better Boundaries: Owning and Treasuring Your Life* (Oakland, CA: New Harbinger Publications, 1997).

**+Brown, E. B., *Living Successfully with Screwed-Up People* (Grand Rapids, MI: Fleming H. Revell, 1999).

Brown, N. W., *Children of the Self-Absorbed: A Grown-Up's Guide to Getting Over Narcissistic Parents,* 2nd ed. (Oakland, CA: New Harbinger Publications, 2008).

Engel, B., *Divorcing a Parent: Free Yourself from the Past and Live the Life You've Always Wanted* (New York: Fawcett Columbine, 1990), www.beverlyengel.com.

——, *The Emotionally Abused Woman: Overcoming Destructive Patterns and Reclaiming Yourself* (New York: Fawcett Columbine, 1990), www.beverlyengel.com.

———, *The Emotionally Abusive Relationship: How to Stop Being Abused and How to Stop Abusing* (Hoboken, NJ: John Wiley & Sons, 2002), www.beverlyengel.com.

———, *Loving Him Without Losing You: How to Stop Disappearing and Start Being Yourself* (New York: John Wiley, 2000), www.beverlyengel.com. This book is also appropriate for men.

Evans, P., *Controlling People: How to Recognize, Understand, and Deal with People Who Try to Control You* (Avon, MA: Adams Media Corporation, 2002.)

**Forward, S., with D. Frazier, *Emotional Blackmail: When the People in Your Life Use Fear, Obligation, and Guilt to Manipulate You* (New York: HarperCollins Publishers, 1997).

**Forward, S., with C. Buck, *Toxic Parents: Overcoming Their Hurtful Legacy and Reclaiming Your Life* (New York: Bantam Books, 1989).

Jeffers, S., *Feel the Fear and Do It Anyway* (New York: Ballantine, 2007).

**+Klatte, B., and K. Thompson, *It's So Hard to Love You: Staying Sane When Your Loved One Is Manipulative, Needy, Dishonest, or Addicted* (Oakland, CA: New Harbinger Publications, 2007).

**Lerner, H., *The Dance of Anger: A Woman's Guide to Changing the Patterns of Intimate Relationships* (New York: Perennial Currents, 2005). This book is also invaluable for men.

Miller, A., *The Enabler: When Helping Hurts the Ones You Love* (Tucson, AZ: Wheatmark, 2008).

Neuharth, D., *If You Had Controlling Parents: How to Make Peace with Your Past and Take Your Place in the World* (New York: Cliff Street Books, 1998).

**Savage, E., *Don't Take It Personally! The Art of Dealing with Rejection* (Oakland, CA: New Harbinger Publications, 1997), www.queenofrejection.com.

Stenack, R. J., *Stop Controlling Me! What to Do When Someone You Love Has Too Much Power Over You* (Oakland, CA: New Harbinger Publications, 2001).

Young, J. E., and J. S. Klosko, *Reinventing Your Life: The Breakthrough Program to End Negative Behavior . . . and Feel Great Again* (New York: Plume, 1993), www.schematherapy.com.

Power Tool 3: Communicate to Be Heard

**+Klatte, B., and K. Thompson, *It's So Hard to Love You: Staying Sane When Your Loved One Is Manipulative, Needy, Dishonest, or Addicted* (Oakland, CA: New Harbinger Publications, 2007).

Linehan, M. M., *Skills Training Manual for Treating Borderline Personality Disorder* (New York: Guilford Press, 1993), behavioraltech.org. This manual is written for clinicians who use dialectical behavior therapy (DBT), but it has useful worksheets for those with BPD.

**+Lundberg, G. B., and J. S. Lundberg, *I Don't Have to Make Everything All Better* (New York: Viking, 1999).

Wainwright, G. R., *Teach Yourself Body Language* (Chicago: McGraw-Hill, 2004).

Power Tool 4: Set Limits with Love

**Black, J., and G. Enns, *Better Boundaries: Owning and Treasuring Your Life* (Oakland, CA: New Harbinger Publications, 1997).

Engel, B., *The Jekyll and Hyde Syndrome: What to Do If Someone in Your Life Has a Dual Personality—or If You Do* (Hoboken, NJ: John Wiley, 2007).

Katherine, A., *Boundaries: Where You End and I Begin* (Center City, MN: Hazelden, 1991).

**+Klatte, B., and K. Thompson, *It's So Hard to Love You: Staying Sane When Your Loved One Is Manipulative, Needy, Dishonest, or Addicted* (Oakland, CA: New Harbinger Publications, 2007).

Lerner, R., *Living in the Comfort Zone: The Gift of Boundaries in Relationships* (Deerfield Beach, FL: Health Communications, 1995).

Power Tool 5: Reinforce the Right Behavior

**Aguirre, B. A., *Borderline Personality Disorder in Adolescents: A Complete Guide to Understanding and Coping When Your Adolescent Has BPD* (Beverly, MA: Fair Winds Press, 2007).

**Pryor, K., *Don't Shoot the Dog! The New Art of Teaching and Training*, rev. ed. (New York: Bantam Books, 1999).

**Sutherland, A., *What Shamu Taught Me About Life, Love, and Marriage: Lessons for People from Animals and Their Trainers* (New York: Random House, 2008).

Specialized Materials

People with BPD

Anderson, S., *The Journey from Abandonment to Healing* (New York: Berkley Publishing Group, 2000).

**Chapman, A. L., and K. L. Gratz, *The Borderline Personality Disorder Survival Guide: Everything You Need to Know About Living with BPD* (Oakland, CA: New Harbinger Publications, 2007).

Kreisman, J. J., and H. Straus, *Sometimes I Act Crazy: Living with Borderline Personality Disorder* (Hoboken, NJ: John Wiley & Sons, 2004).

Moskovitz, R., *Lost in the Mirror: An Inside Look at Borderline Personality Disorder*, 2nd ed. (Lanham, MD: Taylor Trade Publishing, 2001).

Couples Issues

Eddy, W. A., *Splitting: Protecting Yourself While Divorcing a Borderline or Narcissist* (Milwaukee, WI: Eggshells Press, 2003), www.bpdcentral.com, 888-357-4355. A companion CD is also available.

Fruzzetti, A. E., *The High-Conflict Couple: A Dialectical Behavior Therapy Guide to Finding Peace, Intimacy, and Validation* (Oakland, CA: New Harbinger Publications, 2006).

Kreger, R., and K. A. Williams-Justesen, *Love and Loathing: Protecting Your Mental Health and Legal Rights When Your Partner Has Borderline Personality Disorder* (Milwaukee, WI: Eggshells Press, 2000), www.bpdcentral.com, 888-357-4355.

Lewis, K., and P. Shirley, *You're My World: A Non-BP's Guide to Custody* (Milwaukee, WI: Eggshells Press, 2001), www.bpdcentral.com, 888-357-4355.

Paleg, K., and M. McKay, *When Anger Hurts Your Relationship: 10 Simple Solutions for Couples Who Fight* (Oakland, CA: New Harbinger Publications, 2001).

Thayer, E., and J. Zimmerman, *The Co-Parenting Survival Guide: Letting Go of Conflict after a Difficult Divorce* (Oakland, CA: New Harbinger Publications, 2001).

Parents with a Borderline Child

**Aguirre, B. A., *Borderline Personality Disorder in Adolescents: A Complete Guide to Understanding and Coping When Your Adolescent Has BPD* (Beverly, MA: Fair Winds Press, 2007).

Greene, R. W., *The Explosive Child: A New Approach for Understanding and Parenting Easily Frustrated, Chronically Inflexible Children,* revised and updated (New York: Harper, 2005).

McVey-Noble, M. E., S. Khemlani-Patel, and F. Neziroglu, *When Your Child Is Cutting: A Parent's Guide to Helping Children Overcome Self-Injury* (Oakland, CA: New Harbinger Publications, 2006).

Rubin, C., *Don't Let Your Kids Kill You: A Guide for Parents of Drug and Alcohol Addicted Children,* 3rd ed. (Petaluma, CA: NewCentury Publishers, 2007).

Winkler, K., and R. Kreger, *Hope for Parents: Helping Your Borderline Son or Daughter Without Sacrificing Your Family or Yourself* (Milwaukee, WI: Eggshells Press, 2000), www.bpdcentral.com, 888-357-4355.

Children Exposed to BPD Behaviors

Johnston, J. R., K. Breunig, C. Garrity, and M. Baris, *Through the Eyes of Children: Healing Stories for Children of Divorce* (New York: Free Press, 1997).

**+Lawson, C. A., *Understanding the Borderline Mother: Helping Her Children Transcend the Intense, Unpredictable, and Volatile Relationship* (Northvale, NJ: Jason Aronson, 2002).

McKay, M., K. Paleg, P. Fanning, and D. Landis, *When Anger Hurts Your Kids: A Parent's Guide* (Oakland, CA: New Harbinger Publications, 1996).

Rashkin, R., *An Umbrella for Alex* (Roswell, GA: PDAN Press, 2006), www.pdan.org. This is a book for children about a parent with mood swings.

+Roth, K., and F. B. Friedman, *Surviving a Borderline Parent: How to Heal Your Childhood Wounds and Build Trust, Boundaries, and Self-Esteem* (Oakland, CA: New Harbinger Publications, 2003), www.survivingaborderlineparent.com.

Biography

These people were not officially diagnosed with BPD, but their stories are highly indicative of BPD.

Rossi, M., *Courtney Love: Queen of Noise* (New York: Pocket Books, 1996).

Smith, S. B., *Diana in Search of Herself: Portrait of a Troubled Princess* (New York: Times Books, 1999).

Spungen, D., *And I Don't Want to Live This Life: A Mother's Story of Her Daughter's Murder* (New York: Ballantine Books, 1996).

Self-Harm and Suicide

Blauner, S. R., *How I Stayed Alive When My Brain Was Trying to Kill Me: One Person's Guide to Suicide Prevention* (New York: William Morrow, 2002).

Ellis, T. E., and C. F. Newman, *Choosing to Live: How to Defeat Suicide Through Cognitive Therapy* (Oakland, CA: New Harbinger Publications, 1996).

Levenkron, S., *Cutting: Understanding and Overcoming Self-Mutilation* (New York: W. W. Norton, 2006).

McVey-Noble, M. E., S. Khemlani-Patel, and F. Neziroglu, *When Your Child Is Cutting: A Parent's Guide to Helping Children Overcome Self-Injury* (Oakland, CA: New Harbinger Publications, 2006).

Co-occurring Disorders

Brown, N. W., *Children of the Self-Absorbed: A Grown-Up's Guide to Getting Over Narcissistic Parents,* 2nd ed. (Oakland, CA: New Harbinger Publications, 2008).

Carter, L., *Enough About You, Let's Talk About Me: How to Recognize and Manage the Narcissists in Your Life* (San Francisco: Jossey-Bass, 2005).

Conyers, B., *Addict in the Family: Stories of Loss, Hope, and Recovery* (Center City, MN: Hazelden, 2003).

Fast, J. A., and J. Preston, *Loving Someone with Bipolar Disorder: Understanding and Helping Your Partner* (Oakland, CA: New Harbinger Publications, 2004).

Wexler, D. B., *Is He Depressed or What? What to Do When the Man You Love Is Irritable, Moody, and Withdrawn* (Oakland, CA: New Harbinger Publications, 2005).

Miscellaneous

**Goleman, D., *Emotional Intelligence: Why It Can Matter More Than IQ* (New York: Bantam Books, 1995).

LeDoux, J., *Synaptic Self: How Our Brains Become Who We Are* (New York: Viking, 2002).

Lieberman, D. J., *How to Change Anybody: Proven Techniques to Reshape Anyone's Attitude, Behavior, Feelings, or Beliefs* (New York: St. Martin's Press, 2005).

BPD Organizations

National Education Alliance for Borderline Personality Disorder (NEA-BPD)
www.neabpd.org
The NEA-BPD works to raise public awareness, provide education, and promote research about BPD, as well as enhance the quality of life of those affected by BPD. It offers family education programs, annual conferences, regional meetings, and educational and research materials.

The NEA-BPD also offers a twelve-week Family Connections program that teaches people with BPD and their family members coping skills based on dialectical behavior therapy (DBT). This course is taught only in certain cities, and participants are required to pay a fee. The program is also available by telephone. For information, see the organization's Web site.

The NEA-BPD's extensive Web site contains information about upcoming conferences, grants, family programs, video and audio resources, and much more. Of special interest is the video and audio archive of presentations from clinicians with expertise on BPD.

Personality Disorders Awareness Network (PDAN)

www.pdan.org

PDAN works to increase public awareness about the impact of BPD on children, relationships, and society.

Florida Borderline Personality Disorder Association

www.fbpda.org

This organization promotes awareness, education, and research about BPD. It cultivates an atmosphere of support among professionals, consumers, and families throughout the state.

BPDWorld

www.bpdworld.org

This site offers resources in the United Kingdom.

Association d'Aide aux Personnes avec un Etat Limite

www.aapel.org

This is the site of a French BPD organization.

Selected Online Resources

Some of the best resources for people interested in BPD can be found on the Internet. Depending on the site, the information on the Web can be the most up-to-date. And, of course, the information is instantly accessible.

If you search the phrase "borderline personality disorder," you'll find an overwhelming number of options. Following are some of the most notable online resources that have stood the test of time and offer current, useful information.

Online Support Groups

Something magical happens when a person with a borderline family member meets someone else in the same situation, whether it's in real life or online. Books and clinicians may say, "It's not you, it's the disorder," but it's hard not to feel like a failure when someone you love is insistent that everything is your fault.

When other people say, "That's exactly what's happening to me," and then describe a parallel experience, it becomes much easier to understand the dynamics going on, put aside feelings of hurt and guilt, and start problem solving.

The Welcome to Oz Online Community for Family Members with a Borderline Loved One

www.bpdcentral.com

Welcome to Oz (WTO) was founded by Randi Kreger in 1995. With 16,000 members, it is the largest and longest-established family forum about BPD. Conversations take place via e-mail. The experiences of WTO members became the basis for *Stop Walking on Eggshells, The Stop Walking on Eggshells Workbook,* and this book.

Because WTO is large, it can support both large, mixed groups and smaller, specialized groups for people in different types of relationships. These include grandparents (WTOGrandparents), siblings (WTOSiblings), adult children (WTOAdultChildren1), and Christians (WTOChristian). There is also a men-only group (WTOMenOnly) and a women-only group (WTOWomenOnly).

Individuals with a borderline partner can select groups based on the status of their relationship. There are groups for people who wish to remain in the relationship (WTOStaying), those who wish to leave (WTODivorcing), and those who are not sure (WTOTransition). Other groups include WTOCoParenting 1 (includes stepparents) WTOGLBT, WTOLifeAfterLeaving, and WTOProfessionals (for clinicians who wish to add to their professional knowledge).

Members can subscribe to these groups at www.bpdcentral.com and by sending a blank message to [name of group]-subscribe@yahoogroups.com.

Facing the Facts Message Board

www.bpdfamily.com, click on "Message Board"

BPDFamily.com is in a message-board format, similar to a real-life bulletin board where members make posts and others reply, creating "threads." The mission of the board is to provide support, education, and actionable tools. It also helps members keep a healthy perspective.

Like Welcome to Oz (WTO), Facing the Facts is organized into different sections for those in different types of relationships: parents, partners, children, and so on. It also offers the following areas: General BPD Questions and Resources, Workshops, Book Reviews, Taking Personal Inventory, Rebuilding Our Life, and "NON Stop" (for fun and off-topic discussions).

NUTS (parents Needing Understanding, Tenderness, and Support
to help their child with borderline personality disorder)

www.parent2parentbpd.org

NUTS consists of parents and grandparents whose children (adult or minor) have BPD, with or without a formal diagnosis. This group, established in 1996, is operated by a dedicated and experienced mother, Sharon, who has appeared several times in this book. Parents discuss a variety of topics, including the effect of BPD on their own emotions and on those of other family members. There is a small monthly membership fee.

Selected Sites on the World Wide Web

BPDCentral

www.bpdcentral.com

BPDCentral was established by author Randi Kreger in 1995. It offers a wide variety of information about BPD, including articles, essays, and interviews with experts; excerpts from books and booklets; links and resources; answers to common questions; basic and advanced information about BPD and the effects of borderline behavior on family members; and much more.

Facing the Facts: When a Loved One Has Borderline Personality

www.bpdfamily.com

This is an extensive site about BPD for family members. It contains articles and a reliable resource list of links, support groups, and books.

Borderline Personality Disorder Demystified

www.bpddemystified.com

This is a detailed, up-to-date site by Robert O. Friedel, MD, author of *Borderline Personality Disorder Demystified*, a leading BPD psychiatrist.

Borderline Personality Disorder: Reliable Resources for Family Members

www.bpdresources.net

This site features independent book reviews and interesting excerpts from the books. It also features interviews with the authors.

Touch Another Heart: Empathy and Listening Skills for Emotional Intimacy

www.touch-another-heart.com

This is an interesting, informative site about empathic acknowledgment, which is a key way to improve communication with individuals who have BPD.

My Trip to Oz and Back

www.mytriptoozandback.com

Subtitled "A True 'Retrospective' Story of My Relationship with a Person with BPD," this site is a reproduction of a woman's fifty-page letter to her borderline partner. Her experiences are representative of most people with a borderline partner.

Borderline Personality Disorder from the Inside Out

www.borderlinepersonality.ca

A. J. Mahari, who has appeared in this book many times, is a prolific writer who comes from not only the perspective of a person with BPD but also the perspective of a family member. The site includes links to Mahari's e-books and YouTube videos.

BPDRecovery

www.bpdrecovery.com

This is an extensive site for people with the disorder, which features a message-board community.

Middle Path: Awareness, Compassion, and Support for Borderline Personality Disorder

www.middle-path.org

This is an online resource for people with BPD.

BPD Awareness

www.bpdawareness.org

Subtitled "Shades of Grey," this site is dedicated to increasing awareness of BPD. It sells BPD awareness EMBRACElets.

Behavioral Tech, LLC

www.behavioraltech.com

Behavioral Tech, LLC, founded by Marsha M. Linehan, PhD, trains mental health care providers and treatment teams to use dialectical behavior therapy (DBT). This site has a searchable database of U.S. clinicians trained in DBT.

Borderline Personality Disorder Resource Center

www.bpdresourcecenter.org

This site is associated with the Borderline Personality Disorder Resource Center (BPDRC) at New York–Presbyterian Hospital. This site provides a great general introduction to BPD.

Schema Therapy

www.schematherapy.com

This site presents information about the treatment method founded by Jeffrey Young, PhD.

About Psychotherapy

www.aboutpsychotherapy.com

This is an extensive, far-reaching site about therapy and the therapeutic process.

Notes

Chapter 1: Welcome to Oz

1. K. Winkler and R. Kreger, *Hope for Parents: Helping Your Borderline Son or Daughter Without Sacrificing Your Family or Yourself* (Milwaukee, WI: Eggshells Press, 2000), 8.

2. R. Kreger and K. A. Williams-Justesen, *Love and Loathing: Protecting Your Mental Health and Legal Rights When Your Partner Has Borderline Personality Disorder* (Milwaukee, WI: Eggshells Press, 2000), 9–11.

3. Perry Hoffman, phone interview with the author, March 2007.

4. National Education Alliance for Borderline Personality Disorder, "Borderline Personality Disorder: Awareness Brings Hope," available at www.borderlinepersonality disorder.com/awareness/awareness-files/BPD-FACT-0508.pdf.

5. *Diagnostic and Statistical Manual of Mental Disorders (DSM-IV)*, 4th ed. (Washington, DC: American Psychiatric Association, 1994).

6. P. D. James and S. Cowman, "Psychiatric Nurses' Knowledge, Experience and Attitudes Towards Clients with Borderline Personality Disorder," *Journal of Psychiatric and Mental Health Nursing* 14, no. 7 (October 2007): 670–78.

Chapter 2: Understanding Borderline Personality Disorder

1. *Diagnostic and Statistical Manual of Mental Disorders (DSM-IV)*, 4th ed. (Washington, DC: American Psychiatric Association, 1994).

2. S. Anderson, *The Journey from Abandonment to Healing* (New York: Berkley Publishing Group, 2000), 1.

3. A. J. Mahari, "Relationships: The Borderline Dance—'I Hate You, Don't Leave Me,'" available at www.borderlinepersonality.ca/borderrelationshipshatedontleave dance.htm.

4. Robert O. Friedel, interview with the author, August 2007.

5. B. A. Aguirre, *Borderline Personality Disorder in Adolescents: A Complete Guide to Understanding and Coping When Your Adolescent Has BPD* (Beverly, MA: Fair Winds Press, 2007), 53.

6. Kathleen, interview, *The Infinite Mind with Dr. Fred Goodwin*, WNYC AM 820, November 21, 1999.

7. A. Miller, *The Enabler: When Helping Hurts the Ones You Love*, (Tucson, AZ: Wheatmark, 2008), 56.

8. Chris, www.mytriptoozandback.com.

9. A. J. Mahari, "Borderline Resistance to Help and 'Truth,'" available at www.borderlinepersonality.ca/borderresisthelp.htm.

10. B. Strain and B. Ann, "The Influence of Gender Bias on the Diagnosis of Borderline Personality Disorder," *Dissertation Abstracts International* (2003): 2, 941.

11. A. Brandt, "Anger and Gender Expression," available at www.ezinearticles.com/?Anger-and-Gender-Expression&id=416607.

12. L. G. Berzins and R. L. Trestman, "The Development and Implementation of Dialectical Behavior Therapy in Forensic Settings," *International Journal of Forensic Mental Health* 3, no. 1 (2004): 93–103.

13. Mary Gay, phone interview with the author, February 2007.

14. Jim Breiling, e-mail to the author, March 2007.

15. National Alliance on Mental Illness, "About Mental Illness," available at www.nami.org/Template.cfm?Section=By_Illness&Template=/TaggedPage/TaggedPageDisplay.cfm&TPLID=54&ContentID=44780.

16. R. O. Friedel, "Substance Abuse Treatment in Patients with Borderline Disorder," available at www.bpddemystified.com/index.asp?id=46.

17. U. Feske, P. H. Soloff, and R. E. Tarter, "Implications for Treatment and Prognosis of Borderline and Substance Use Disorders," *Psychiatric Times* 24, no. 1 (January 1, 2007), available at www.psychiatrictimes.com/Substance-Abuse/showArticle.jhtml?articleID=196902120; Borderline Personality Disorder Demystified, www.bpddemystified.com.

18. M. C. Zanarini, F. R. Frankenburg, E. D. Dubo, A. E. Sickel, A. Trikha, A. Levin, and V. Reynolds, "Axis I Comorbidity of Borderline Personality Disorder," *American Journal of Psychiatry* 155 (December 1998): 1733–39.

19. C. Levin, "Narcissistic Personality Disorder Treatment," available at www.mentalhelp.net/poc/view_doc.php?type=doc&id=479&cn=8.

20. B. Engel, *The Jekyll and Hyde Syndrome: What to Do If Someone in Your Life Has a Dual Personality—or If You Do* (Hoboken, NJ: John Wiley, 2007), 71.

21. Ibid., 52.

22. National Institute of Mental Health, "Bipolar Disorder," available at www .nimh.nih.gov/publicat/bipolar.cfm#bp1.

23. Robert Friedel, e-mail to the author, May 2007.

24. Marsha M. Linehan, interview, *The Infinite Mind with Dr. Fred Goodwin,* WNYC AM 820, November 21, 1999.

Chapter 3: Making Sense of Your Relationship

1. J. Young and M. First, "Schema Mode Listing," available at www.schematherapy .com/id72.htm.

2. M. Dombeck, "Personality Disorders: Defense Mechanisms," available at www.mentalhelp.net/poc/view_doc.php?type=doc&id=4054&cn=8.

3. D. Goleman, *Emotional Intelligence: Why It Can Matter More Than IQ* (New York: Bantam Books, 1995).

4. Ibid., 81–82.

5. L. J. Siever, "Neurobiology of Impulsive-Aggressive Personality-Disordered Patients," *Psychiatric Times* 19, no. 8 (August 2002), available at www.psychiatrictimes.com/ display/article/10168/47131.

6. Chris, www.mytriptoozandback.com.

7. Ibid.

Chapter 4: Risk Factors of BPD

1. John M. Harlow, "Passage of an Iron Rod through the Head," *Boston Medical and Surgical Journal* 39 (1848): 389–93 (republished in *Journal of Neuropsychiatry and Clinical Neuroscience* 11:281–83).

2. "Museum Partnerships: Science in the Community," available at www.pfizer. com/brain/etour4.html; J. H. Lienhard, "Gage's Brain," available at www.uh.edu/en-gines/epi929.htm; F. G. Barker, II, "The American Crowbar Case and Nineteenth Century Theories of Cerebral Localization," available at www.neurosurgery.org/ cybermuseum/pre20th/crowbar/crowbar.html.

3. R. O. Friedel, *Borderline Personality Disorder Demystified: An Essential Guide for Understanding and Living with BPD* (New York: Marlowe & Company, 2004), 98.

4. D. Goleman, *Emotional Intelligence: Why It Can Matter More Than IQ* (New York: Bantam Books, 1995), 23.

5. W. C. Henderson, "Putting Limits on Teen Drivers," *Time,* October 15, 2006, available at www.time.com/time/magazine/article/0,9171,1546345,00.html.

6. National Institute of Mental Health, "Teenage Brain: A Work in Progess," available at www.nimh.nih.gov/health/publications/teenage-brain-a-work-in-progress .shtml.

7. P. J. Howard, *The Owner's Manual for the Brain: Everyday Applications from Mind-Brain Research,* 3rd ed. (Austin, TX: Bard Press, 2006), 747.

8. Friedel, *Borderline Personality Disorder Demystified,* 73.

9. H. P. Lefley, "From Family Trauma to Family Support System," in *Understanding and Treating Borderline Personality Disorder: A Guide for Professionals and Families,* ed. J. G. Gunderson and P. D. Hoffman (Arlington, VA: American Psychiatric Publishing, Inc., 2005), 136.

10. Sharon, phone interview with the author, May 2007.

11. Perry Hoffman, phone interview with the author, March 2007.

12. J. M. Bailey and A. Shriver, "Does Childhood Sexual Abuse Cause Borderline Personality Disorder?" *Journal of Sex and Marital Therapy* 25, no. 1 (1999): 45–57.

Chapter 5: Treating BPD

1. J. M. Carver, "The 'Chemical Imbalance' in Mental Health Problems," available at www.drjoecarver.com/clients/49355/File/Chemical%20Imbalance.html.

2. Table adapted from R. O. Friedel, *Borderline Personality Disorder Demystified: An Essential Guide for Understanding and Living with BPD* (New York: Marlowe & Company, 2004), 135–50, table available at www.bpddemystified.com/index.asp?id=21.

3. Blaise Aguirre, interview with the author, April 2007.

4. B. Pologe, "About Psychotherapy," available at www.aboutpsychotherapy.com.

5. National Association of Cognitive-Behavioral Therapists, "Cognitive-Behavioral Therapy," available at www.nacbt.org/whatiscbt.htm.

6. M. M. Linehan, K. A. Comtois, A. M. Murray, M. Z. Brown, R. J. Gallop, H. L. Heard, K. E. Korslund, D. A. Tutek, S. K. Reynolds, and N. Lindenboim, "Two-Year Randomized Controlled Trial and Follow-up of Dialectical Behavior Therapy vs. Therapy by Experts for Suicidal Behaviors and Borderline Personality Disorder," *Archives of General Psychiatry* 63, no. 7 (July 2006): 757–66.

7. Marsha M. Linehan, interview, *The Infinite Mind with Dr. Fred Goodwin,* WNYC AM 820, November 21, 1999.

8. Ibid.

9. M. Baugh, "Distress Tolerance," available at www.dbtsf.com/distress-tolerance.htm.

10. M. M. Linehan, *Skills Training Manual for Treating Borderline Personality Disorder* (New York: Guilford Press, 1993), 115–33.

11. D. St. John and N. Blum, "The STEPPS Group Treatment Program for Borderline Personality Disorder," available at www.uihealthcare.com/topics/medical departments/psychiatry/stepps/index.html.

12. Ibid.

13. "Innovative Therapy Fosters Full Recovery for Patients with Borderline Personality Disorder," available at www.medicalnewstoday.com/medicalnews.php?newsid =53869.

14. J. E. Young, J. S. Klosko, and M. E. Weishaar, *Schema Therapy: A Practitioner's Guide* (New York: Guilford Press, 2003).

15. Robert Friedel, e-mail to the author.

16. Andrea Corn, interview with the author, June 2007.

17. James Holifield, interview with the author, February 2007.

18. Perry Hoffman, phone interview with the author, March 2007.

Chapter 6: Finding Professional Help

1. June Peoples, interview, *The Infinite Mind with Dr. Fred Goodwin*, WNYC AM 820, November 21, 1999.

2. R. Moskovitz, "Why Do Many Professionals Still Treat People with BPD As If They Can't Get Better?" available at www.borderlinepersonality.ca/drm09.htm.

3. Marsha M. Linehan, interview, *The Infinite Mind with Dr. Fred Goodwin*, WNYC AM 820, November 21, 1999.

4. Kathleen, interview, *The Infinite Mind with Dr. Fred Goodwin*, WNYC AM 820, November 21, 1999.

5. Rachel Reiland, e-mail to the author, 1997.

6. A. J. Mahari, "Is Your BPD Loved One Serious About Therapy?" available at www.bpdfamily.com/tools/articles8.htm.

7. J. G. Gunderson and C. Berkowitz, "Family Guidelines," available at www .neabpd.org/guidelines.shtml. Edited slightly with permission.

8. B. D. Beitman in T. DeAngelis, "Where Psychotherapy Meets Neuroscience," *Monitor on Psychology* 36, no. 10 (November 2005), available at www.apa.org/monitor/nov05/neuroscience.html.

9. T. DeAngelis, "Where Psychotherapy Meets Neuroscience," *Monitor on Psychology* 36, no. 10 (November 2005), available at www.apa.org/monitor/nov05/neuroscience. html.

10. Robert Friedel, interview with the author, August 2007.

11. B. A. Aguirre, *Borderline Personality Disorder in Adolescents: A Complete Guide to Understanding and Coping When Your Adolescent Has BPD* (Beverly, MA: Fair Winds Press, 2007), 51.

12. American Academy of Child and Adolescent Psychiatry, "Comprehensive Psychiatric Evaluation," available at www.aacap.org/cs/root/facts_for_families/comprehensive_psychiatric_evaluation.

13. Aguirre, *Borderline Personality Disorder in Adolescents*, 22, 12.

14. J. G. Gunderson, with P. S. Links, *Borderline Personality Disorder: A Clinical Guide* (Washington, DC: American Psychiatric Publishing, Inc., 2001), 182.

15. R. L. Trestman, "Optimism Grows for Combined Treatment of Severe Personality Disorder," *Psychiatric Times*, October 1, 2004, news section.

16. A. J. Mahari, "Is Your BPD Loved One Serious About Therapy?" available at www.bpdfamily.com/tools/articles8.htm.

17. Andrea Corn, interview with the author, June 2007.

18. K. Kersting, "Axis II Gets Short Shrift," *Monitor on Psychology* 35, no. 3 (March 2004), available at www.apa.org/monitor/mar04/axis.html.

19. Ibid.

20. New York State Psychiatric Association, "Questions and Answers About Psychiatry," available at www.nyspsych.org/webpages/qa.asp.

21. National Education Alliance for Borderline Personality Disorder, "About Borderline Personality Disorder," available at www.borderlinepersonalitydisorder.com/FAQ.shtml.

22. Byron Bloemer, interview with the author, May 2007.

23. Blaise Aguirre, interview with the author, April 2007.

About Power Tools

1. J. O. Prochaska, J. C. Norcross, and C. C. DiClemente, *Changing for Good: A Revolutionary Six-Stage Program for Overcoming Bad Habits and Moving Your Life Positively Forward* (New York: Avon, 1994).

Chapter 7: Power Tool 1: Take Good Care of Yourself

1. "Post-traumatic Stress Disorder (PTSD): Symptoms, Types and Treatment," availableatwww.helpguide.org/mental/post_traumatic_stress_disorder_symptoms_treatment.htm; K. McKeever, "PTSD a Risk Factor for Long-Term Disease," available at www.medicinenet.com/script/main/art.asp?articlekey=87135; "Depression (Major Depression)," available at www.mayoclinic.com/health/depression/DS00175/DSECTION=2.

2. E. Savage, *Don't Take It Personally! The Art of Dealing with Rejection* (Oakland, CA: New Harbinger Publications, 1997).

3. D. Carnegie, *How to Stop Worrying and Start Living* (New York: Pocket Books, 2004).

4. Chris, www.mytriptoozandback.com.

5. C. DeRoo and C. DeRoo, *What's Right with Me: Positive Ways to Celebrate*

Your Strengths, Build Self-Esteem, and Reach Your Potential (Oakland, CA: New Harbinger Publications, 2006).

6. Andrea Brandt, *The Anger Zone,* www.theangerzone.com.

7. D. J. Lieberman, *How to Change Anybody: Proven Techniques to Reshape Anyone's Attitude, Behavior, Feelings, or Beliefs* (New York: St. Martin's Press, 2005), 12.

8. M. D. Lemonick, "A Frazzled Mind, a Weakened Body," *Time,* January 20, 2003, available at www.time.com/time/magazine/article/0,9171,1004080,00.html.

9. Ibid.

10. K. Mahr, "How Stress Harms the Heart, available at www.time.com/time/health/article/0,8599,1669766,00.html?iid=sphere-inline-bottom.

11. H. E. Marano, "The Rewards of Shut-Eye," Psychology Today Online, April 25, 2003, available at www.psychologytoday.com/articles/pto-20030425-000002.html.

12. Ibid.

13. P. Maruff, M. G. Falleti, A. Collie, D. Darby, and M. McStephen, "Fatigue-Related Impairment in the Speed, Accuracy and Variability of Psychomotor Performance: Comparison with Blood Alcohol Levels," *Journal of Sleep Research* 14, no. 1 (March 2005): 21–27.

14. M. Carmichael, "Stronger, Faster, Smarter," *Newsweek,* March 26, 2007, available at www.newsweek.com/id/36056.

15. J. Phelps, *Why Am I Still Depressed? Recognizing and Managing the Ups and Downs of Bipolar II and Soft Bipolar Disorder* (New York: McGraw-Hill, 2006).

Chapter 8: Power Tool 2: Uncover What Keeps You Feeling Stuck

1. B. C. Berg, *How to Escape the No-Win Trap* (New York: McGraw-Hill, 2004), 7–9.

2. Ibid., 21.

3. Ibid., 10.

4. D. Goleman, "Feeling of Control Viewed as Central in Mental Health," *New York Times,* October 7, 1986, available at query.nytimes.com/gst/fullpage.html?res=9A0DE1D61731F934A35753C1A960948260&sec=health&spon=&pagewanted=all.

5. B. Engel, *The Emotionally Abusive Relationship: How to Stop Being Abused and How to Stop Abusing* (Hoboken, NJ: John Wiley & Sons, 2002), 10–11; B. Engel, *The Jekyll and Hyde Syndrome: What to Do If Someone in Your Life Has a Dual Personality—or If You Do* (Hoboken, NJ: John Wiley, 2007), 89.

6. J. M. Carver, "Love and Stockholm Syndrome: The Mystery of Loving an Abuser," available at drjoecarver.makeswebsites.com/clients/49355/File/love_and_stockholm_syndrome.html.

7. B. Klatte and K. Thompson, *It's So Hard to Love You: Staying Sane When Your*

Loved One Is Manipulative, Needy, Dishonest, or Addicted (Oakland, CA: New Harbinger Publications, 2007), 45.

8. For more information about this, see P. T. Mason and R. Kreger, *Stop Walking on Eggshells: Taking Your Life Back When Someone You Care About Has Borderline Personality Disorder* (Oakland, CA: New Harbinger Publications, 1998), 172–74.

9. S. Jeffers, *Feel the Fear and Do It Anyway* (New York: Ballantine Books, 1987), 18.

10. Klatte and Thompson, *It's So Hard to Love You,* 50.

11. Perry Hoffman, interview with the author, March 2007.

12. Debra Resnick, interview with the author, February 2008.

13. Berg, *How to Escape the No-Win Trap,* 23.

14. J. J. Messina and C. Messina, "Tools for Handling Control Issues: Developing Detachment," available at www.coping.org/control/detach.htm.

15. "Codependent with You," music and lyrics by John Forster, ©1991 Limousine Music Co. (ASCAP). All rights reserved.

16. A. Miller, *The Enabler: When Helping Hurts the Ones You Love* (Tucson, AZ: Wheatmark, 2008), 37.

17. E. B. Brown, *Living Successfully with Screwed-Up People* (Grand Rapids, MI: Fleming H. Revell, 1999), 217, 218.

18. "Tools for Handling Control Issues: Developing Detachment," available at www.coping.org/control/detach.htm; "Tools for Personal Growth: Accepting Personal Responsibility," available at www.coping.org/growth/accept.htm.

Chapter 9: Power Tool 3: Communicate to Be Heard

1. B. Pologe, "Couples," available at www.aboutpsychotherapy.com/Tcouples.htm.

2. H. Mills "Anger vs. Fear," available at www.mentalhelp.net/poc/view_doc.php?type=doc&id=5806&cn=116.

3. Chris, www.mytriptoozandback.com.

4. A. J. Mahari, "BPD: The Power and Control Struggle," available at www.borderlinepersonality.ca/borderpowercontrolstruggle.htm.

5. P. Chard, "Out of My Mind," *Milwaukee Journal Sentinel,* May 23, 2006, 3E.

6. Available at www.merriam-webster.com.

7. S. Heller, *The Complete Idiot's Guide to Conquering Fear and Anxiety* (Royersford, PA: Alpha Publishing, 1999), 74.

8. P. T. Mason and R. Kreger, *Stop Walking on Eggshells: Taking Your Life Back When Someone You Care About Has Borderline Personality Disorder* (Oakland, CA: New Harbinger Publications, 1998).

9. C. Bojrab, "Everything You Always Wanted to Know About Psychotropic

Medication but Were Afraid to Ask," CRGA (Children's Resource Group Associates) Continuing Education Seminar, Indianapolis, Indiana, November 16, 2007.

10. P. Bierma, "Depression and Verbal Abuse," available at www.ahealthyme .com/topic/depverbal.

11. Mason and Kreger, *Stop Walking on Eggshells*, 166.

12. J. G. Gunderson and C. Berkowitz, "Family Guidelines," available at www .neabpd.org/guidelines.shtml. Edited slightly with permission.

13. L. J. Bookbinder, Touch Another Heart: Empathy and Listening Skills for Emotional Intimacy, www.touch-another-heart.com.

14. See Roundstone International, Inc., "Communication," available at www .roundstoneintl.com.

15. L. J. Bookbinder, "5. Controlling the Urge to Help," available at www .touch-another-heart.com/ch5.htm.

16. G. B. Lundberg and J. S. Lundberg, *I Don't Have to Make Everything All Better* (New York: Penguin Group, 1995), 82.

17. Ibid., 84.

18. A. Mehrabian, "'Silent Messages': A Wealth of Information About Nonverbal Communication (Body Language)," available at www.kaaj.com/psych/smorder.html.

19. S. Dingfelder, "BPD Tied to Enhanced Emotion Recognition," *Monitor on Psychology* 37, no. 11 (December 2006), available at www.apa.org/monitor/dec06/bpd .html.

20. B. A. Aguirre, *Borderline Personality Disorder in Adolescents: A Complete Guide to Understanding and Coping When Your Adolescent Has BPD* (Beverly, MA: Fair Winds Press, 2007), 48.

21. Mehrabian, "'Silent Messages'"; Jan Hargrave, interview with the author, June 2007; "Tools for Communication: Nonverbal Communication Issues," available at www.coping.org/dialogue/nonverbal.htm; T. Loo, "Using Body Position to De-fuse Angry People," available at ezinearticles.com/?Using-Body-Position-to-Defuse-Angry-People&id=158056; "Nonverbal Communication: The Hidden Language of Emotional Intelligence," available at www.helpguide.org/mental/EQ6_nonverbal_ communication.htm; G. R. Wainwright, *Teach Yourself Body Language* (Chicago: McGraw-Hill, 2004), 6–17.

22. Gunderson and Berkowitz, "Family Guidelines."

23. Gunderson and Berkowitz, "Family Guidelines."

24. E. B. Brown, *Living Successfully with Screwed-Up People* (Grand Rapids, MI: Fleming H. Revell, 1999), 149.

25. "Invalidation," available at www.eqi.org/invalid.htm#Examples%20of%20 invalidating%20expressions.

26. Sharon, interview with the author, February 2008.

Chapter 10: Power Tool 4: Set Limits with Love

1. Jack, interview with the author, January 2007.

2. D. R. Bellafiore, "Boundaries in Relationships," available at drbalternatives .com/articles/si7.html.

3. J. Black and G. Enns, *Better Boundaries: Owning and Treasuring Your Life* (Oakland, CA: New Harbinger Publications, 1997), 10–13.

4. Debra Resnick, interview with the author, February 2008.

5. J. Adams, *Boundary Issues: Using Boundary Intelligence to Get the Intimacy You Want and the Independence You Need in Life, Love, and Work* (Hoboken, NJ: John Wiley and Sons, 2005), 7–9.

6. B. Engel, *The Emotionally Abusive Relationship: How to Stop Being Abused and How to Stop Abusing* (Hoboken, NJ: John Wiley & Sons, 2002), 108.

7. Suzanne Roberts, interview with the author, July 2008.

8. S. Forward, with D. Frazier, *Emotional Blackmail: When the People in Your Life Use Fear, Obligation, and Guilt to Manipulate You* (New York: HarperCollins Publishers, 1997), 39–40.

9. Ibid., 150.

10. P. T. Mason and R. Kreger, *Stop Walking on Eggshells: Taking Your Life Back When Someone You Care About Has Borderline Personality Disorder* (Oakland, CA: New Harbinger Publications, 1998), 62–63.

11. G. B. Lundberg and J. S. Lundberg, *I Don't Have to Make Everything All Better* (New York: Penguin Group, 1995), 11–12.

12. Blaise Aguirre, interview with the author, April 2007.

13. J. G. Gunderson and C. Berkowitz, "Family Guidelines," available at www .neabpd.org/guidelines.shtml. Edited slightly with permission.

14. Perry Hoffman, interview with the author, March 2007.

15. Freda Friedman, interview with the author, April 2007.

16. Gunderson and Berkowitz, "Family Guidelines."

17. Freda Friedman, interview with the author, April 2007.

18. A. Mehrabian, "'Silent Messages': A Wealth of Information About Nonverbal Communication (Body Language)," available at www.kaaj.com/psych/smorder.html; Jan Hargrave, interview with the author, June 2007; "Tools for Communication: Non-verbal Communication Issues," available at www.coping.org/dialogue/nonverbal. htm; T. Loo, "Using Body Position to Defuse Angry People," available at ezinearticles. com/?Using-Body-Position-to-Defuse-Angry-People&id=158056; "Nonverbal Communication: The Hidden Language of Emotional Intelligence," available at www. helpguide.org/mental/EQ6_nonverbal_communication.htm; G. R. Wainwright, *Teach Yourself Body Language* (Chicago: McGraw-Hill, 2004), 6–17.

19. Sharon, interview with the author, February 2008.

20. Gunderson and Berkowitz, "Family Guidelines."

Chapter 11: Power Tool 5: Reinforce the Right Behavior

1. A. Sutherland, *What Shamu Taught Me About Life, Love, and Marriage: Lessons for People from Animals and Their Trainers* (New York: Random House, 2008).

2. K. Pryor, *Don't Shoot the Dog! The New Art of Teaching and Training* (New York: Bantam Books, 1984), 120.

3. Sharon, interview with the author, February 2008.

4. Sutherland, *What Shamu Taught Me about Love, Life, and Marriage.*

5. Ibid., xiii.

6. Pryor, *Don't Shoot the Dog!*

7. See www.clickertraining.com/node/484 for more information.

8. Sutherland, *What Shamu Taught Me about Love, Life, and Marriage*, 118–19.

9. Rita, interview with the author, February 2008.

10. Pryor, *Don't Shoot the Dog!* 133–34.

11. J. G. Gunderson and C. Berkowitz, "Family Guidelines," available at www.nea bpd.org/guidelines.shtml. Edited slightly with permission.

12. Ibid., 2.

Index

abandonment, 25–26, 33, 34, 35
    fear of, 43, 53–54, 123, 168
abuse, 207
    of children, 18, 74, 91–92
    emotional, 149–50, 153–54
    physical, 176–77
    substance, 38, 41, 43, 45–46
    verbal, 175
acceptance, 87–88, 138–39
Adams, Jane, 204, 205
Adolescent Dialectical Behavioral
    Therapy Center (MA), 29, 41
adolescents, with BPD, 41, 42
aggression, 39, 43–44, 53, 80
    impulsive, 58–59, 165–67
Aguirre, Blaise, 29, 41, 83, 113, 114, 122–23,
    183
alprazolam, 83
American Psychiatric Association, 24
American Psychological Association,
    117–18
amygdala, 69, 70–71, 168
Anderson, Susan, 25
anger, 43, 54, 115–16, 133, 137–38, 174, 185
    central nervous system and, 167

    as DSM trait, 34, 35
    gender and, 42–44
anxiety, 28, 33, 175
aural dyslexia, 165
authenticity, 159

Baugh, Michael, 89
behavior
    abusive. *See* abuse; limits
    aggressive, 39, 43–44, 53, 80
    impaired, 33, 35
    incompatible, 236–37
    praising, 238–39
    rewarding, 237–38
    unwanted, 235–36
Behavioral Tech Web site, 91
Bellafiore, Donna R., 198
Benham, Elyce, 209
Berg, Barbara Cowan, 147–48, 153–54
Berkowitz, Cynthia, 102, 176, 184–85,
    238–39
Better Boundaries (Black/Enns), 199–200
bipolar disorder, 47–48
bitterness, 203
Black, Jan, 199–200

267

About the Author

RANDI KREGER has brought the concerns of people who have a family member with borderline personality disorder (BPD) to an international forefront through her best-selling books, informative Web site, and popular online family support community.

Her book *Stop Walking on Eggshells,* co-written with Paul Mason, has sold more than 350,000 copies worldwide. Her second book, *The Stop Walking on Eggshells Workbook,* was published in 2002 and met similar acclaim.

Her Web site, BPDCentral (www.bpdcentral.com), is one of the longest-established and largest sites about BPD. It serves as a gateway for her popular Welcome to Oz (WTO) online support community for people who have a loved one with BPD.

Kreger speaks and gives workshops about BPD internationally.